THE SUN AT NOON

THE MACMILLAN COMPANY
NEW YORK · BOSTON · CHICAGO
DALLAS · ATLANTA · SAN FRANCISCO

MACMILLAN AND CO., LIMITED
LONDON · BOMBAY · CALCUTTA
MADRAS · MELBOURNE

THE MACMILLAN COMPANY
OF CANADA, LIMITED
TORONTO

LUCIUS CARY, VISCOUNT FALKLAND

Reproduced by permission of Country Life, London,
from a photograph of the original painting

THE SUN AT NOON

THREE BIOGRAPHICAL SKETCHES

by *Kenneth B. Murdock*

Elizabeth Cary, *Viscountess Falkland*, 1585–1639
Lucius Cary, *Viscount Falkland*, 1610–1643
John Wilmot, *Earl of Rochester*, 1647–1680

THE MACMILLAN COMPANY
NEW YORK   1939

PRINTED IN THE UNITED STATES OF AMERICA
AMERICAN BOOK—STRATFORD PRESS, INC., NEW YORK

TO

THE TUTORS

OF

LEVERETT HOUSE

1931–1938

PREFACE

I HAVE called the narratives in this book "biographical sketches" in the hope that no one will be misled into supposing that they are intended to be "scholarly" or "exhaustive." My concern has been with the relation of my three subjects to some major interests of their time, and I have omitted data of importance for the scholar but irrelevant to my present purpose. I have not attempted literary criticism of what Rochester and the Falklands wrote, nor have I tried to discuss or even to mention all their works. I have not hunted for the sources of their learning, illuminating as such a search might prove. My object has been simply to expose a part of what they may be presumed to have thought and to tell enough of their major experiences and problems to show how far what they did was determined by certain of their ideas and feelings.

I have tried to ground the book solidly on a wide and careful study of sources and secondary materials, but I have included few footnotes, limiting them in general to brief comments on controversial questions or to material directly supplementing the text. I have, however, supplied a list of the authorities on which I have depended most and from which I have most often quoted, and I have kept a fully annotated manuscript of the entire book, so that if any reader chances to be interested in the authority for any passage I can, I hope, supply it.

I am grateful to the President and Fellows of Harvard College for a grant which enabled me to spend six months reading and seeking material in England; to the authorities of the Bodleian, the British Museum, the London Library, and the Harvard College Library, for many courtesies and much help; to Canon William Charles Emeris for permission to read and

vii

PREFACE

quote briefly from Elizabeth Cary's manuscript "Mirror of the Worlde"; to the Right Honorable Earl Spencer for allowing me to have copies made of the Falkland letters owned by him; to Professor Daniel Thompson and Miss Rhoda Welsford of the Courtauld Institute of Art, for their aid in supplying illustrations; to Eleanor E. McLaughlin and Richard B. Schlatter, who investigated special points for me; to John Rackliffe, who has shared with me some of his studies in the seventeenth century; and to the members of my family who supplied helpful criticisms of my work. I am particularly indebted to Mr. Kurt Weber, who has most generously allowed me to use some of the material he has collected for his dissertation on Falkland, which will, I hope, soon be published, and will, I feel sure, consider many matters I have not treated, and set right my errors in what I have. Most of all, it is a pleasure to acknowledge, even thus inadequately, my obligation to two long-suffering colleagues, Walter E. Houghton and Perry G. E. Miller. They patiently examined my manuscript, showed me how to include much that I should otherwise have overlooked, and saved me from many mistakes that I should otherwise have made.

K. B. M.

Leverett House
Cambridge, Massachusetts
August, 1938

CONTENTS

ILLUSTRATIONS

THE SUN AT NOON

I

INTRODUCTION

"The Sun at Noon"

"Though in the wayes of fortune, or understanding, or
conscience, thou have been benighted till now, wintred
and frozen, clouded and eclypsed, damped and benummed,
smothered and stupified till now, now God comes to thee,
not as in the dawning of the day, not as in the bud of the
spring, but as the Sun at noon"—

JOHN DONNE

AN ECCENTRIC poetess, choosing poverty for piety's sake and
defying husband, family, and the law, in order to believe as
she liked; a scholar, deserting his books in an attempt to make
high principles count in politics and war; the most notorious
rake of a dissolute court, following profligacy with all the
thoughtfulness of a philosopher—these three are the subjects
of this book. Unlike as they seem—and were—there are good
reasons for making them companions of the printed page.
They all lived in seventeenth-century England, and in Oxfordshire; two of them were linked by blood, and all by mem-
bership in the same social class; but their real kinship lies in
the fact that their lives were shaped by warfare for a common
goal. Elizabeth, Lady Falkland; Lucius, Viscount Falkland;
and John, Earl of Rochester, in their separate ways and in suc-
cessive generations, contended with a single dilemma created
for them by the intellectual climate of their times. Beset by con-

1

flicts of opinion they each sought for an object of faith, some general principle more potent than the promptings of flesh and proof against the vicissitudes of earth.

Many men in the seventeenth century, as before and since, derived their warmest satisfactions from religious assurance, the gift of God to His dependents, and it was this that John Donne wrote of as "the Sun at noon." That "Sun" Elizabeth Cary thought she saw, and the vision made her contemptuous of adversity; John Wilmot, two generations later found, in what he felt to be its rays, relief from his anguished scorn for the material bounties of existence. Toward it Lucius Cary groped, although by seeking it with his mind alone he achieved only a cold reflection of it—a reflection so pale and distorted that when he tried to live by its light he was beset by confusion. All three of these characters in their pursuit of an ultimate "truth" by which to live, yearned to see "the Sun at noon." They took different roads and came to different ends, but the aspiration was alike for all.

To appreciate how they felt and acted is also to catch glimpses of what others in their day did and suffered. They represent three periods in the same century and thus their deeds and beliefs may give hints of both the nature and the development of ideas immensely important in the seventy-five years before 1680. In those years new experiences, discoveries, and theories, in religion, politics, economics, and science, unsettled men's minds about what their fathers had held to be certainties, but the fathers bequeathed to the sons at least their conviction that somewhere such certainties must exist, and this conviction survived even when the old objects of belief did not. Flushed with confidence in the powers of the mind, supplied with new learning and trained in new logical methods, seventeenth-century Englishmen exalted "reason," sometimes at the expense of "faith" and sometimes, like Falkland, as the surest means of attaining it. Some found what they needed; others were led by what they construed as "reason" to doubts too powerful to combat, and some of these, like Rochester, succumbed at last to what could be felt as "faith," thus deserting their contemporaries and going back to where Lady Cary, three-quarters of a century before, had begun.

No single formula sums up all the ideas of a period as varied and as active as the seventeenth century, and no one intellectual problem, however far reaching, can serve as a clue to the entire labyrinth of its intellectual history. Surely, however, the ways in which "reason" was thought about; the experiments made in applying it to the concerns of daily living —religious, political, and economic; the attempts to reconcile it with Christian beliefs and the long tradition of divine revelation; and most of all the struggle to exalt it to fill the place of a "Sun at noon," account for much in the thinking of the seventeenth century in England—for more, it may be, than can be related to men's speculations on any other group of questions. Sir Thomas Browne said, that in past ages, before Christianity, men lived "in that disadvantage of time, when" they "could say little for futurity, but from reason: whereby the noblest minds fell often upon doubtful deaths and melancholy dissolutions." But there were "doubtful deaths and melancholy dissolutions" among Browne's contemporaries and some of them still labored under a "disadvantage of time" and could say little for futurity or for anything else "but from reason." They were often troubled because "reason" somehow still left them a prey to feeling or was made by them into something so lofty as to be quite useless in a selfish world. "It is the body that makes the clothes warm, not the clothes the body: and the spirit of man makes felicity and content, not any spoils of a rich fortune wrapped about a sickly and uneasy soul," thought Jeremy Taylor. "Reason" may be so interpreted as to leave its servants as badly off as Taylor's old man who was "cold and paralytic under a load of sables and the skins of foxes." Lady Elizabeth Cary, her son, and the outrageous Earl

3

of Rochester, all puzzled about "reason" and "faith" because they wanted "felicity and content." How they fared was partly the result of their own natures, partly forced upon them by the vagaries of chance, and still more by the pressure of their times, dictating doctrines to them and entangling them in necessities they could not evade. What they underwent, many others did also. They were an exceptional trio, perhaps, in that they were in their own right admirable or at least interesting individuals and their lives were more strikingly dramatic than most even in their lively age, but essentially what gave them happiness and grief, what they did and failed to do, what they lost and won, was just what rejoiced or distressed many of their contemporaries and spelled for them victory or defeat.

Nor are the careers of Rochester and the two Carys of interest simply as sidelights on a complex chapter of intellectual history. The riddles that vexed them crop up now and then to plague men even today. The solutions they found, thought they found, or hoped to find are still in use. There is less talk of "faith" and "reason" now than in the seventeenth century and many scoff where Falkland prayed, but current needs and satisfactions often look curiously like old ones, disguised with new names. Churches and their teachings may be renounced; the sanctity of reason may be suspect; Donne's "Sun at noon" may be eclipsed, but men still seem happiest when they think they possess some basic criterion by which to measure values in their lives and others'. Whatever it be—a political platform, an economic theory, a psychological system, a reverence for scientific "fact"—it is easy to centre a creed about it, and though its devotees may strive to defend it by "reason" they are likely to regard it with the adoration of faith. They may succeed better or worse than the characters in this book; those characters may be praised or ridiculed because their immediate concerns and their vocabularies are out of date; but the chances are that some knowledge of them may aid understanding of the present. The moral, if moral there be, is not to be pointed

4

here. If anything applicable to the twentieth century is to be discerned in lives lived in the seventeenth, it is for the reader to interpret the record by whatever variety of "reason" or whatever "faith" best pleases him.

II

"PASSION AND INFIRMITIES"

The Pilgrimage of Elizabeth Cary,
Viscountess Falkland, 1585?–1639

AMONG all Clarendon's splendid portraits of the great figures of the Civil War, the finest is that of Lucius Cary, Viscount Falkland. On it Clarendon lavished all his skill in effective eulogy; in it is the full warmth of his hero-worship. Little that Falkland cared for or did, lay outside his biographer's sympathy. But Falkland's mother, Lady Elizabeth Cary, was dismissed as "a lady of another persuasion in religion, and of a most masculine understanding, allayed with the passion and infirmities of her own sex."

Yet she was in her day a genuine, if eccentric, force. Her friends had reason to curse her amazing absent-mindedness, and her financial irresponsibility amounted to genius, but good Catholics tried hard to see her as a persecuted saint. Others merely laughed at her for her lack of beauty and her poverty, but learned men from the universities sought out her grubby lodgings to talk theology with her. Books were dedicated to her, and her knowledge and wit were celebrated by more than one contemporary; even statesmen respected—or feared—her political skill and powerful friends when she presented petitions at court; she was buried at last in Queen Henrietta Maria's own chapel.

6

She provoked her son, the most moderate of men, to write sharp letters; she cost him many pounds and many hours of worry, but she commanded from him, as from Clarendon, respect for her mind. To him she bequeathed much of her own defiant insistence on the necessity of a sure basis for faith. He became a scholar, a rationalist, and a leader in a group of thinkers who helped to chart out a central, if shallow, channel in the troubled intellectual waters of the seventeenth century, and his interests were largely moulded by her. Her strength and high courage, constantly qualified by "passion and infirmities"; her wisdom, mixed with a rash zeal that often eclipsed it; were too striking to ignore.

She has a right to be remembered because she helped to shape the life of a man greater than she, and also because what she lived through illustrates what many of her contemporaries had to survive. Her way was individual, but it was in part typical of the way of other Catholic converts in her time. If her adventures came from her own folly, they were also often forced upon her by the tangled loyalties of the world in which she dwelt. Her story helps to explain her son's, and lights up part of the intellectual history of a complex period—a period so complex, indeed, that it defies most attempts at general "synthesis" of ideas or events, and drives the intellectual historian back to the individuals who were the badly matched units out of which its intricate pattern was patched together.

In 1602 she was seventeen years old, and in that year she was married.[1] Romance was absent. Her husband, Sir Henry Cary, son of the Master of the royal Jewel House, was nine years older than she, and was interested in her because she was the only child of a rich man. Her father was Lawrence Tanfield, a

---

[1] *Life* gives the year of her birth as 1585 or 1586 and says she was married at fifteen (pp. 1, 7, 22). *Complete Peerage*, V, 240, gives the date of the marriage as 1602. This agrees with *Life*, p. 11, which says that she was married "seven years without any child," since her eldest seems to have been born in 1609 (*Complete Peerage*, VI, 556).

rising lawyer, who had a respectable fortune. Cary was a
"compleat courtier," of the new type soon to flourish under
James I and Charles I. Such men observed the external
forms of the old chivalric supporters of the throne, but their
motives smacked of the increasingly capitalistic atmosphere of
the time, and service at court was for them as much a profit-
making enterprise as a duty imposed by family or tradition.
Cary's unreasoned devotion to the sovereign was bound up
with an acute sense that fidelity might bring him wealth and
power. He was brave and, within limits, able; but he was
not one to marry for love if he could marry for money. If
this was a defect, his loyalty was, at least on the surface,
admirable. Late in life he broke his leg hunting at Theobald's
Park with the royal party, and the story goes that, as he lay in
great pain on the ground where he had fallen, Charles I came
quickly to his side to offer help. Good courtiers always stood
in the presence of the Lord's anointed, and Sir Henry Cary
somehow wrenched himself to his feet, breaking his leg in a
new place as he did so.[2] His injuries cost him his life. The
splendid tribute to convention was a fitting last act for a
Cavalier—and yet, perhaps like most of the newer breed of
Cavaliers, Sir Henry Cary saw the King less as an object for
disinterested and ideal devotion than as the concrete symbol
of the order of things by which such men as he lived, following the career of a courtier as a profitable, or potentially
profitable, profession. Thus he looked at Elizabeth Tanfield
on the day of his marriage with no flush of romantic adoration.
She was just a girl in her teens, with a good complexion, and
very fair, but short and fat—her merit was that she was an
heiress. Naturally enough, he left his wife with her family
after the wedding, and for at least four years seems to have
seen her rarely if at all—certainly not to have lived with her.

---

[2] *Life*, p. 46. Other accounts of Cary's death do not mention his rising
to greet the King, but there seems no necessity to question the story.

She had been piously brought up, and was, in a day still reverent toward absolute authority, ready to dedicate herself faithfully to one man, even if he paid little attention to her and could not be transformed, even in imagination, into an ardent lover of her very moderate charms. She had been reared in a household where his scale of values was accepted, and where high place at court was a mark of success. Her father, later to be Chief Baron of the Exchequer, and her mother, Elizabeth Symondes, were well versed in the ways of the world. To marry an only child to an older man she had hardly seen, was, for the sake of profit or place, an obvious move in the game they knew best.

One of Elizabeth's emotions on becoming a married woman must have been hope that she might in her new status have freedom she had been denied before. The day of her wedding meant the payment of a debt of £300, which she had run up to her father's servants, largely because of her imperious need to enjoy at least one form of liberty—liberty in so trivial a matter as the right to read in bed.

She learned to read very early, and to love it. A modest measure of literary interest was proper enough for a gentleman's daughter, but she "spent her whole time in reading, to which she gave herself so much that she frequently read all night; so as her mother was fain to forbid her servants to let her have candles." The rule was only wise, but little Elizabeth had a will of her own. She bribed the servants to bring her candles, in spite of her mother, promising to pay eventually half a crown for each. By the time she was twelve she owed thus £100—for eight hundred candles—and £200 for other things which her maids had secretly supplied. Neither as a child nor as a woman was she ever kept from having her way merely because she could not pay for it—provided, of course, someone would trust her for the amount. As a little girl she must have been intensely annoying to her parents, and for the Tanfields there was probably only slight compensation in the fact that their self-willed daughter was not only stubborn and disobedient but richly talented.

At four or five they tried to have her taught French. She studied for a few weeks, and then decided it was not worth her while. Soon she discovered that she really did want to read French books, and went unaided to work and taught herself. Similarly she learned Spanish and Italian, then Latin, and even Transylvanian. While she was still young, perhaps even before her marriage, she translated Seneca's epistles, proof that she had instructed herself to some purpose. She was the only person by whom she could be taught. Her independence of character, her insistence on her own way of doing things, must have made her the despair of any tutor, but what she wanted to know she managed to learn alone, even the art of needle-work—an accomplishment probably more welcomed by her father and mother than her skill in languages and her incorrigible love for books. "She was," says her daughter, "skilful and curious . . . never having been helped by anybody: those that knew her would never have believed she knew how to hold a needle unless they had seen it."

However little her family cared for her bookishness, there were those who did. In 1597 Michael Drayton, in dedicating to her two poems in his *Englands Heroicall Epistles*, praised her wisdom, her reading, and her skill in languages. And her great-uncle, Sir Henry Lee, she thought, could also appreciate her learning. For him she wrote between 1598 and 1602, a translation of Abraham Ortelius's *Le Miroir du Monde*, an epitome of geography published in Amsterdam when she was thirteen. The little work exists today in a manuscript copy in the church at Burford, Oxfordshire, where she was born. It was, Elizabeth told Lee, but a "humble presente, the fruites and endeuours of" her "younge and tender yeares." But she confidently assured him that there would be more. "As riper years shall afforde mee better fruites with greater iudgemente," she remarked, "I shall be euer ready to present

you with the best of my trauailes." The translation was work-
manlike and literal, and writing it must have stretched Elizabeth's imaginative horizon far beyond the rolling hills about
Burford, and past the towers of Oxford, eighteen miles away to
include such glamorous realms as China, India, and "Turkie."
She read of "America," of which "it is not certainly knowne
whether it be compassed with the sea, or ioined to Asia on the
north side. The which by gods helpe we hope to know, shortly
by the diligent search of the curiouse Englishmen." This
touched on one of the central romantic dramas of the day,
and a little girl's patriotism might well have been stirred by
the news that America "(except some little) is vnder the
Kinge of Spaine his Dominion" and that "these saide countries be . . . full of golde." As for England, it "is the best ile of
all Europe," which no doubt she had believed from her cradle,
but Ireland was peopled with "barbarouse" beings who were
"very much geuen to musick" and valued "liberty more than
riches"—statements she was sooner than she realized to be
able to test for herself. Then there was "admirable Rome," and
whole new seas and continents of which to dream. Small wonder that she tried to make Ortelius her own by translating
him.[3]

Geography was not all. When she was twelve her father

---

[3] The ms. translation of Ortelius was given to the church at Burford by
Viscount Dillon, Sept. 14, 1925. The dedication is to "my singular good
unckle Sr Henry Lee" and is subscribed "Your euer obediente Neece E. Tan-
felde." The ms. is not, according to a note inserted in it, in Elizabeth's hand.
Comparison of it with Abraham Ortelius, *Theatre de L'Univers* ([Antwerp],
1581) shows that it translates an abridgement of this work. Such an abridgement was printed in 1598 at Amsterdam, as *Le Miroir Dv Monde, ov, Epitome dv Theatre D'Abraham Ortelius* (cf. G. Atkinson, *La Littérature
Geographique Française de la Renaissance*, Paris, 1927, #390). I have not
seen *Le Miroir*, but Elizabeth's title for her ms. is "The mirror of the Worlde
translated Out of French," so that there can be no doubt as to the book she
used. For Sir Henry Lee, cf. Sir E. Chambers, *Sir Henry Lee, An Elizabethan
Portrait* (Oxford, 1936), especially pp. 206-208, 224. He was fond of his
grand-niece, Elizabeth, bought her a jewel as a wedding present, and left her at
his death "a cup of agate and another of ivory trimmed with silver."

gave her Calvin's *Institutes* to read. By now, surely, he must
have decided that whether he liked it or not, she was a scholar,
and to be treated as one. No doubt he expected her to be impressed by the great Swiss reformer; no doubt she was, but she
felt free to criticize. So, against the book which was then dictating most of English theological thought, "she made . . .
many objections, and found in him . . . many contradictions."
Her astonished father declared, how truly he was soon to learn
to his sorrow, "This girl hath a spirit averse from Calvin."

Even in his own profession of the law, this startling child
had a grain of wisdom to offer him. He took her once to see
him try a woman accused as a witch. The prisoner, in her terror, was confessing freely that she had bewitched this person
and that to death. But Elizabeth Cary somehow scented the
truth, and "so she whispered her father, and desired him to
ask" the accused "whether she had bewitched to death Mr.
John Symondes. . . . He did so, to which she said 'Yes,' just as
she had done to the rest." But John Symondes, Elizabeth's
uncle, was alive and in the courtroom. The poor woman could
only say " 'Alas, sir, I knew him not; I said so because you
asked me,' " and to Tanfield's, " 'Are you no witch then?' "
replied with protestations of innocence. She had, she said,
been threatened if she would not confess, and promised mercy
if she would. Thanks to Elizabeth Tanfield she was freed, perhaps slightly to the annoyance of the learned judge, set right
in his own courtroom by the wit of a ten-year-old girl.

Just why, even after she was married, her parents felt she
must not be allowed to write to her husband in her own
words, is hard to understand. If any girl of her age could have
been trusted with a pen, she could, but for some time her
elders saw to it that the letters Cary received ostensibly from
his wife were written for her. Possibly the Tanfields felt her
erudition might frighten a man of the world, or that such
heretical views as her opinion of Calvin would offend a conventional Protestant. And they may well have feared lest her

self-willed independence might be so revealed as to make him repent of his bargain. It was no secret to his mother. "Dame Katherine Lady Paget" had a vivid sense of her own importance. She expected those about her to fawn upon her, but in her new daughter-in-law she met her match. Elizabeth "for the most part" talked to her own mother on her knees, a custom she kept up as long as Lady Tanfield lived and even through long conversations, though she was always "but an ill kneeler, and a worse riser." But she saw no reason to be humble before her mother-in-law, and when she visited her she did little to gratify the older woman's craving for attention. She preferred to read. Her outraged hostess saw to it that except for one serving maid and for Jane, one of Henry Cary's sisters, the household left her quite alone.[4] Moreover Lady Katherine took away all Elizabeth's books, and grappled to her heart an enduring dislike for her son's wife.

Sir Henry Cary had set off in 1604 with permission to travel for seven years. He served in the wars in the Low Countries and when "twelve hundred Hollanders and Englishe menne rann from fower hundred Italions" was one of four who "did charge those fower hundred." He was taken prisoner, and it was nine months before he was in London again. Out of the adventure he won a reputation for valor, and a few lines of praise from Ben Jonson. On the other hand, a ransom had been exacted and its payment helped to begin the financial difficulties which beset him through his life.

Presumably he began to live with his wife in 1606 or 1607. He had been confused by her letters. Those sent in her name, but written by others, had been followed by some of her own, perhaps smuggled out by her in spite of her vigilant elders, and the genuine ones struck him as so good that he could not believe they were actually from his wife, so much did they improve on those which had been professionally written and

---

[4] That the kind sister-in-law was Jane seems clear from *Life*, pp. 21, 34, and *Complete Peerage*, I, 431.

signed with her name. When he learned the truth, his respect for her increased; her story of how she had been treated in his absence must have roused his chivalrous instincts; and their married life began with at least some basis in sympathy on his part.

Their first child, a daughter, was born in 1609. In the next fifteen years there were ten more "born alive." Almost continually she was "as long as she lived with" Sir Henry "either with child or giving suck." Lucius, her eldest son, born in 1610, was the prospective heir and her father took him from her at birth, to bring him up in his own house. The other babies she nursed herself, and most of their education they had from her. What time remained she spent innocently enough, reading history, poetry, and plays—going to the theatre whenever she could—and writing much of her own. When her mother-in-law had taken her books away she had begun to make verses and she kept up the habit. Throughout her life she published little, but there is some reason to think that a play, Mariam, printed in 1613, was hers, and her family and friends saw enough of her unprinted work to be sure she was worthy of a place among the wits.[5]

Mariam, if she did write it, suggests that her claims as authoress were rather for fluency and diligence than for imaginative power or poetic inspiration. It does, however, show some real ability to visualize history in dramatic terms, and a strong taste for moralizing on married loyalty.

"When to their Husbands they themselves doe bind,
Doe they not wholy giue themselues away?
Or giue they but their body not their mind,
Reseruing that though best, for others pray?
No sure, their thoughts no more can be their owne,
And therefore should to none but one be knowne."

---

[5] For the authorship of Mariam see A. C. Dunstan's notes in the Malone Society edition of The Tragedy of Mariam, 1613 (Oxford, 1914).

So far as in her lay, Elizabeth Cary tried to live up to this ideal. It was not easy to be Sir Henry's wife, for "he was very absolute," but "to her husband she bore so much respect, that she taught her children as a duty to love him better than herself . . . though she saw it was a lesson they could learn without teaching." However absorbing the nursery was, she could not, as Lady Cary, or after 1620 as Viscountess Falkland, stay always in it. "Being most fearful of a horse," but her husband "loving hunting, and desiring to have her a good horsewoman" she managed for years to "ride so much and so desperately as if she had had no fear but much delight in it; and so she had, to see him pleased, and did really make herself love it" as long as they were together, "but after (as before) she neither had the courage nor the skill to sit upon a horse."

She had no interest in clothes and "dressing was all her life a torture to her," but she had to dress well to content her husband, and dress she did. More accurately, she let her maids dress her. Poor maids! No sooner was she supposed to be ready for their hands than her mind would jump off to a book, or a train of thought started by her last eager talk with some learned theologian, and away she would go in a restless march about the room. For the servants, there was nothing to do but to chase her, and, as she walked, to stick in a pin here, to set a ruff there, to curl and weave the amazing structure she wore on her head, while her short figure kept up its uneasy journey and for a few blessed moments she forgot children and household. For the maids it was but one more proof of their mistress's eccentricity. For her, her dressing was, however annoying and distracting, at least another concrete means of showing her complete devotion to her husband. The whole story is written in the few lines which record how, after she was estranged from him, she showed "extraordinary great carelessness . . . of herself" and "never went out of plain black, frieze, or coarse stuff."

It was easy, relatively, to flounce over hedges on the back of a horse, or to glitter in the candlelight at court, clad as fashion demanded, but the chorus in *Mariam* made it the duty of a wife to share her mind with her husband. Here there were difficulties for Elizabeth Cary. She could, to be sure, sympathize with Sir Henry when he had surrendered to the crown one of his properties; she could approve and rejoice in his successes at court. He bought estates, was keeper of Marylebone Park, and Comptroller of the Household, sold his Mastership of the Jewel House for a good price, became a member of the Privy Council, and finally in 1620 was created Viscount Falkland. In all this Elizabeth Cary and he could share, but beneath the surface there was discord. He was a Protestant and an Anglican, if for no other reason than that it was expedient to be so. She had been brought up to be the same, but mere inheritance and training could not curb her conscience. As she read and thought it came to be more and more Rome and not Canterbury toward which she looked for that ultimate infallible authority which, true child of her age, she felt must inhere in some one all-embracing and solely valid church.

Early in her married life she read Hooker's *Ecclesiastical Polity*, the classic defense of the English church, but just as Calvin's logic had failed to convince, so Hooker's sweet reasonableness did not persuade. Indeed, it raised doubts instead of answering them. When her husband's brother, Adolphus, came back from Italy, he spoke well of Catholicism there, and introduced her to St. Augustine and others of the church fathers. Quickly she turned from history and poetry to theology. Her uncertainty increased, and for weeks at a time she refused to go to an Anglican service. She sought advice from Richard Neile, Dean of Westminster, and later Archbishop of York, and went often to his house. She met there not only the Dean but "many of the learnedest . . . divines." All they could do was persuade her "she might lawfully remain as she was, she never questioning for all that but that to be in the Roman Church were infinitely better and securer." It was a poor compromise for anyone as keen-witted as she, and her questionings were not resolved in action for more than twenty years. On the one hand was her duty as the wife of a Protestant courtier in a Protestant court; on the other her faith that there was a single way of truth and her discontent at not being able to follow it. It is fortunate that the children she bore, nursed, and taught, left her little time for religious speculation.

It was a serious thing in the reign of James I to flirt with Rome. The monarchy was welding to itself a powerful ecclesiastical structure; Catholic powers were potential enemies of England—many a good citizen could remember the Armada —and Protestantism of a radical sort was enlisting supporters from plain men who hated Catholicism and even the national church. Social cleavages, political divisions, even patriotism itself, were being linked with questions of where to worship and how. Could Lady Cary, because she believed in Catholic doctrine, ally herself with the perpetrators of the Gunpowder Plot? Could she risk her husband's fortunes by making herself a target for hot-headed Puritans, eager to snatch any weapon against the bishops and the court, and fanatically confusing taxes, laws, and policies of state which they disliked, with the government's failure to adopt their own extreme brand of Protestantism? She was caught in one of the central dilemmas of her time, between intellectual conviction and expediency, between loyalty to an ideal and loyalty to her husband, between the pursuit of Heaven and the race for favor with the King. The end was to be disastrous, but for the time she made herself the good wife and resolutely closed her heart to the protests of her relentless mind.

In 1622 her husband was appointed Lord Deputy of Ireland. It was an arduous post, but it was a great one, and one which might bring personal profit for a skilful courtier. Cary set out with high hopes. But it cannot have been easy for his wife to move her family from England to Ireland, where, as she had read in Ortelius, the people, however fond of music, were "rude" and "grosse." Moreover it was expensive. Sir Henry could not scrape up enough, and Lady Cary gave up to him a jointure settled upon her by the terms of her marriage contract. This outraged her father, who must have remembered all too well the improvident little girl who ran herself into debt to the servants, and may have been one reason why he disinherited her, making Lucius, her son, his heir instead.[6]

So, beset with uncertainties in belief, thronged about with all her children (except the eldest who married just before she left England), still loving books, still relatively uninterested in practical worldly affairs, but none the less loyally intent on being a good wife to a Lord Deputy and a good mother to his children, she set out in 1622 for Dublin. Fortunately she had put behind her some of the ills of her early married life. For a while she had been racked by melancholic fits, and there had been an ugly time when she had completely lost her reason. Now she had schooled herself into some sort of control of nerves and mind. She had taught herself the trick of sleeping whenever she wished—a blessed protection against accusing thoughts which might attack her in Ireland. It was a land of Catholics, and her husband was the agent of a Protestant king. When Lord Falkland, almost as soon as he took up the Deputyship, proclaimed harsh measures against Papists, she must have winced. When the government at home virtually rebuked him, since a Spanish match was being arranged for the prince, she must have been relieved, even if sympathetic toward her lord.

She was far too active, and her mind was far too fond of planning, for her to be merely passive as the Lord Deputy's wife. So she plunged into a large scheme for training Irish children in trades. She gathered as instructors "several sorts of linen and woollen weavers, dyers, all sorts of spinners and

---

[6] Lord Falkland insisted later that the disinheriting of his wife was because of her religious views. CSP, Ireland, 1625–1632, p. 248. But cf. p. 51 post.

knitters, hatters, lacemakers," and as pupils "beggar children (with which that country swarms) more than eight score prentices, refusing none above seven years old, and taking some less: these were disposed to their several masters and mistresses, to learn those trades they were thought most fit for, the least amongst them being set to something, as making points, tags, buttons or lace, or some other thing: they were parted in their several rooms and houses, where they exercised their trades; many rooms being filled with little boys or girls, sitting all round at work." The broadcloth they made was so good "that her lord being Deputy wore it." But "she had great losses by fire and water (which she judged extraordinary, others but casual); her work-house . . . was burnt; her fulling-mills carried away, and much of her things spoiled with water; all which" later "she took to be the punishment of God for the children's going to" the English church. Others, more reasonably, "thought it rather that she was better at contriving than executing, and that too many things were undertaken at the very first."

If Viscount Falkland needed proof of his wife's energy and zeal he had it now, but he had, too, alas, good evidence that her activity would be expensive. She never could handle money without grave risk of losing it; she never saw the practical hazards in any plan to which she gave her heart. Her daughter's comments are revealing. She was easily cheated, "though she were not a little suspicious in her nature." It was "the ill order she took for paying money" which did most harm. She had "the worst memory in such things in the world" but "wholly trusting to it (or them she dealt with), and never keeping any account of what she did, she was most subject to pay the same things often (as she hath had it confessed to her by some that they have . . . made her pay them the same thing five times in five days); neither would she suffer herself to be undeceived by them that . . . saw her do it . . . and the same unwillingness she had to see she was cozened in all things on which she was set with such violence (as she was on all the things she undertook, which were many), which violence in all occasions made her ever subject to necessities, even when she had most, and made her continually pawn and sell anything she had, though it were a thing she would need almost within an hour after, to procure what she had a mind to at the present."

An idealist, she was too limited by circumstance to act as she would have liked. So she managed, little by little, to cheat herself into believing that she could make a world in which the ideal might be all and the means simply taken for granted, the obstacles ignored, and the dangers forgotten. Success came only in so far as blind energy could prevail over petty material hindrances. In her daughter's incisive phrase, "she always seemed scarce able to do small things; but great ones, by the grace of God, she sometimes did." Her retreats into her own thoughts made her absent-minded, and her memory was picturesquely bad. Much of life was pleasanter forgotten than remembered—after all, she did keep accurately in mind what she read in her beloved books. She had a hot temper, and self-control she got only by fighting for it. Her unworldliness can be admired, her innocence was lovable, and her character appeals in the same way as an enthusiastic child's. But the charm of such a temperament is felt most by those who live safely at a distance, and risk nothing on its vagaries. If Falkland managed to keep his temper while the same bills were paid over and over again with his money and while fire and water, in the absence of all precautions against them, helped to reduce his slender resources, he deserves a martyr's crown. His wife's good works must have eaten up as much as he could easily make from the perquisites of the Deputyship, and he maintained later that in his life with her she cost him more than he had from the jointure she gave him. It is small wonder that in 1625 it seemed best for the Viscountess to go back to England, leaving him in Dublin to follow the trade of a politician, without having to turn so much of the profit over to God by way of Elizabeth Cary's diligent but fumbling hands.

Possibly Lord Falkland might have kept his wife with him, in spite of the danger to his purse, had there been no other reasons for her returning to England. But her eldest daughter, who three years before had married Lord Home, at the age of thirteen, was soon to be confined. Also the Viscount seems to have been afraid of war in Ireland. Two more babies had been born since the Falklands came to Dublin, and even in peace it was not a place where there could be much security for infant children and a wife. Possibly, too, the Lord Deputy may have dreamed that once in London Lady Elizabeth might persuade the great at court to give him more than he had been able to get by his letters, though he was soon to be convinced that women had no place as suitors with the ministers of the King. Finally in the background was always the ghost of his wife's Catholic leanings. If that ghost had showed itself even once to him, it would have frightened him into wanting to put her at a safe distance, lest his own faith and loyalty be made suspect by her beliefs.

Leaving Dublin was for her in every material sense the beginning of disaster. Spiritually it opened the way at last to fulfilment of her ideal. It began a new scene, really the final act of her life, and appropriately the curtain rose on storm and death. Her ship was caught in a gale and once driven back to Ireland. She sat for hours on the hatches, in the wind and spray, little Henry at her breast, and managed to save him even when a wave stunned and almost drowned him. Great ladies, at least those whose husbands left England, had then to be made of stern stuff. So had mothers; within a few months Elizabeth Cary sat by the deathbed of her eldest daughter, and watched her die from a miscarriage brought on by an accident on the journey from plague-ridden London into Oxfordshire. But even in this there was material for her web of dreams, for

21

her daughter in her last hours thought she was visited by heavenly apparitions. So did her mother, to whom such visions were as real, and more important, than anything in Whitehall or Dublin Castle.

Indomitably the Viscountess went on. She had a family to care for, for she had brought back with her not only little Henry, but the two next youngest children, as well as Victoria, now the eldest daughter. Lady Falkland found time, none the less, to plunge into her husband's business, her mind full of great schemes to aid him. But he was ungrateful. Just what she was trying to do, is not clear, but he wrote to Conway, thanking him for his favors to her, and saying that he heard she had done well in standing off his enemies at court—adding, a bit grudgingly, "though it was but an act of duty in her." This was in January, 1626. By April Cary was writing to Conway, declaring he had never doubted his wife's good intentions, but insisting he never thought well of her as a negotiator, nor made use of her for that purpose, "for," he adds, "I conceive women to be no fit solicitors of state affairs, for though it sometimes happens that they have good wits it then commonly falls out that they have over-busy natures withall." He says he would rather have her go back to her mother's than gain a great suit at court, and threatens that if Conway cannot persuade her to join Lady Tanfield, he, Cary, "must have it done some other way." A week later, still writing to Conway, he is even more explicit, complaining that from his wife's efforts to get court favors for him he has received nothing but "diminutions."

She was certainly not giving all her thought to his service, but was preparing ruin for herself, and brewing confusion for him and for her family. Once more in England, in touch with scholars and books, with a Catholic queen on the throne—to whom she had paid her respects as soon as she landed—her old doubts about religion floated up again. Her husband's Protestantism, whether dictated by principle or policy, was staunch.

She was eager, as always, to be a good wife, but there were her religious scruples to appease. Hopefully, but unrealistically, she dreamed of staying in the Church of England, but drawing as near as possible to the practice of the Catholics. To John Cosin, later Bishop of Durham, she proposed that he hear confession from her. He temporized, and declared he must have time to prepare himself. He had no wish to have his gown smirched, in the eyes of the politicians, by anything suggesting Catholic sympathies. But Elizabeth Cary, headstrong and now bent on action, would not wait. Lady Denbigh, Buckingham's sister, was toying with the idea of going over to Rome; at Lord Ormond's Catholics gathered; often with them "that worshipfull the Lady Faulkland" took part in "much good talke." She was now too much in earnest to delay, and too sharp-witted to be put off with compromise. She could not have all that she wanted as an Anglican. Wildly she imagined that she might safely become a Papist if she did not announce it publicly, thus quieting her conscience but not, she fondly believed, prejudicing her husband's interests. Lady Denbigh, not finally to turn Catholic for many years, tried to restrain her, but she was never docile when her heart was set on anything. She saw that if she were to act at all she must act alone, and calmly announced her decision to Lady Denbigh. That shrewd dame saw how serious the consequences might be, and decided to keep her friend a prisoner till she repented of her rashness. To Lady Cary she said, "Well, I have you now in the court, and here I will keep you; you shall lie in my chamber, and shall not go forth." But her captive was equal to the occasion, and pretended meekly to be content to stay. Lady Denbigh left her alone for a few minutes, and away she went. The same day she was formally received into the Church of Rome. The rites were administered by Father Dunstan in no more dignified setting than Lord Ormond's stable. Wise heads knew of laws against those who lent houses for such uses, but stables were free ground. So, at last in the bosom of her chosen church, but in the eyes of her family and indeed to some extent of the state, a heretic and apostate, she came back to Lady Denbigh, and mildly said she was now content to stay her prisoner.

This was the turning-point in Lady Cary's tragi-comic life. She had followed her heart, her conscience, and her mind, but she had set herself to swim against the tide. Never again was she to be in any real sense the wife of the man whose children she had borne, and to whose service she had so long loyally devoted her eager if blundering enthusiasm. Never again was she to be secure or comfortable in a material sense. Idealism was fixed directly counter to worldly benefits; she had chosen a minor martyrdom; the rest of her life was to be an atonement to the conventions she had defied. Her penance was to be in hardship, poverty, and worry; her satisfactions were to be solely those of the spirit.

Her poor husband was in straits enough without this last blow from a strong-willed wife. In October he wrote Sir Julius Caesar about the desperate state of his affairs, for his whole property was threatened by a suit in Chancery. In December he had news of his wife's apostasy, and he blazed forth angrily. She was now, for him, one "whom now I may say I have long unhappily called wife." She must, he proclaimed, be sent back to her mother, who might yet save her from the priests.

All this was gall to her. She had been steadfast in faithfulness to her husband, but now he wrote cruelly, called her a serpent in his bosom, and virtually cast her off. There was no hope left that her following of conscience could avoid becoming a public scandal, for Lady Denbigh, in order that her own course in the affair might seem above reproach, promptly told the tale to her brother, Buckingham, and he informed the King. What popular opinion would demand was quite clear, and Secretary Coke brought the errant lady royal commands that she was to stay a prisoner in her own house until the

King's further pleasure should be known. This was only annoying, but her husband and his agent used more brutal weapons. Her allowance was stopped; her children taken from her, together with all the servants but one, faithful Bessie Poulter; and the house was stripped of everything that could be moved, even beer, coal and wood. She was not seriously disturbed by Dr. Cosin's woe, as he cast "himself on the ground," and wept "even to roaring," but it was painful to think of the fury of the man with whom she had lived for more than twenty years. She wrote him that it was the King who had made her declare herself a Catholic. Presumably she meant that the King's notice of her private act had made it a matter of public concern. Such a defense could hardly satisfy her raging lord and master.

Fortunately there were powerful friends. The Queen herself looked kindly on this strange Englishwoman who had joined her own church, and took Elizabeth Cary's oldest daughter into her service. Lady Buckingham wrote in the Viscountess's defense; Conway and others did all they could. But the battle raged, and Lady Cary, alone with her thoughts, lost herself in her "deep and sad passion," consoling herself characteristically by writing a life of Edward II, with perhaps some ironic thoughts about the natures of royal favorites.[7]

Her father had died, but her husband demanded that she go to her mother. The King so ordered. She won a delay, and said that her mother now refused to give her any relief. She would like to go back to her husband in Ireland; if that could not be she begged that she might be banished to live in Essex near her "sister Barrett," now Lady Newburgh, the sister-in-law who alone in the Cary household had been kind to her

---

[7] For the ascription to Lady Falkland of *The History of the Life, Reign, and Death of Edward II. King of England . . . Written by E. F. in the year 1627* (London, 1680) see D. A. Stauffer, "A Deep and Sad Passion" in *The Parrott Presentation Volume* (ed. H. Craig; Princeton, 1935), especially pp. 311–314. The author of the *History* says it was written "to out-run those weary hours of a deep and sad Passion."

when she was a bride visiting her mother-in-law. Piteously she declared that she had no meat, no clothes, no drink, no money. By April 1627, her husband was openly writing about her "feminine wily pretences" and threatening a divorce; in May her mother wrote her that she must live with her husband in the religion to which she had been bred, giving up her present "ungodly lyfe." " 'I will not exsept of you," said Lady Tanfield, "and if by any exterordenary devis he cold compell you, you shall fynd the worst of it." The most she would offer was "for my part you may lyve wher you ples, if in essexe, then shall you have som such pore stuf from London as I can spar, and if you shold lyve at Cote [Coates], ther is yet som stuf that may sarve your turn."

Elizabeth Cary now wrote directly to the King, telling him her mother would do nothing for her, and imploring him to order her husband to pay her enough weekly for food, shelter, and clothes. Incidentally she tried to lay at least one bit of malicious gossip, and showed she had learned something of the price she must pay for her faith. "I heard by a person of quality," she writes, "that your Majesty was pleased to believe that I altered my . . . religion upon some court hopes . . . yet judge me not so foolish as to understand so little in the state of this time, as to think promotions likely to come that way. . . . I desire nothing but a quiet life, and to reobtain my lord's favour, which I have done nothing to lose but what I could not, with a safe conscience, leave undone. . . . I had rather sustain any misery than petition to be supplied contrary to my lord's will, to which I have and will submit me as far as till I be obliged in conscience not to suffer myself to perish."

She made part of her case, at least, and in June Charles I directed that Falkland's agent take steps to care for his master's deserted wife. To this it was answered that if Lady Falkland would go to Oxfordshire, her mother would give up her house there to her, and Lord Falkland would allow her £500 a year. But a few weeks later her husband wrote to the Lord Treasurer, saying nothing of £500. Instead he coldly promised that if his wife would go to her mother's house at Coates, he would pay her through her mother "such allowance as I will make her." Acidly, he wished that she had a conscience to be touched. For him she was "replete with serpentine subtelty . . . conjoined with Roman hypocrisy." The news of her hardships did not touch him, and he retorted that for all of him "such an imposture pirdigall" as he knew her to be, "might eat hashes with hogs or live of alms."

By July 20 the King was insisting that something be done. Even if Catholic converts were to be publicly frowned upon, it was not likely to bring him credit to have a lady of his court actually starve, and it was poor policy to press too far anyone for whom the Queen and the Duchess of Buckingham would plead. Lady Cary, too, had begun to take a sturdier tone, and she told Conway cogently enough that though she did not like to have her husband displeased, "where the question is whether he should be displeased or I starved, it will admit no dispute."

Accordingly she tried to earmark for herself the proceeds of a suit her husband had brought for revenues he thought were due him for certain pipestaves. Nothing could have irritated him more, or have added more to the complicated position of his affairs in London. She was put off with a promise that the King would find some other way to help her.

At last, in September, there was definite prospect of some final agreement as to "her present necessity." To Conway she wrote fulsome thanks—quixotically including a request that he do something to save from prison a Catholic taken in her house. She was still so deep in her cloud-cuckoo land that she did not fully realize her plight. She was an offender against orthodoxy, lifted precariously out of downright want by the good offices of a few friends. Yet she was so sure of her own righteousness that she was blind to the absurdity—even dan-

27

ger—of trying to be at the same time an advocate for another, caught in the very net of prejudice in which she had snared herself.

On October 4 the Privy Council commanded Falkland to provide for his wife "meat, drink, and all other necessaries . . . and nine servants to attend her" at Coates; to supply "furniture and horses . . . wearing-clothes and wearing-linen . . . and one hundred pounds per annum . . . over and above, for her private expenses"; or, in lieu of this, to give her £500 a year. In addition, he was to pay her debts, amounting to £272-15-6, with such various items as £50-0-0 each owed to the Countess of Buckingham and to Lady Hastings, £15-0-0 to the chandler, £4-10-0 to the baker, £3-12-0 to the brewer and £6-13-6 to the butcher.

Her daughter has it that once the Privy Council had ordered her husband to care for her up to £500 a year, she refused to accept that sum from him. This is hardly probable, though it would fit in well with her zeal for principle and her contempt for mere money. In any case, even in the face of the Council's order, sent to him on October 31, Lord Falkland was stubborn. By May, 1628, he had not obeyed. The King ordered the Council to subtract from his salary the amount he had been ordered to pay his wife. He insisted that her "humour" was "so vast, that an Indies will no more suffice her vanity than the meanest limited portion." He would not and could not pay as he had been commanded, but did agree, in spite of his straitened circumstances, to allow her £300 a year. But he begged that she be forbidden to come within ten miles of the court.

The whole sordid chapter was nearing its end, however, and in August, 1629, Falkland was recalled from Ireland, with heavy charges about his conduct as Lord Deputy resting against him. He was in a tight place financially, and though he wrote vigorously in his own defense, his enemies were as outspoken. Back in London he can have had little time to devote to his wife's affairs—even to such as were subjects of public comment, as was her joining in November a party of fourteen hundred knights, ladies, and gentlemen, and one hundred and fifty priests, for a pilgrimage to Saint Winifred's well. Bad as this was in her husband's eyes, it was less serious than his need of money and the threats of his enemies. He concentrated on defending himself against the charges urged against him, and on trying once more to make profits at court. He contrived to hold his own, at least, and by November, 1629, he was again on the Privy Council and had been defended by the Lords Justices of Ireland, who wrote of his virtues as Lord Deputy.

He was still too poor to keep up a proper establishment. For the most part he lived with his relatives and friends. As for his wife, when the Queen herself intervened to bring about peace in the family, he generously agreed. They lived together, if at all, only for a short time one summer, but she had the satisfaction of believing that her lord was no longer displeased with her, and he achieved enough superficial tolerance so that he could talk of some day letting her have a chapel for her own priests. On the tragic day of his fall in Theobald's Park, she hurried to him. Through the hours when bad surgeons and primitive medical methods tortured him to death, she was by his side. She was to see how a Cavalier could die, and if she still remembered his cruelty to her, she could at least be proud now of his courage. In all his torment he made but one complaint, "Oh, softly," during the probing of his gangrened leg. She longed to have him share the joys she had found in religion, and talked much to him of her faith. When he was urged to say he was still a Protestant, lest the world think he had yielded to her, he was too proud to reveal his heart, and dismissed his questioners with: "Pray do not interrupt my silent meditation." She clung to the belief that he died convinced of Catholic truth, and his daughter believed that his wife prevented his making public profession of his change of faith, lest it injure the future of his children. However, neither to Lady Cary nor to anyone else did he give any sure sign. It was probably enough for him to be able to wrap himself in memories of loyalty to two kings and of unflinching support of his class and calling, and then to die stoically unafraid of what lay beyond the world in which to be a gentleman and a courtier had been all.

Of course, the imps of comedy can make much of Elizabeth Cary's life from 1625 to 1633. For them Lord Falkland is just a stiff-necked, stupid, would-be statesman, tied to a stubborn and extravagant wife, trying in vain to assert authority over her, and, because the Queen bade him, meekly making peace with her. The same imps would have much fun with Bessie Poulter, the only one of Lady Falkland's servants whom she could keep in the lean years. Bessie was Scottish, and was sure priests were witches, but she believed her mistress was a saint, and she became a Catholic out of loyalty not to God but to Lady Falkland. They were a strange pair. The one, dining with Lord Ormond's servants because the larder was bare at home, and smuggling back to her mistress such table scraps as she could get; the other, writing poems to the Virgin, or on the lives of St. Agnes and St. Elizabeth, reading constantly, patiently translating Cardinal DuPerron, sleeping in a chair when there was no bed, so absent-minded that sometimes she could not remember what she wanted or where she was. Thus, once when she burned her hand, she called for beer. She knew she wanted something—what she could not think. She used to forget the faces of her friends, to forget even that she was living in a tumble-down cottage, with no furniture except a flock bed on the ground, an old hamper which did as a table, and a wooden stool. She would fancy she was still mistress of an establishment, and would clap her hands and call for the servants when there was no one to hear but the faithful Bessie. She was beset by creditors, and when she had money she would give it to them gladly and as forgetfully as in Ireland.

When she had nothing, she was annoyed at being troubled. She built up an elaborate rationalization so that she preferred to beg from her friends rather than to borrow, which irritated them and made her lot no easier. She was an ardent Catholic but was too forgetful to remember Fast Days and often had to be reminded of her duty. She was generous to a fault and money meant nothing to her unless it were spent for what she needed or, better, given to further God's work as she understood it. She was "never in her greatest scarcity . . . able to refuse a little (when she had it) to those that it would relieve. . . . Whatsoever she had had in the morning, she would have had nothing left at night, unless she should have found none that did need, or would ask; . . . she was almost . . . certain to go to bed without money . . . unless some friend of hers had got it out of her hands to keep it for her." Her only care for outward appearance came from her wish not to offend her critical children, but where their prejudices were not likely to be outraged she did not in the least mind the ridicule of smart London. Dumpy in figure, wearing rusty black, with neither money nor maids to dress her as she once had dressed, discarding, in order to save expense, even her "chopins" ("high slippers for low women" which she wore to increase her stature), she padded about London on foot, importuning courtiers and even the King himself. At home she had her books and her writing, and she could always sleep. When she was with scholars—and some still came to see her—she talked volubly, interrupted only by frequent fits of coughing. If there was no one to talk to, she could always spin verses, or lose herself in clouds of speculation and devout meditation.

But poor Bessie Poulter, bewildered by the sight of a mistress who acted so little like a great lady and gave such clear signs of being "fey," would have had no patience with the imps of comedy. For her the whole strange play in which she had a minor part was no farce, and if she could not understand the blazing individual idealism which had reduced Lady

Falkland to poverty, she could at least see, beneath the drab costume and setting, the true quality of a generous woman who had brought her up, taught her, and, in bad days when there was nothing in the house but fish, had contented herself with the water in which they were boiled in order that her poor Scottish waiting-woman might have what little solid food there was.

Her husband dead, Lady Falkland began again a weary campaign for something to live on. One resource was her eldest son—Lucius, now Viscount in his turn. He was not a Catholic, but like his mother was absorbed in books and fascinated with ideas. They disagreed—perhaps they were too much alike—and she was usually too proud to let him know how poor she was. For his part he knew her too well to help her except with caution, lest her carelessness of money waste his own slender fortune. As he wrote the King, he did not wish to bind himself to pay any fixed allowance but to do what he could for his mother "in free gifts." For she had, as he said, "no over-frugal disposition," an understatement which was, he added, the most that it became him to say. Knowing her, he felt that a little which she did not expect would help her more than larger sums which she could count on and so might recklessly spend.

Her husband's death ended one of Elizabeth Cary's major loyalties. There was left her church, and into its service she plunged with the same energy, and the same disregard of practical considerations, that had marked her whole uneasy life. She yearned to bring her children into the fold. Lucius was either a Protestant, or, worse, one whose rationalistic approach to the whole problem was leading him to question the authority of any church. He put her off by saying he could not yet make any final decision; she turned her zeal to his brothers and sisters. One was a lady-in-waiting to the Queen. The others she had in her charge. Shrewdly she saw that she could not press them too hard. For one thing it would have been unsafe to do so, lest she rouse once more the wrath of official English Protestantism. Quite as important was her sense that her oddities might easily make her, in their eyes, just a ridiculous bore. They had been taken from her in 1625. She was not rich enough to keep them with her now, though whenever she could she had them share her modest lodgings. But, however cautious she was in not trying openly to convert them, she was ready to fight anyone who sought to fix them in a way of belief other than hers.

It was thus that William Chillingworth, remembered still as an advocate of tolerance, one of the great so-called "rationalists" of his century, suddenly became for her a villain in the piece. He had been converted to Catholicism, and so endeared himself to her; he was a close friend of her eldest son; he could and did pose as her firm ally. But he turned back again from Catholicism, and justly or not she believed he wanted to win her children for Protestantism or godlessness. Matters came to a crisis when Patrick and Henry, the two youngest, were staying with Lucius Cary at Great Tew. Chillingworth, the agent of error, was there; it was for her as the champion of truth and light to protect her boys. The little drama was her last defiance of the practical world she lived in; the last proof of her unconquerable zeal. However petty its theme, it was, in terms of character, a fitting last appearance for her in the strong light of court and state.

She hit on the mad idea of saving her two little sons from Chillingworth's evil influence, by kidnapping them from Great Tew. She had no means of supporting them; she must have known that it was a serious matter to offend even a young Viscount Falkland; and she was surely aware of what view the government would take if she, a Catholic, snatched two brothers from a Protestant lord, if there were the slightest reason to suspect—and there was much—that they were stolen in order to be delivered to the Church of Rome. Nor was it easy to plan a kidnapping without money. But such considerations were not of the kind to hold Elizabeth Cary back. Bessie Poulter might wring her hands, but her mistress's "working head" was active again, and all her maid could do was tremble in her kitchen and mutter her newly learned Catholic prayers as charms against the trouble she feared must come from her lady's mad determination to serve her God.

One day a messenger, Harry Auxley, brought a letter to Anne Cary, Lady Falkland's daughter, who was with her two younger brothers at Great Tew. The hand was disguised, fortunately, since Chillingworth peeked suspiciously at it, but Anne knew whose it was, and loyally followed the instructions in the letter. The next morning at three, when it was still dark, the little boys got up, ostensibly to wake their sisters who had talked of rising early since they had that day "much business." The children took care for an hour to be noisy enough to assure everyone that they were in the house, and then bolted. The young Carys had something of their father's courage, and whatever their fears of lonely roads and strange men, they ran breathlessly into the half-light of the morning. A mile from the house they found Auxley and one George Spurrier, "whose persons were no way promising nor apt to encourage the children," waiting with horses. Guided by them they set off for Abingdon, vastly excited by the adventure, but dreading every sound that suggested pursuit. At the sight of a coach or horse, they rode off the road; in Oxford, they dismounted, and without hats or cloaks, tried to look like boys of the town. These devices worked and they got undetected to Abingdon, where they were to be met by a gentleman, Alexander Smyth, and by him taken down the river in a boat to London. But the boatmen were drunk and they had perforce to decide to stay in Abingdon for the night. Their escorts quarrelled, and let out the secret that they were stolen children. "The town was raised, and the constable came to seize on them." One of their attendants somehow disarmed the suspicions of the constable, who was fortunately an old friend, but the narrowness of the escape proved there was no safety in Abingdon. So at ten o'clock of a dark night they set out in a boat, "with watermen not only not able to row, but ready every minute to overturn the boat with reeling and nodding." Somehow they got to London, as overjoyed as Lady Falkland at the safe outcome of the risky adventure she had planned for them.

The kidnapping, of course, had been quickly discovered, and there was no doubt as to who was behind it. So, in May, 1636, Elizabeth Cary was haled before the Privy Council. For all her absent-mindedness, her wits were quick. She had hidden the children out of her own house, and she was quite able to face cross-examination. She admitted she had sent for the boys, and "had disposed of them as she had thought good," denying that there was in this anything for which she could be held. She made a perfect case for the legality of her act. She was told that to send children to Catholic seminaries was against the law. Actually the children were in London, but astutely she saw that to admit this might make it harder for her to keep them hidden or later to smuggle them out. She therefore asked blandly that the Lords of the Council prove that she had sent them to seminaries, and added that even to send them to France would have been no crime and no proof that they had been committed to priests. She clearly hoped that if pursuit were diverted across the Channel her sons might be safe for the time at least in England. When the Lords pointed out that it was illegal to leave the country without license and attempted to prove it by showing the orders to port officers to let no one sail who had not the proper papers, she glibly said such orders were all very well but were not addressed to her, but simply to officers of the state. If she had sent her children abroad, the sending was no crime; if the officers had let them sail, the officers not she should be questioned. This was too much. One of the Lords asked angrily if she meant to teach them law. Her retort was that she only wanted them to remember what they knew already, adding mildly that she was, after all, a lawyer's daughter. Quite off the track by now, her inquisitors pressed her to give the name of the man who had taken her sons to France. She said—quite truthfully—that she did not know it. The "collapsed lady" was too much for the Lords of the Privy Council. They issued a warrant referring her to Chief Justice Bramston, and, in the event that she did not satisfy him, committing her to the Tower.

The Chief Justice treated her civilly, but got no information whatever. By now she must have been thoroughly enjoying this game with the pompous officers of the state, whose skill was less than a match for her wit, and she asked Bramston gravely, "how she was to be conveyed to the Tower, to which she stood committed, if he were not satisfied. He acknowledged he knew not what more to say to her . . . and offered her his coach home." He was not eager, apparently, to press the case. He summoned Lady Cary's daughters, but when they came they were told he was busy. They did not wait, and "they never heard more from him." The Council voted to examine their mother again, and declared that if she continued to give "uncertain and illusory answers" and to "use the like subtilties as heretofore," she should be sent a prisoner to the Tower. But there is no record that she ever did tell them what they wanted, or that the threat of imprisonment was ever carried out. Apparently in January, 1637, the Council did vote that she should be "confined to such place as" the Lord Treasurer should think fit, but this probably amounted to no more than her being required to live where the authorities could find her. In any case, by then the boys were safe overseas and she cared nothing for the mutterings of the King's baffled officers.

Indeed, there is reason to believe that they were more afraid of her than she of them. The men who had escorted the children on their way to London, and one Mrs. Mullens, in whose care they were for a time, were examined. One of them was jailed. Lady Cary promptly threatened to sue her husband's brother-in-law, Lord Newburgh, one of the examiners, for the false imprisonment of her servant. He knew her mettle, and said the sentence had been the Chief Justice's. He denied it; the officers of the law turned tail before the irate old lady. The man was released, search for the boys failed, they got to France and into Catholic hands, and their mother's last skirmish with the state ended in triumph.

By 1639 England was swiftly drawing to a social and political crisis, but six of Lady Cary's children were Catholics, and four of them were in the Benedictine order.[8] Archbishop Laud's complaints to the King had failed; his zeal to call her before the High Commission for her crimes, came to nothing. Alone with Bessie Poulter, she could rest unworried by troubles of state, now that her work was done. When Lucius Cary came to London she could flare up once more into long, eager theological debates; her eyes must still have quickened when there was printed an attack on, or an able defense of, her faith. In the writings of Blosius, a Flemish Benedictine monk, she found a new subject for her skill as a translator. But her cough was growing steadily worse; she was definitely "in a consumption," and the days when she could be active and keep her dowdy figure a familiar one at court, were past. Yet she could still manage to supply yarn and wool for the poor, her neighbors, to work on, and this must have raised ghosts of her Irish sojourn and the days when her crowded workshops in Ireland had been her joy.

There is no reason to suppose she was unhappy. Childish griefs, mockery, revilings from her husband, threatenings from bishops and judges, hunger, dingy houses—all these she could laugh at now. She had found "the Sun at noon," a faith by which she could live, and it had kept her uncowed by all

---

[8] Anne and Elizabeth were Catholics as early as July, 1634, and Mary, at least by Dec. 1635. *CSP, Domestic, 1634–1635*, p. 159; *Id., 1635*, p. 578.

that she had to bear. Was she not safe in the hope her church held out? Had she not been the loyal wife of a brave man, whose abuse she had repaid, as she saw it, always with good? Had she not dreamed that he died reconciled not only to her but to her church? Had she not brought her children and his into the right path? And along the way there had been much that was good to look back upon. Books, plays, her own verses, the dedication to her of *Englands Helicon* and of Marston's *Works*—it was happiness to remember these. It was happiness to know that the Queen herself had always been kind and comforting, and to have her Majesty's grant to pay some of her many debts. There were still a few in London who would gladly call her friend. In her sickness, there was even Lady Morison, mother of her son's wife, a Protestant, but a kind and gracious woman, to ease her last hours. Proud of her service of her own beliefs, mercifully not quite aware of what her self-will had cost others, she cared not at all for having been frowned on at court, for having been called a disgrace to her family, or for the fact that a grave archbishop ordered her translation of part of DuPerron to be publicly burned. She had lived well. What was there to fear in death? There was not even agony, and in October, 1639, she slept quietly out of a world where her idealism had meant strife, into one in which, she believed, the weakest saint might be rewarded for staunchness in faith.

ELIZABETH, VISCOUNTESS FALKLAND

*Reproduced by permission of W. A. Call, Monmouth,
from a photograph of an effigy on the Tanfield tomb
in the church at Burford, Oxfordshire*

III

THE "TERCEL GENTLE"

The Boyhood of Lucius Cary, 1610–1630

AT NINETEEN Sir Lucius Cary, Lady Falkland's eldest son, was committed to a London jail.[1] It was his first taste of what it meant to be a rebel; it was the price of an illusion. He had fancied that when his pride was hurt and his standard of justice outraged, he might trust to his courage to see him through. But the Lords of the Council, his father among them, saw only folly in such youthful dreams. It was well for a boy to be ready to fight; it was well for him to cherish a sense of his dignity and rank, but it was nonsense for him to stand out against a royal decree. Honor and justice were, in such cases, what the King's will made them. The individual who insisted on his own definitions was at best a fool and at worst an enemy of the state.

Sir Lucius Cary was neither, but he had laid himself open to suspicion, and an order of the Privy Council on January 17, 1630, directed the Warden of the Fleet Prison to keep him in custody until further order. There were even threats of a Star Chamber action. Some months before, Cary had been deprived of the command of a company of foot, given him

---

[1] There is no record of the exact date of Cary's birth, but 1610 is commonly accepted. It accords with Clarendon's account and with what is known of the dates of birth of his brothers and sisters.

earlier by his father, then Lord Deputy of Ireland. The company had now been assigned by the Irish Lords Justices to Sir Francis Willoughby. Lucius, smarting at the slight put upon him, promptly challenged Willoughby, who was also in London, to a duel.[2]

"Sir," he wrote, "Yf I had knowne certeinly afore the other daye that youe had my company, and afore yesterdaye where your lodginge was, youe had afore nowe heard from me. Now I heare youe are to goe towardes Ireland on Mundaye, to which I shalbe a little Remora.[3] I only desire youe to excuse me that I send a sarvant of myne, and not a freind, on such a buisines, for it is toe short a tyme toe make a freind in, and I have none ready made. I doe confesse youe a brave gentleman (and for myne own sake I would not but have my adversary be soe), but I knowe no reason why, therfore, youe showld have my company, any more then why therfore you showld have my breeches, which yf every brave man showld have, I should be fayne shortly toe begg in trowses. I dowght not but youe will give me satisfaction with your sworde, of which yf you will send me the lengthe, with tyme and place, youe shalbe sure (accordingly toe the appointment) toe meete

LUCIUS CARY."

Willoughby was probably older than Sir Lucius, and more experienced. He was surprised by the challenge, and might well either have laughed at it, or have trusted his sword to teach its author more meekness. Instead, perhaps touched by Cary's spirit, he tried to smooth things over by politeness. He pointed out that he had not asked for the company and

---

[2] For Willoughby, see Gardiner, *History*, VIII, 255, X, 53. He was probably the Sir Francis knighted at Dublin, Oct. 30, 1610; W. A. Shaw, *Knights of England*, II, 150.

[3] "Remora" in Cary's letter means simply "delay, hindrance"; "trowses" were "originally a close-fitting article of attire for the buttocks and thighs"— garments to be worn under breeches. See *New English Dictionary*, "trouse."

so had intended no injury. He hinted that it was the duty of a good courtier simply to obey. He himself, he remarked piously, had "lost better fortunes by following his Majesty then any" he had yet received. He went further, and virtually warned Cary that the challenge was in effect rebellion against "an ackt of his Majesties, whoe dowghtles will mayntayne it."

The answer to this was a visit from Captain Rainsford, an Oxfordshire friend of Cary's, now acting as his second.[4] He left no doubt of Sir Lucius's temper. "He tells me," Willoughby wrote, "that youe rest unsatisfied . . . becawse I have accepted of that company which was . . . taken from youe by his Majesty. . . . Further he tells me that, in regard youe can not strike at the hande, youe must and will strike at the stone that lies lower." Then, with one last reminder that Cary's only complaint was against his royal master, Willoughby agreed to a duel at Bristol.

Apparently the meeting never took place. The story leaked out, and both Cary and Rainsford were promptly imprisoned. Willoughby may have told the secret, feeling that there was no reason why he should delay his sailing for Ireland and risk a wound from an impetuous boy with a fancied grievance and more courage than sense. Perhaps Sir Lucius was so angry that he talked too freely. In any event the damp

---

[4] Rainsford seems to have been Francis Rainsford, knighted as "a captain" in 1632 (Shaw, II, 200). See E. A. Buckland, *The Rainsford Family* (Worcester, 1932?), *passim*. He was "cousin german" of Sir Francis Nethersole, whom Cary knew, and was a connection of the Rainsfords who sold Great Tew to the Tanfields in 1610 and were connections of Cary's mother, through the Lees. Francis Rainsford's brother, Sir Henry, married Anne Goodere, in whose father's household Michael Drayton was a page and protégé. Drayton's dedication in 1597 praising Cary's mother (p. 10 *ante*), then only twelve, and his calling her his "honoured Mistres," suggest that he may for a time have been her tutor or in some other capacity a member of the Tanfields' household. This might indicate that the Gooderes were somehow linked with the Tanfields, and they were probably connected with the Carys, through the Manners family. Ben Jonson is said to have visited Rainsford's family; by 1630 Cary knew Jonson. Cf. W. Berry, *Pedigrees of Hertfordshire Families* (London, n.d.), p. 188; J. Donne, *Poems* (ed. H. J. C. Grierson; Oxford, 1912), II, 144-145.

walls of the Fleet stood to keep such as he out of mischief, and inside them he had time to digest his lesson. His company he had likened to his breeches—the fact was that the breeches were the King's to dispose of as he chose. Cary had had to be taught that even if one did not strike against the royal hand itself, one could be bruised by the stone that the hand moved.

Londoners who heard of the affair no doubt fed the legend that Viscount Falkland's eldest son was "very wild, and also mischievous, as being apt to stabbe and doe bloudy mischiefs." His challenge was in terms that seemed "to make too bold with the king." His mother, probably, was too absorbed in her own precarious career to be greatly concerned, and after all she had never been hesitant about defying the law when her principles were at stake. But her husband, fighting hard to get back prestige at court, beset by debts, scheming for profit, and largely dependent on royal favor, must have regarded his son's disgrace with disgust. It was bad enough to be cursed with a Catholic wife; must he put up with a graceless boy who had not yet learned the elements of political decorum? He could not protect himself by disowning Lucius, for a marriageable son was an asset, and he had long hoped that a rich bride for him might repair the family fortunes. But who was likely to take a husband from jail, or marry a young knight sentenced by the Star Chamber?

Fortunately Viscount Falkland was no novice at court, and not the man to waste time in idle rage. He went busily to work. Richard Boyle, the Earl of Cork, had been his friend in Ireland. His daughter, Katherine, was about to marry the son of Viscount Ranelagh. To him Falkland talked on January 26, about "Lucius his imprisonment and his entended Starr Chamber menace," after which he noted his "confidence the conclusion wylbe fayre, but to be kept secrett." The next day the Warden of the Fleet had a warrant "to set at liberty the person of Sir Lucius Cary." On February 1, Falkland saw

Ranelagh again—it would be bad if the Earl of Cork, who was rich and still had unmarried daughters, should get too black a picture. Five days later Falkland proudly wrote that Lucius's freedom had been achieved "with honor to boath of us," and entered in his minute book: "The Kinges favour and countenance to me."

Ranelagh was not the only courtier to whom Falkland talked. The way to get things done at Whitehall was to interest those whose rank and wealth made their words count with the King and Council. He knew that the way to succeed with "courtiers' affections" was to "solicit . . . with importunity." Buckingham, Falkland's old benefactor, was dead, but he had made new allies.[5] Moreover, in this case he appealed directly to the King. His petition to his sovereign was shrewdly calculated to tickle Charles I's vanity, and exposes vividly some central items in Falkland's worldly creed.

"I had a son," he wrote, "until I lost him, in your Highness's Displeasure, where I cannot seek him, because I have not Will to find him there." Fatherhood was less than loyalty. Lucius was now no son, but merely "a wild young Man . . . Prisoner in the *Fleet*." But, according to his father, he was ready to "bow and humble" himself before the King. This being so—or alleged—would royal Charles display the "Glory of the supremest Powers," forgiveness? "When it is extended in the greatest Measure," the letter goes on, "it converts the greatest Offenders into the greatest Lovers. . . . If now Your Majesty will vouchsafe, out of Your own Benignity, to become a second Nature, and restore that unto me which the first gave me, and Vanity deprived me of, I shall keep my Reckoning of the full Number of my Sons with Comfort . . . else my weak old Memory must forget one." This was the

---

[5] The Duchess of Buckingham, Catherine Manners, was Viscount Falkland's second cousin, and his sister, Frances, married Sir George Manners, the duchess's uncle. (F. Harrison), *The Devon Carys* (N. Y., 1920), II, 399, 401, 415; I. Eller, *History of Belvoir Castle* (London, 1841), chart facing p. 1.

true vein. A courtier had to know how to be servile, how to set a Stuart as high as Nature, and how to profess that to disown a son were better than to risk a royal frown.

Probably Charles cared very little about Sir Lucius Cary's offense, and was ready enough to overlook it. It was all the more easy after being flattered, and easier still since it was clearly profitable to keep the good will of any man with powerful connections and friends. The King had many critics, Englishmen who seemed flirting with disloyalty, and this made doubly precious those who, as long as they had favors, were uncritically devoted and wrote petitions showing a healthily unreasoning awe of the sovereign's divine right. So the King was pleased to be gracious and "on representation made to him . . . stopped . . . further punishment." Sir Lucius was set free, and Falkland could dismiss from his "weak old Memory" all recollection of his son's "Vanity." But he did not dismiss the fact that his son had not been paid in full for the time he held his command, and more than two years later the Viscount was busily writing to collect the "Arreares dicw to Lucius Cary and his Company for the haulf yeare endeing . . . Sept. 1629."

Trivial as the whole affair was, it sets in relief some features of Sir Lucius Cary's character when he was barely twenty. His courage and his hot sense of his own rights, are both obvious. So are his inexperience of the world, and his "Vanity" in supposing that the will of a Stuart king might be treated by a courtier otherwise than as law. One sentence in his father's petition poses the dilemma implicit in Lucius Cary's whole life, and bites deep into a basic problem of the age in which he was to make of his short career a noble failure. In his father's words his fault had been "measuring his Actions by his own private Sence." That had been his mother's fault too, though she had at last submerged her "private sense" in her faith in the infallibility of her church. It was to be the fault of many Englishmen in the next twenty years, led by "private sense" to heresies, violence, and civil war. It was to be peculiarly the fault—or the central merit—of Lucius Cary. His imperious individualism was to lure him to worship of reason and passionate allegiance to a free quest for truth in a world in which reason and love of truth were frail weapons against circumstance.

But in 1630 all this lay ahead. His ten days in the Fleet may have sowed doubts of the justice of kings and courts, but until then, at least, his experience had been pretty well limited by the courtier's horizon. For the first twelve years of his life, until 1622, he had lived chiefly in Oxfordshire, in Burford, where he was born, or in Great Tew, making the most of whatever small boys could learn in country villages. Dogs, horses, hawks; hunting, fishing; the life of farms, hard-worked tenants and the chances of drought and flood; peaceful parish churches echoing the rhythms of the Book of Common Prayer; great estates of country gentlemen and noblemen; vistas of gentle landscape; glimpses of busy Oxford with its growing colleges and clusters of students—all these were in his pattern of impressions. More practical were the lessons taught by the household in which he lived. Sir Lawrence Tanfield, his mother's father, had taken him at birth to be brought up as his heir. Of his own mother and father he saw little in the days when she was doing her best to be a good wife and Sir Henry was using every means to improve his fortune and his rank, coming at last to be a Viscount instead of a mere knight, and Lord Deputy of Ireland instead of a lesser gentleman in the King's household. But about ways of advancing in the world, Tanfield and his wife were tutors as able as Sir Henry Cary, and their methods were justified by success. In 1607 Tanfield was made Chief Baron of the Exchequer, proof of his value in official circles. He had wealth and managed to keep it, and all signs point to his having lost no chance to increase it. Whether he was, in fact, a cruel landlord, guilty of extortion, fond of bribes, and willing to cheat even his relatives for profit, may not be proved, but his poorer neighbors accused him of all this and more. Even three centuries after his death villagers in Great Tew, to whom the name Falkland means a sign over an inn door, remember the "unjust judge," whose deeds were so evil that for years his restless ghost used to drive in a coach and six around a tree in the park at midnight. Such posthumous fame testifies to the sinister light in which his contemporaries saw him, and some of them, at least, thought his wife as bad. If she was harsh to her errant daughter, she was, if the stories are to be believed, even more merciless to her tenants.

Fortunately no boy of twelve was likely to understand fully how rising lawyers and prosperous landowners grew rich, and got themselves hated by the country folk. For Lucius Cary, wealth meant only handsome houses, "lands, money, howshould stufe, juells and plate," good clothes and good living, things which he was not so eccentric as to dislike. Similarly, when he saw his father and mother he was not likely to waste time in ethical speculations about Sir Henry Cary's career or his mother's anxious searchings of her conscience. Naturally, in 1620, he must have been delighted at the news that his father had been created Viscount, because thereby he became heir to a title, and titles had great value in the eyes of a gentleman's son.

There were duller things to think of, too. Studying, for example, with this or that writing master or tutor. He seems to have been entered at St. John's College, Cambridge, when he was eleven. Whether he actually went to the university or not, is not clear. If he did, he did not stay long, for in 1622 he went joyfully to join his parents on their pilgrimage to Ireland.[6] It was a progress of great pomp, preceded by his

---

[6] T. Baker, *History of the College of St. John the Evangelist, Cambridge* (ed. J. E. B. Mayor; Cambridge, 1869), I, 206n., 263, says Cary was a member of St. John's in 1621. *Id.*, I, 531-532, prints a letter to him from the college and his reply, Jan. 16, 1642. In the letter he speaks of himself as a St.

elder sister's wedding to Earl Home in the presence of the King. There he had a chance to admire his father's noble bearing; his mother, painstakingly adorned by her maids; the splendor of a ceremony at court; the glitter of a life that was new to him. If he was sorry to have his thirteen-year-old sister go off to Scotland, there was abundant chance to forget it in the magnificence of the journey westward to the coast. Eight coaches and two hundred horsemen powdered the weeds by the roadside with dust, while six carts creaked under the weight of the goods necessary to furnish and equip the Lord Deputy and his family. Those carts Lucius may have remembered later, for they linked themselves with the richest experience of his youth. They were furnished by Sir Richard Morison, Lieutenant of the Ordnance, whose son became Cary's closest friend.

The Carys landed at Howth, late in the evening of Friday, September 6, 1622. The Lord of Howth entertained them that night, and the next afternoon, half-way to Dublin, they were met by a delegation headed by Sir Adam Loftus. On Sunday the Lord Deputy was installed with proper ceremony. The Lords Justices went in procession from Dublin Castle to Christ Church, with the King's sword, symbol of the Deputy's authority, "borne before them by Sir Charles Coote." After them rode Falkland himself, attended by Lord Wilmot of Athlone. In Christ Church the Bishop of Meath preached, the sword of office was delivered to Viscount Falkland, and he ended the ritual by making his first use of his new powers in knighting "Mr. Cary Lambert, second son of Lord Lambert." Finally the whole assembly returned to the Castle "in solemnity of estate." All this was calculated to impress Lucius with his father's importance, just as he must have been impressed with his mother's quite different achieve-

---

John's man and of the college as "the seed-plott" for his "fruites." He writes "Yet S^r as little Learning as I brought from you, and as little as I have since encreased and watered what I did bring . . . ," which seems to mean that he actually studied in Cambridge for a time.

ments if she showed him the two sonnets William Basse had
written on her leaving England. The verses were not distinguished; neither was the poet, and he probably wrote them
as a shrewd bid for patronage from a woman who might be
generous to a wit who lived by the favor of the great. Still,
it was something to be assured that the praises of Lady Falkland would precede her to Ireland, and that she was

> "everywhere
> In worth, but where the world of worth doth fayle."

A mother thus flattered for her familiarity with the Muses,
and a father bred "from . . . youth in courts and camps, the
schools of honor and vertue," with a "reputation every way
becominge a gentleman," who had "obteyned unsought a degree of high honor from the bounteous hands of" his sovereign—these were surely the most immediate influences on
Cary in his early teens.

Dublin, of course, had the zest of a new scene, spiced with
the romantic sense of strange, even dangerous, unknown
things not far away. From the towers of the Castle where
the Deputy and his family lived one could look back to Howth
and the sea; there were the woods of Clontarf, the slopes
above Merrion, and farther, the Killiney hills. There were
town streets, tilled fields, and, beyond, barren wild country
sure to be peopled in Lucius's mind with the Irish of whom
he had read, and his mother once had written, some of them
barbarous, and many of them unruly subjects for an English
Lord Deputy.

Nor was Ireland, with its new sights and sounds, its splendid dogs, and such terrifying excitements as the fall of one
of the Castle towers, to be summed up by Dublin. At Youghal
was Richard Boyle, the great Earl of Cork, growing richer
day by day, powerful in politics and wide-awake to the usefulness of a well-disposed Deputy in Dublin. He was open-
handed to the Falklands. Two casts of falcons came from him

to the Viscount; there was gold for Lady Cary to sink in her
trade school, and for Lucius, a grey "barbary" horse and a
"tercel gentle"—a male falcon. Boyle's coming to Dublin to
visit the Lord Deputy was a great event, and it was even more
exciting for Lucius to set out with his father and mother to
visit him. The Earl met them at Limerick. Thence they went
to Kilmallock, to Moallo, and to Cork, and at Bandonbridge
the whole party was entertained for four days by Sir Francis
Slingsby and by Boyle. There was a side trip to Kinsale, and
while the Earl went back to Youghal to prepare a proper
reception, his guests visited Cloyne. On August 26, 1624, they
were greeted at Youghal by the Earl with forty gentlemen
and a hundred horsemen, and rode grandly through the town,
with the sword of the Deputyship carried before Falkland by
his host. For four days the Carys and the Earl of Thomond,
Lord President of Munster, and "all their traynes" sampled
Boyle's opulent hospitality.

Of special interest for Lucius, and in another way for his
father, were the Earl of Cork's children. Sarah, the second
daughter, was a widow at fourteen; Lettice, Cork's "dear,
dear daughter, one of the best women in the world," was close
to Lucius's age; Katherine was a little girl of ten, and Dorothy
was only six. Falkland was most concerned with the daughters,
for he was already hoping to marry his son to one of them.
Of the sons, Francis and Roger were still infants, Lewis was
only five, but Richard was eleven and old enough to be a
companion for Lucius. Their boyish acquaintance seems to
have ripened into friendship, and to Elizabeth Clifford, who
married Richard Boyle in 1634, Cary wrote letters even in
the last troubled months of his life. Katherine Boyle, too, later
Viscountess Ranelagh, made a friend of the English boy she
met in her father's house in 1624 and after his death wrote
warmly of him.[7]

---

[7] Her letter is in *State Papers Collected by Edward, Earl of Clarendon*
(Oxford, 1767–1786), II, 166-167.

During the visit at Youghal Richard Boyle took momentarily the centre of the stage, for, young as he was, the Lord Deputy saw fit to knight him—a graceful return for hospitality and an adroit way of winning his father's favor. After the ceremony, held in the "dining chamber," the boy, now Sir Richard, gave Falkland another falcon, and his father presented a black mare—together, incidentally, with £40 as the fee for the knighthood. Lucius had been honored the day before by admission as a Freeman of the Corporation of Youghal, and now Richard gave him a "tercel gentle."

The "tercel gentle"—the second Lucius had had from the generous Boyles—was a symbol for one side of his youth. A bird of prey, disciplined to the rules of a calling, taught to live by chase of the weak, bred to kill with grace and to please its masters as well as satisfy its own thirst for blood, was a reasonable model for a boy nurtured to be a courtier, schooled by such experts as Sir Lawrence Tanfield and his own father in the art of taking wealth and power where they were to be had. Such men as Viscount Falkland had the hawk's swiftness in striking where there was ready prey, but like trained birds hunted within the rules of a game in which greed was masked by an outward show of decorous forms and linked with unblinking reverence for the masters whose bounty fed and housed them.

At night, while Lucius and Sir Richard slept, and the hawk sat motionless on its perch, the Earl and the Viscount talked busily, about politics, plans for more profit from Irish lands, and about a wife for Lucius. Romance was not up for discussion. Viscount Falkland had been charmed into matrimony only by his wife's wealth, and he was not the man to waste time on ideas of young love. The Earl of Cork had money and he had daughters. Lucius was heir to a title. Why should not Lettice, or Katherine, or even little Dorothy or the child-widow Sarah, be betrothed to him? True, he was small, not handsome, and "of no great strength," but these things concerned only his bride, whose wishes mattered less than finance. In January Falkland had sent the Earl letters from the King, who was pleased to hope that the marriage "in treaty" between one of the Boyle daughters and Lucius Cary might be arranged. Lord Carew also lent his persuasions. But the Earl was rich because he drove good bargains. His record reads: "I offered his Lordship with my thirde daughter, the Lady Lettice Boyle . . . eight thousand pounds . . . so as his Lordship would procure the Lord Chief Baron Tanfield, his lady's father, to pass over his estate upon Lucius Cary" and provided Falkland would "convey to his son and the heirs male" of the marriage "£5000 lands per anno in England and . . . make my daughter for her jointure a good house fully furnished with a thousand pounds land per anno in England." Tanfield's part was easy, and he did will his property directly to his grandson, passing over his daughter, Viscount Falkland's wife and Lucius's mother. The Earl of Cork's demands might well have explained this, but probably his daughter's imprudence in giving up part of her jointure to her husband and possibly some dawning suspicions of her Catholic yearnings played their part in his decision. But this was not enough to buy Lettice, and the stipulations about lands and a house in England were beyond Falkland's means in 1624 or later. The bargain fell through, and Lucius left Youghal as free as he came. His father, a hawk who had missed his prey, had to try new flights.

At home again in Dublin, Lucius was knighted by his father early in 1626. Since he was fourteen he had commanded his troop of foot. This he delighted in, since his blood and the tradition of his class led him to exalt the virtues of the soldier, and his small stature no doubt made him the more eager to prove his "clear and keen temper" in arms. None the less, writing to Sir Francis Nethersole, he contrasted unfavorably his life in Dublin "in a hermitage" with Sir Francis's in the court of the Queen of Bohemia at The

Hague. The Lord Deputy's castle was not so great a place as the King's palace at Whitehall, or even so gay as the court of Elizabeth, James I's daughter, exiled from Bohemia to Holland.

The duel of 1630 was prepared for, in part, by Lucius Cary's training as a "tercel gentle" in Ireland. His readiness for adventure, his fondness for his sword, his liking for his rank and privilege as captain of a company, were all signs of his breeding. But to plan a duel at the clear risk of offending the King argued a state of mind not so easily explainable by the standards of the well-trained hawk. Viscount Falkland himself was outraged by the King's injustice about Lucius's company, and said so, discreetly, to his friends, but he flew free only with his master's leave and made no open gesture of defiance. Somewhere his son had acquired a taste for trying his wings as his own instinct demanded, not as a falconer chose. Moreover, throughout his life he was to show impulses quite foreign to court followers of his father's stripe. When, at eighteen or nineteen, he came back to England, he promptly chose his friends "by other rules than were prescribed to the young nobility of that time . . . He admitted some few to his friendship for the agreeableness of their natures and their undoubted affection to him" but "his familiarity . . . for the most part was with men of the most eminent and sublime parts, and of untouched reputation in point of integrity. . . . Such men had a title to his bosom." Before long scholars at Oxford were to wonder at his "immenseness of wit," "solidity of judgment," "vast knowledge," and his "infinite . . . fancy bound in by a most logical ratiocination." His father and his foster-father had little place for such qualities in their scheme of things. "Agreeableness" in friends was welcome, of course, but better still was usefulness. "Eminent parts" in statecraft or money-making were to be prized, but the sublime was at a discount. And "untouched reputations in points of integrity" were often less to be admired than repu-

tations for unscrupulous profiting within the law. Good
courtiers, to be sure, liked wit and had a taste for easily
turned verses; to know how to fill a letter with dextrous rhetoric might even be useful, as Falkland found it when he addressed the King; but it took more than such talents to make
up for the silliness of cherishing "wit and fancy and good
parts in any man" to the ridiculous extreme of overrunning
one's income in order to be a bountiful patron of learning and
the arts.

It was fitting enough, and a sign of noble nurture for Cary
to be at eighteen "master of the Latin tongue," to have read
"all the poets, and other of the best authors with notable
judgment," or to use French "as if he had spent many years
in France." What mystified his father, what certainly he
never learned from Baron Tanfield or the Earl of Cork, was
his innocence of any "other ambition than of knowledge";
stranger still was his scorn for "those arts, which must be
indulged in the transactions of human affairs." Men of business and the new courtiers, like Falkland, Tanfield, and the
politicians at Dublin Castle, who made a paying business out
of the King's service, lived by those arts. What hope was there
for a young knight, even a Viscount's son, who deserted them
for bookish will-o'-the-wisps? Such desertion led all too easily
to such inanity as his headstrong challenge to a duel in the
face of the King's certain displeasure.

Just how intractable his son was, Viscount Falkland was
not to discover until after the affair with Willoughby, but
part of Lucius's life in Ireland had initiated him in the vice
of study, and fixed the dangerous habit of thinking for himself. In this side of his training it was not the Viscount but
his wife who counted most. If he was reckless in following
his own lights, so was she; if he was later too careless of money,
so had she been; if he came more and more to seek for truth
in books, her example taught him how. Her efforts to make
her children love their father better than herself failed with

53

Lucius. Before 1625, when her husband sent her back to London, her eldest son had three years in Ireland with her, long enough for him to absorb much from her spiritual zeal, her intellectual exploration, her reckless readiness to doubt as well as to believe, her moral integrity burning up through her eccentricities, and her helpless incompetence with pounds and pence. After 1625 when her claiming of her right to believe as she chose brought upon her the wrath of the husband whom she always hoped to placate and made her name a hissing in Dublin Castle, her son was without her daily influence, but he never forgot what she had taught, nor did he stifle in himself the traits that were most like hers.

Of course a Viscount's son had to be educated, and Lucius Cary studied at Trinity College, Dublin, and graduated in 1625. To do so he had to satisfy the authorities that he could translate any part of the Greek Testament, and turn the first two psalms from Hebrew into Latin. Ramist dialectics— Temple, the provost of Trinity, was an ardent disciple of Ramus—logic, physiology, rhetoric, and ethics, had been the staples of his course. So far as his father was concerned, the essential was that the forms should be observed, and that Trinity College should supply a degree and enough knowledge of books to fit a young man to hold his own with such wits as came to court. But Lady Falkland took education more seriously, and no doubt she was troubled by the strong Puritan and anti-Catholic bias of Trinity College. Holy Communion was not celebrated in the chapel, and even though Temple was not a minister, extreme Protestantism was dominant at Dublin University. Reading and pondering, puzzling her way through the Protestant-Catholic controversy, trying to teach herself Irish by poring over an Irish Bible, the Viscountess would stimulate any son of hers to look for more at the University than the privileges granted him as a nobleman's heir or the pleasures of riding with retainers, leading a troop of infantry, being called Captain, and demonstrating his superiority over the less aristocratic by his skill in the forbidden sport of hawking.

For Lucius, with a mother busily examining into her own religious allegiance, and a father staunch in his Anglicanism and his hatred for Irish Catholics, four years at Trinity presented problems he could not ignore—problems that before long ate into the fabric of English life and for a time absorbed Cary's intellectual energies. Some of his classmates may have yawned through Samuel Ward's and Joshua Hoyle's lectures on theological controversies, but he must have listened intently to them, since they touched topics that were important not simply in the abstract but as actual realities bound up with the daily life of Lord and Lady Falkland and their son.

No doubt Lucius had other instruction than that of the college. Most noble households boasted a few dependents who served as tutors and chaplains. Possibly Cary travelled abroad with some one of them; he is said to have done so under "the tutelage and protection of a discreet person," and the same account suggests that this "discreet person" did much to change him from a "wild youth" into a reformed character "as to life, manners, and learning." If the story is true the journey may have taken place either between July, 1625, when he took his degree, and March, 1626, when he was knighted at Dublin, or after the later date and some time before he returned to England in 1628 or 1629.[8]

During his teens he learned the joys of intimate friendship. Sir Richard Morison, who had supplied the baggage carts for the Falklands' pilgrimage to Dublin, had known the Lord Deputy for years. They both had served with Essex in Ireland in 1599, had been knighted by him there, and both had been in the House of Commons in 1620. Morison was in

---

[8] Clarendon, *Life*, I, 42, says Cary returned to England when he was about eighteen, *i.e.*, 1628; but Cary wrote that he "lived seven yeares in Ireland," which would make it 1629. L. Cary, *Discourse of Infallibility* (2d. ed.; London, 1660), p. 175.

Ireland for part at least of Falkland's Deputyship. In 1622 he had a company of Irish foot, and in the next year he was Governor of Wexford and Waterford. In 1624 he was to have a patent for the presidency of Munster, but this was held up, partly by Falkland's agency, and conferred instead on Sir Edward Villiers, apparently only after the Duke of Buckingham had agreed to recompense Morison. Shortly before the latter's death in 1625 he was made Receiver of the Composition Rents in Munster, and added to the Irish Privy Council. His old acquaintance with Falkland and his contact with Irish politics must have brought him into close touch with the Lord Deputy's household, and thus his son Henry came to know Lucius Cary. When the elder Morison died, his son seems to have taken over the command of his company in Ireland, and must have been there for most of the time that Cary was. Certainly he was in 1627, though in October of that year he was knighted in London and immediately afterward was given leave to go to France to broaden his military experience. Possibly Lucius went abroad with his "dearest and almost only friend." In any case by 1629 they had achieved an "immortal friendship."

Cary is said to have studied for a time at Exeter College, Oxford, and possibly this was before July, 1629, when the death of his grandmother, Lady Tanfield, left him heir to her English estates.[9] Surely he must have been in England soon after she died. Probably Morison was, too. At all events they kept in close touch with each other.

Their intimacy became the theme of one of Ben Jonson's best poems, to the "immortal memory and friendship of that noble pair, Sir Lucius Cary and Sir Henry Morison"—

---

[9] For the date of Lady Tanfield's death I rely on information generously supplied by Mr. Kurt Weber. Cf. K. B. Murdock, "An Elegy on Sir Henry Morison, by Lucius Cary" in *Harvard Studies and Notes in Philology and Literature*, XX (Camb., 1938), p. 30, note 3.

"Two names of friendship, but one Starre:
Of hearts the union. And those not by chance
Made, or indenture, or leas'd out t'advance
The profits for a time."

The poet saw in them a noble tradition of disinterested affection. He deliberately contrasts his heroes with those for whom acquisitiveness and the code of business transcended friendship. Their union rested, he declared, on their moral worth. Morison was not only a soldier and a perfect patriot, a faithful friend and a virtuous son to a widowed mother, but a very type of the good. So was his friend. There could be

"Nothing perfect done,
But as a CARY, or a MORISON."

Lucius Cary himself praised Sir Henry for his military prowess, for his strict honor toward women, for his good looks, and above all for his wit. He was near Cary's age, at the most only a year or two older, and by right of family he was in touch in England with a circle in which literature and learning bulked more largely than they did in the households of Cary, Tanfield, or Boyle, always except for Lucius's mother. Viscount Falkland had good blood in his veins; his sisters had married well; and his son was connected with many great houses. But Morison's mother was a Harington, and the Haringtons were exceptionally fortunate in their affiliations. In 1684 it was said that they were allied to "eight dukes, three marquisses, seventy earls, nine counts, twenty-seven viscounts, and thirty-six barons, among which" were "sixteen Knights of the Garter." In this galaxy or linked to it were several of the writers and patrons who gave the age its literary glory.

His relation with Morison, then, brought Cary not only friendship but a chance for a broadened horizon and an opportunity to establish himself as an apprentice in the company of wits. It led also to tragedy and taught him that even courtiers' sons, heirs to titles, must taste the bitter kernel at the heart of life. Cary made a friend of Morison only to lose him; all the new-found delight in comradeship with a youth whom he devotedly admired and the excitement of entering with him a world quite unlike anything Dublin had offered, were smoothly blotted out by death. Morison died at Carmarthen, in Wales, probably of smallpox, soon after July, 1629. In that year Lucius Cary, nineteen years old, tapped two sources of maturity. His grandmother's death gave him the independence of manhood, with an income and estates; the loss of his friend made him suddenly conscious of the fleeting quality of fortune.

To Morison's sister he wrote a long elegy on her brother and his friend. It is not a great poem, but it is revealing of Cary, and it makes a fitting end for the story of his boyhood, just as the event that called it forth went far to turn him from a boy into a man.

The praise of Morison is largely hyperbole, but beneath the rhetoric there are the clear outlines of what his friend had treasured most in him. He was a true friend, not merely "freind-seeming" or one of those "who neuer loue, except they loue for ends"—a breed familiar to any boy brought up in the Lord Deputy's house. Morison was handsome, without being womanish. He was brave and modest, contemptuous of vulgar fame. He had

> "Soe infinite a witt, that had there all
>   That from him with out heede did drop and fall"

been collected, it would have put other authors to shame. He was, Cary thought, expert in prose and verse, skilled in statesmanship and the art of war. No woman was worthy of him, and to none did he speak falsely, so that at his death there were by him no "Oenones haples left."

All that he had Cary vowed he would have given up for Morison. He would have died that his friend might live. To save him he would have renounced his "pedegree." A friend was more precious than any kinsman, even a father. Are not fathers loved because they are friends? To care for relatives because they are relatives is to forego "free will"—they deserve no love unless their "worth" demands it.

The elegy does credit to Cary's education. There is a sprinkling of classical references, and a variation on a phrase in Lyly. There are Biblical allusions, of course. Peru and the lands of the "great Mogul," Sir Lucius had heard of; he knew something about Wales and a silver mine there. Reason, and philosophy, which was chiefly useful to "pump out passions," were more than empty names. Cary, like Jonson in his ode on Morison, dipped into Seneca—perhaps by way of his mother's translation—and made much of the idea that life is to be measured not by years but by "witt and worth." Among contemporary writers Sandys was named, but the chief rôles as wits were reserved for John Donne, extolled as poet and poet alone, and for Jean-Luis de Balzac, held up for his skill in prose letters. As type of soldier and statesman there was Prince Frederick Henry of Orange, just then fresh from victories against Catholic Spain.

Lucius Cary had the tastes of his class. The erudition was of the sort it valued, and bits of the imagery and diction in the elegy smack of the horseman and the country landowner. Morison is praised for despising "all below him," and Cary's assurance that the social order, which allowed him rank and wealth, was in tune with a divine plan, comes out in his calm assertion that those born to beggary bear it contentedly and value riches less than poverty. The assumptions of the noble and the rich are exalted to infallible authority. But mixed with this there is a loftier strain. Though the verses are bookish, and deferential to fashionable poetic conventions, they are tinctured with thoughtfulness about religion and philosophy, and with reverence for unworldly standards. Incomes and estates could not be undervalued except by someone "strangely . . . compos'd," but even they should be sacrificed for friendship. The estimate of Morison is redolent of traditional idealisms as to honor, courage, and chivalry in the best sense.

Moreover, the elegy is, for all its inexpertness, instinct with emotion.

> "This, next to the Gospell, I beliue:
> What euer can not loue, can not griue,"

Cary wrote. This leads him, in his sorrow, to put folly above sober sense, and to feel that the "chayre or stoole," incapable of feeling, is happier than man who suffers because he loves. None the less, the elegy insists on unselfish devotion, as food for the spirit. Deeply shocked by Fate, Cary is ready to hate life—but there is always love to reckon with. As "executor" to Morison's affection he swears to dedicate himself to his friend's mother, aunt, and sister, and to cheat despair by a new consecration to friendship.[10]

The elegy was written just before the challenge to Willoughby and helps to explain it. Granted that boyish hotheadedness goes far to account for his defiance of authority, injured pride and boldness do not tell the whole story. The clue lies in the poem, with its idealistic reverence for honor, valor, and good faith as strictly personal virtues. If in loyalty to Morison and his "worth" lesser loyalties to property and "pedegree" could be forgotten, might there not be forgetfulness of loyalty to the sovereign when justice and honor were at stake? If Cary was fit to replace Sir Henry in the

---

[10] Who the aunt was is not clear. One of Lettice Morison's aunts seems to have been for a time in the service of Elizabeth of Bohemia, and may be referred to here. Cf. J. A. Manning, *Memoirs of Sir Benjamin Rudyard* (London, 1841), pp. 143-144, and Sir G. Bromley, *Collection of Original Royal Letters* (London, 1787), pp. 142-143.

eyes of his mother and sister could he begin by weakly sacrificing his own confidence of right?

He was, in 1630, groping for security, for a standard that might resolve the contradictions of which his mind was full, without giving up his worship of the good embodied in his friend. His parents had come to typify discord, and their quarrel struck at the roots of religious certainty. Books told of virtue and honor, and courtiers talked of loyalty, but money-making and luxury counted most in daily experience. Sir Henry Morison, Cary felt, had been perfect, but he had died. His lovely and pious sister was an inspiration toward faith and decency, but among courtiers poverty was not atoned for by virtue. Where was the true? Was there anything to be said for the critics of the King and the bishops, the murmurers about rebellion? Should he follow his mother and silence doubts by submission to faith; could he be content as his father was with a career in which observance of the traditional forms of chivalric service of the King was made to serve the ends of profit-seeking and speculation in a changing economic order? Or should he renounce his "pedigree" and seek his fortune with those who had no use for the court; should he listen to the new "religionists" who insisted that all reason and wisdom were caught in their net of strict Biblical interpretation? Since his own parents could not agree as to the best way, could anyone? He was forced into independence of attitude, less because he was rich enough to choose for himself than because he had no single code by which to arbitrate the conflicts of allegiance that ensnared his boyhood.

There was probably, then, a hint of bitterness behind his challenge in 1630, and certainly a passionate feeling that ultimate validity, for the moment at least, inhered only in his "private sense." There were deeper motives, too, for his insistence on his individual dignity. Unlike Morison, he was not handsome, or charming to women, but undersized, awkward, with coarse, straggling, black hair, and a harsh "untuned" voice. If he was to pass for a hero it must be by dint of deeds, not looks. And to be less than brave meant to be unworthy of his friend. Thus he came to make an ideal of daring. His "little person . . . was quickly found to contain a great heart . . . and a nature so fearless, that no composition of the strongest limbs, and most harmonious and proportioned presence and strength, ever more disposed any man to the greatest enterprise; it being his greatest weakness to be too solicitous for such adventures." For all his later love for peace, he never lost his taste for hazardous physical activity.

He got no glory out of the affair with Willoughby. Ten days in the Fleet, and forgiveness won by his father's pleas, were nothing to be proud of. Yet he had been unfrightened and faithful to himself. Nor did proof that the royal authority held the whip hand convince him that fashionable loyalties, right or wrong, must be inviolate. There were higher sanctions. There were emotions, there was love. He had not learned to cheat himself in deference to convention. The chief allegiance it imposed—at least that most immediately realizable—was to his father. Within a few months he was to renounce even that, and to prove once more how fervently he worshipped his "private sense."

IV

"QUICKSILVER FIXED"

Young Manhood at Great Tew, 1630–1639

Soon after his release from the Fleet, Lucius Cary married against his father's will. In his challenge to Willoughby he had done no more than Lord Falkland could repair and forgive; this new sin, less serious in the eyes of the state, cut off once and for all his relation with his father. To the elder Cary it seemed arrant folly, blind impracticality worthy of his prodigal wife; it was weakness, selfishness, slavery to passion. Even to forget was beyond his generosity.

Lucius's challenge had been a gesture toward an ideal of justice, however much mixed with pride and an exuberant insistence on proving himself too brave to swallow a slight even at the King's bidding. His newest exploit was an offering on the altar of love. In the society in which he had grown up, young men might woo, perhaps, as they liked, but they married, as Lord Falkland had done, for pounds and pence. This was no way for one who had seen in Sir Henry Morison a model of disinterested virtue. Beneath the worldliness of a social structure in which wealth was becoming the test of merit, there were still alive romantic theories of absolute nobility, conceptions of honor as better than profit, of truth to heart and mind as superior to slavery to money. To such theories Cary and Morison, neither yet forced to make a living, had managed to be faithful. Ben Jonson celebrated their friendship as unmarred by any sordid truckling to the new economic order that was eating away the old standards with such subtle corrosives as rising prices, concentration of wealth, and the exigent loyalties of a capitalistic scheme. Only fools could hope to prosper long with the values of Jonson's poem, but Lucius Cary was in 1630 still fool enough—or young enough—to try. He had enough of his mother in him to make it easier for him to spend money than to take thought as to what he could do without it.

His father had had definite plans for him. Just as he had tried, years before, to marry him to Lettice Boyle, because her father was rich, so in May, 1629, he had schemed for his betrothal to the daughter of the Lord Treasurer, Richard Weston. Weston was suspected of being a Catholic, but his wealth and power outweighed Falkland's Protestant scruples. The Lord Deputy was failing in Ireland, and knew there was talk of displacing him. He probably hoped, by using Lucius as a link with Weston, not only to fatten his purse but to "continue Lord Deputy still." The negotiations may still have been going on when Lucius was jailed, and even if they had broken off, Falkland was not the man to give up merely because one venture collapsed. He must have looked on his son's delivery from prison as important chiefly because it made him once more eligible for a rich match.

But this was in London, and for months a little drama had been playing in Tooley Park, Leicestershire, with Lettice Morison, Sir Henry's sister, as its heroine. What she was like as a girl it is hard to tell, since she became the victim of a pious biographer, who reduced her personality to the stereotyped pattern of female sainthood. We read of her obedience, of her eagerness for books, of how she "wrought a purse for her own Almes and would importunately begge her Mothers . . . money to fill it, that she might empty it again to the poor." Verse makers chimed in and expatiated on her colorless piety. But, however good she was, it seems that she was

beautiful—allowing for the conventions of contemporary por-
traiture, Janssen's painting confirms that. No doubt Lucius
Cary appreciated her goodness and, idealizing her brother's
virtues, was ready to idolize hers. But it is to be hoped that
she had more warmth than her devout panegyrists have permitted her; indeed, had she not had, it is most unlikely that
she could have charmed a young man who, for all his serious
tastes, cannot yet have been ready to sacrifice the flesh completely to the spirit.

Charm him she did. Before Sir Henry Morison died, Lucius
wrote verses to her, now lost, choosing the device of a
"feigned elegy," written as if she had died. It was an excellent
way of praising her, sparing both her blushes and his. By
the time he wrote his poem on her brother, he was calling her
his "dearest Sister," an earnest, at least, of his sense of close
relation to her, and the lines ended with his vow to devote
himself to her as well as to her mother and aunt. He was as
good as his word, and regardless of his father's ambitions,
turned from pretended brotherhood to frank courtship. They
were married early in 1630.[1] She brought him no wealth, but
the "riches" of her "piety, wisdom, quickness of wit, discretion, judgement, sobriety, and gravity of behaviour . . . seemed
Portion enough to him." A poetaster allowed himself to
write:

> "Her riper years did call her to the bed
> Of one who did Her, not her dowrie, wed.
> No shaft with gold tipt, no dart shot from eyes;
> No fires were here seen which from fancie rise.

---

[1] The marriage license was dated 1629, *i.e.*, before March 25, 1630; H. Har-
topp, ed., *Leicestershire Marriage Licenses* (London, 1910), p. 80. On April 12,
1630, Lord Falkland mentions his son's marriage, though this may possibly
refer only to plans for a match; T. Lewis, *Lives of the Friends and Contemporaries of Clarendon* (London, 1852), I, 196. The wedding took place
before May 22, 1630; *Hist. Mss. Comm., Report on Manuscripts in Various
Collections*, V (Hereford, 1909), 133.

Between these curtains, and this nuptial sheet,
Male virtue did with female virtue meet,
A soul with soul, and mind here match'd with mind,
The marriage torch held by a God not blind.
A Husband he, and she a Wife, whose will
After four child-births was a Virgin still."

The chill insipidity of this picture is relieved by Clarendon's assurance that Lucius "passionately loved" his bride. She remained always "dearly beloved," and probably Cupid had more to do with her wedding than divines and pious poets, who preferred to concentrate on such abstract matters as virginity of will, would have cared to admit.

That Lettice Cary was "of the most signal virtue and exemplary life, that the age produced" meant nothing to her father-in-law, since she was poor. He found himself cheated of "all his reasonable hopes and expectation of redeeming and repairing his own broken fortune, and . . . hopes in court." His son, who hated injustice as much in himself as in others, was of "a nature so sincere" that he frankly admitted the wrong he had done his father. He had once more followed his "private sense," and did not repent of that, but was sorry to have injured Lord Falkland. He fondly believed that all could be made right if he kept his bride but gave up his fortune.

He called in lawyers who drew up the necessary papers to make over "his whole estate" to his father's "disposal." But Henry Cary, for all his weaknesses, was not weak enough, even for money, to humble his pride by taking charity from an errant son. "His . . . passion and indignation so far transported him, (though he was a gentleman of excellent parts,) that he refused any reconciliation, and rejected all the offers that were made him of the estate, so that his son remained" comfortably wealthy without wanting to. The interviews between Lucius Cary and his father must have been dramatic. The older man, faced by defeat brought on by his son's self-will, was hurt and desperate; the younger, distressed by his father's pain, was wide-eyed in simple confidence that for love his income would be well lost if Lord Falkland would only accept it. How he proposed to live with his young wife, with nothing on which to support her, seems to have been a question which his generous enthusiasm made him leave unasked. But the Viscount, with the colder eye of an experienced combatant in a hard world, no doubt saw the dilemma, and refused his son's offer not only because he was proud, but because it was idle to imagine that he could gain from sixteen hundred pounds a year if his heir were hopelessly dependent.

Lady Elizabeth Cary pled for her son, but her entreaties broke against her husband's stony rage. The Cary household was irrevocably split. The Viscount and his wife were to be reconciled, outwardly at least, but not the Viscount and his son. Willy-nilly, Lucius and Lettice must stand alone. He decided intelligently that England, London, and the court, where his angry father was, offered little. Action was in moments of crisis always the best way out for him; a soldier's life appealed to his insistent need of compensating for his physique by proofs of valor; warfare had been for his father's generation a conventional school for young noblemen, and sometimes a way to preferment and favor. Naturally he reached again for his sword. "He transported himself and his wife into Holland, resolving to buy some military command, and to spend the remainder of his life in that profession." In camp he could fall back on the code of the hawk, and forget most of the worries about justice or injustice proposed by his "private sense."

Holland was a wise choice. There had been plenty of warlike alarums and excursions there; there might be a chance to fight for the Protestantism to which, in spite of doubts raised by his mother, his training at Trinity College and his wife's pious convictions alike inclined him. Moreover, there

67

was at The Hague a court on which his wife, as a Harington by blood, had special claims. Her great-uncle and great-aunt had been faithful tutors and servants of Elizabeth of Bohemia, who, in 1630, kept up as best she could in exile from her husband's domain the royal dignity of a daughter of James I married to a king without a country. Lettice Cary's aunt had been in her train; Lucius's friend, Nethersole, had been Elizabeth's secretary, and continued to champion her even at the price of jail for his excessive zeal. Others, too, at The Hague must have been ready to look kindly on Lord Falkland's heir. His family was good, and his potentialities as a courtier were not to be sneered at, even though he had, at twenty, signalized himself only by winning the King's brief displeasure and complete estrangement from his father.

Favorable as Holland seemed for the start of a career, Lucius Cary's attempt to become a soldier failed. Apparently he had hopes of a military command which he could not get. Probably his pride reasserted itself, and kept him from taking anything less than he had decided was his due. There was also a momentary interlude of peace, and peace was a bad thing for a warlike boy with his way to make.

In any case, within a short time—certainly less than a year —after May, 1630, when he was at The Hague with his bride, he was back in England with no career even begun. It was a case for taking stock. He had neither his father's backing, nor, presumably, the complete confidence of the King. He was not one of those who could with "court-dog-tricks . . . fawn and fleer" and "make . . . revenue out of legs and faces." His awkwardness, smacking of the hobbledehoy, and his "aspect so far from inviting, that it had somewhat in it of simplicity," fitted him better for the country than for London. His appearance was a "great disadvantage (which in the first entrance into the world is attended with too much prejudice)." This, with his father's hostility, was probably enough to close the door on most opportunities at court. There were left his private income, his country houses, ability to make verses, a taste for books, a hot devotion to his own standards of right and wrong, and a full set of high ideals.

He let his heritage from his mother outweigh what he had from his father, and set out to make the most of his scholarly talents. No doubt this was in part a counsel of despair, but there was some free choice involved. He might still have read for the law, or the church, and have fitted himself for a career like his grandfather Tanfield's, or have set his course toward a bishopric. Even the Lord Falklands of his world could see merit in bishops, commanding the national church in the service of the King, and winning for themselves power and great place. Lawyers, too, might be rich and influential; if they became judges and "lions under the throne" they were sometimes rewarded more richly than Lord Deputies of Ireland. But Lucius Cary chose to study not law or divinity, but Greek. With characteristic energy he swore he "would not see London in many years, which was the place he loved of all the world," but would bury himself in books. So he did, and aided by Patrick Young, the Patricius Junius of later fame, a superlative scholar whom he brought to live with him for a while, he plunged into the classics. Before 1633 he was "master of the Greek tongue . . . and had read not only the Greek historians, but Homer likewise, and such of the poets as were worthy to be perused." He had swerved from his training as a hawk—unless he is to be thought of as Ben Jonson described Goodere's falcon, the bird "sacred to Apollo," who

> "doth instruct men by her gallant flight,
> That they to knowledge so should toure upright,
> And never stoupe, but to strike ignorance."

Such hawks were of a breed strange to Lord Falkland; but Lucius Cary's mother understood them well.

To absorb what there was in the Greek historians and in
Homer about statesmen and their ways, about peace and war,
ethics, heroism, and patriotism, took hard work. Easier and
as effective were lessons on the same themes from the day-by-
day affairs of England. Since Lucius Cary was old enough
to be conscious at all, he must have been, with the Tanfields
and with his father, exposed to some contact with public
affairs.

During the reign of James I he was not old enough to
grasp much of the true inwardness of the increasing friction
between King and Parliament. When it was said in 1618 that
his father was to be Master of the Court of Wards, he was
probably glad because the office was lucrative, and did not
care, if he knew, that the Court of Wards was one of the
institutions most attacked in Parliament for its abuses of
subjects' rights and pocketbooks. It was in Ireland, when he
was old enough to understand better what he saw and heard,
that Lucius Cary's first real insight into current politics must
have come. There, for example, he learned that "Protestant"
and "Catholic" spelled not merely rival forms of worship but
hostile parties in a controversy in which earnest men played
for stakes of life and death. The two words connoted warfare,
in which theology was less important than such immediate
values as patriotism, moral and intellectual freedom, political
fortunes, and the place of England in a world hardly more
torn by swords and gunfire than by the subtler devastations
of intellectual strife. Irish Catholics were rebellious, and Spain
and the Pope were believed to stand behind them. The Lord
Deputy's decrees against Papists were checked because the
Protestant King of England wanted to marry his son to a
princess of Catholic Spain. On the other hand, any favors
to Catholics roused protest. The tight-rope which Falkland
had to walk was stretched between the opposite poles of a
foreign policy according to which England with one hand

beckoned to Spain and with the other gestured toward European Protestantism, particularly in the person of the Elector Frederick. The people remembered the Armada and hated Spain; they adored Frederick and his queen, Elizabeth. His defeat and flight from Bohemia caused widespread agitation in London. Lord Falkland's Protestantism was loudly professed, but his son saw in Ireland other lords and statesmen who were as frank in their devotion to Rome. The surface was chaotic, but even a boy in his teens could feel the pulse of great issues throbbing beneath.

They were dramatized in events. A Spanish ship, fresh from the capture of a Flemish vessel, raided Dublin harbor. Sailors, strangely garbed, and with alarmingly un-English faces "committed many spoils and outrages," sailing away at last only a few hours before the ship bringing Lucius Cary's brothers and sisters from England—rescued from their Catholic mother—was sighted at the harbor mouth. The Lord Deputy fumed helplessly at the insult to him, to Charles I, and to Protestantism. His fury, like his bitter words against his wife, then nearly two years away from him and from the path he saw as truth, taught his son to wonder what war with Spain meant, how patriotism and faith were linked, and how much fire lay behind the thickening smoke of religious dispute.

There were other happenings to ponder. The English defeat at Cadiz, with its unforgettable picture of starved vagabonds masquerading as soldiers, rioting dead drunk under the fierce Spanish sun; the hideous failure of the English at the island of Rhé—such things once heard of stuck in the mind. They shed sidelights on the kind of world young Englishmen were having made for them. So did the personalities Lucius Cary knew best, directly or by reputation. There was his mother, Catholic recusant and a traitor in the eyes of her husband. There was Boyle, the great Irish Lord, made powerful by his use of new capitalistic tools for money-making.

There was Lord Falkland himself, and, far off in London, his patron, the great Duke of Buckingham, arbiter of destinies at court, hated by the people but loved by two kings.

It was all very hard to understand because conflict was everywhere. The shame of Cadiz and Rhé was laid at Buckingham's door, and he was reviled in popular ballads, but when he was murdered Cary's mother wrote a poem in his praise. She was sure that the esteem of two monarchs guaranteed his fame against the "slave" who stabbed him.[2] Scheming courtiers abounded, spreading the "distemper" of a court "diverse from the state." Parliament's temper grew shorter, and the King did not understand why. Echoes from the Palatinate, from Madrid, and from Rome, made strident discord. Out of the heat of controversies, out of disputes at home and intrigues abroad, out of religious feeling, business interests, instinctive allegiances, and the conflicts of classes, were being gathered "the twigs of that rod (a civil war) wherewith" God "intended to whip a wanton nation."

The larger aspects could be seen only with perspective, and even when Lucius Cary had retired to Oxfordshire to study Greek, the panorama was still too close to reveal the complete pattern. But the essentials were tied into his intimate experience. If "the keynote of the seventeenth century was revolt against authority"—a generalization as useful as most— it was a keynote dinned into his ears.[3] Parliament; the Irish; the Puritans denouncing the Bishops; poets discontented with old modes; courtiers with old loyalties tainted by new greed; business men with new scope abandoning old restraints; discontented men murmuring against the shifting of the economic scheme; all in one way or another threatened the ancient sanctions of authority. What of Lucius's mother, her-

---

[2] The poem is in Egerton Mss. at the British Museum (2725, f. 60r.). Mr. Kurt Weber kindly supplied me with a transcript of it.
[3] G. Davies, *The Early Stuarts* (Oxford, 1937), p. xix.

self a rebel? What of his own breaking of the edict against duels? What of his defiance of authority in marrying against his father's wish?

Nor was revolt against authority in family, church, and state, the whole story. Just as religious ideas had been sharply altered since the Reformation, so that Catholic, Puritan, and Anglican waged three-sided war with no single recognized court of appeal, so in philosophy and all forms of thought, change and conflict replaced uniformity and confidence in central harmony. Inevitably men were pushed toward deeper analyses, toward the same sort of close scrutiny of ideas that the new scientists were urging for the study of the physical world. Inevitably the quest for one all-embracing system of truth slackened before the impulse to bring everything to the bar of individual judgment. Had the change in attitude been complete, the strain might have been less. As it was, old definitions and standards lived on, and cropped up awkwardly in prejudices and unconscious responses even where the "modern" had most sway. Philosophic discord is written large in Donne and accents dramatically poem after poem. Ben Jonson and others insisted on concepts of honor, nobility and justice, that were often at odds with what men were actually doing, but survived strongly enough to cause startling inconsistencies in the behavior of society. Lucius Cary himself, the son of a family split by religious difference, relishing the perquisites that a self-seeking courtier could command, still worshipped Morison's moral qualities; longed for feats of arms, but quietly studied Greek; and, though bred to loyalty, obeyed his own sense of justice rather than the King's decree. He summed up in little much of the dilemma of his troubled time. He tried to follow his "own private sense" as a guide through confusion, but his judgment was hobbled by his premises, the axioms from which his reasoning started, and beyond which his conclusions could not soar.

Some of these axioms are plainly to be read in a sermon

preached by John Randol "before Sir Lucius Cary and the
Congregation at Burford" in March, 1631.[4] Randol, "Bachelor in Divinitie, of Brasen-nose Colledge in Oxford," did not,
of course, speak from the dictation of the lord of Burford, but
his doctrine was of the sort that Anglican preachers knew
was palatable to the gentry. The text, Acts xii, 20, was a
springboard for a leap into moralizing on public concerns.
There was praise of Charles I as "a King of peace, in whom
there is no designe of warre." But, said Randol, if Charles
brought peace, God was less kind and chastised his sinful
people with famine, flood, and plague. For one thing servants
were not as docile as they should be, and even if they did not
ride while their masters walked, they were "higher in their
owne imaginations" than in any saddle. There were usurers
and drunkards. Worst of all were "vagrant impes," travelling
from alehouse to alehouse, irreligious miscreants, swearing,
stealing, rioting, and domineering "as if they were the onlie
men, by whom the King and kingdome did subsist." Such,
the unemployed or underprivileged of the time, were but "the
off-scowring . . . of men & beasts . . . the very scumme of
all the land." A shrewder commentator might have hinted
that this was a sign that the social structure of England was
inadequate for its load, but for Randol and probably for most
of his hearers, who had property or work, it meant that idleness and failure to be baptized offended God and so caused
excessive rain, poor crops, and high prices.

England, in Randol's opinion, was to be thankful that she

---

[4] *Noble Blastus: The Honor of a Lord Chamberlaine: And Of a Good Bed-
Chamber-Man: Or The Courtier justified in Conditions of Peace. Being a
Sermon preacht the 27. of March, 1631. before Sir Lucius Cary, and the Con-
gregation at Burford Church in Oxfordshire; With Speciall Relation to the
Coronation-day, and the Plague and Dearth then among the people. By Iohn
Randol Bachelor in Divinitie, of Brasen-nose Colledge in Oxford. London,
Printed for Tho: Lambert neare the Hospitall-gate in Smithfield. 1633.* The
date of the sermon shows Cary was in England again by March, 1631; its
publication in 1633 may well have been occasioned by the death in that year
of his father, a courtier and "Bed-Chamber-Man."

was largely independent of other nations, except the kingdom of God. She might lack silks, but she had native cloth that was warmer; if she lacked spices, she had plenty of juicy meat from native flocks. This truly British assertion of the virtues of a poorly seasoned and unbalanced diet, was part of Randol's plea for the advantages of "England for the English." If she were economically self-sufficient, she could keep out of war, provided her people agreed among themselves. Unanimity of opinion was the nation's "wall and weale." With a good king, noble courtiers, and eligible men to represent some other classes, the state was safe.

Throughout the sermon Randol reiterated his sense that family and breeding were tests of worth, that social upstarts and men of low birth were dangerous if they aspired above their station. The King must be supreme, and accessible to his subjects only through intermediaries, his "noble servants," men by rank and family fitted to intercede at court for their humbler fellow-citizens. A large part of what Randol said— no doubt uttered with full consciousness of what Lord Falkland was and Sir Lucius of Burford might be—was a justification of the courtier's place in the national scheme. There was even a defense of the courtier's habit of taking bribes. Peace and war, order and disorder, prosperity or poverty, so far as worldly agencies could dictate them, depended on the "lord chamberlaines" and "bed-chamber-men" closest to the King, by whom relations between people and sovereign were maintained. Peace was to the interest of these men, since war would be costly for them, and they had, moreover, a responsibility both to the King and to God. They should, of course, love justice, but, just or not, their power was secure. If they did their duty and if the monarch was like Charles I all would be well, provided the people did not think rebelliously, worked, and were godly. Godliness, for Randol, seemed to mean not only reverence for the sacraments but also deference to constituted authority in church and state, together with docile ac-

ceptance of whatever social and economic position it pleased
rulers to allow their subjects.

Later Lucius Cary was to have doubts about courtiers,
bishops, judges, even about the infinite wisdom of absolute
monarchs; later he was to long for peace with melancholy passion. But in 1631 he was no doubt ready to take most of
what Randol said as assured truth. Indeed, he never lost his
confidence in the fitness of a social order in which some were
poor, some rich, some servants and some masters, by right
of birth. Neither he nor Randol was able to foresee how far
new social standards, the groping for power of new elements
in society, the moulding of a changed economic system, were
to go. Just as they still regarded usury as a crime in a time
when, in fact, its milder forms, at least, were becoming an accepted part of good business; so, in spite of new causes for
poverty, they clung to the theory that the idle and poor were
idle and poor by their own fault, and deserved sympathy and
help only in so far as *noblesse oblige* made it proper for
noblemen and landowners to be charitable toward those
who were well behaved. To lay the blame on the sufferers'
sins is a sure anaesthetic for worries about social and economic
ills. Identify the existing order with righteousness, thrift with
holiness, rebelliousness or even poverty with error, and there
is no impulse toward social reform. "Be good and you will
be happy," provided "good" and "happy" are carefully defined, is a comforting maxim, which, properly used, puts the
blame for much misery on those who are miserable and makes
it needless for other hearts to be troubled. The maxim, the
definitions, and the application, were all ready made for the
Randols, the Carys, and other churchmen and prosperous
gentlemen of the 1630's.

His father's death in 1633 interrupted Lucius Cary's leisure
for hearing sermons and speculating on the state of the nation. It tore him away from his placid life in the country, with
his books, his friends, and his young wife. He had to go back

to London to grapple with new responsibilities and problems.

The responsibilities were largely financial. He was now Viscount Falkland in his turn, and that meant heavier expense. He scorned the idea that the great of this world should display their own importance in order "to keep state," and saw shrewdly that it was useless to stand on one's dignity with others unless they were prepared to be respectful. As he put it, "Keeping of state was like committing adultery, there must two go to it." Even so he could not blink the fact that as a Viscount and a gentleman of the King's bedchamber, he must, if he was to fit into the social scheme at all, live more lavishly than as a mere knight. That cost money, and his inheritance from his father was chiefly debts. Unhappy Henry Cary, for all his eager efforts to increase his fortune by colonial speculations, by purchase of estates, by designs on Irish lands, and by constant suits at court, was "no skilful Projector of profit to himself" and died a poor man. His son was left to care for his younger brothers and sisters and his improvident mother, who had already drawn liberally on his income, as well as for his own family.

As for problems, there were his mother's importunities about his religious belief, decisions to make as to whether he should intervene between her and her children to save them from Catholicism, and there was, most immediately, the puzzle as to whether he should go on as a retired country scholar or at last try his luck at court. His father's example showed how easily such an attempt might fail, but the elder Falkland's gallantry in forcing a tortured body to pay final homage to the King, and his stoic dignity in his last hours, threw into relief what was noblest in the courtiers' creed.

For the moment Lucius could postpone decisions and stay on happily in London settling his father's estate. He loved the city and it was full of friends. In their company he must have seen Richard Boyle, Viscount Dungarvan, whom he had known as a boy, act in the "most glorious Masque" given to welcome the King and Queen home from their progress to Scotland. Theatres; great houses; brilliant coaches rocking over the rough pavements of narrow, ill-smelling streets; booksellers' shops; the King and Queen sitting very small and very erect in a gay barge moving down the river; preachers stirring great audiences with the bountiful eloquence of their sermons— here was a feast for eyes tired of the still, green acres of Oxfordshire and the crisp black and white of the printed page. But best of all were the friends.

Lucius Cary had a genius for friendship. In his relation to Morison he had found an emotional security which his parents, after their quarrel, could not give him. Naturally he made of friendship a special ideal, and when he discovered that he had gifts for it, in spite of his unimpressive presence, he gave those gifts full scope. In saying that, at the time of his challenge, he had "no friend," he can have meant no more than that at the moment there was no one in London whom he could ask to be his second in a duel. Certainly he very soon had friends in plenty. "He had great esteem for all men of great parts, though they applied them to ill purposes," and his circle of acquaintances shows the breadth of his tastes. It compassed men of widely different characters, attainments, and interests, and if there were a few given to "ill purposes" there were fewer who lacked "great parts."

When he had come from Ireland in 1628 or 1629 he had had in his own right and by virtue of his companionship with Morison a claim on some of the foremost figures in the world of letters. Ben Jonson had known his father; Lucius's aunt had married Sir George Manners, whose sister-in-law had been the Countess of Rutland, Jonson's friend and a poetess whom he admired. Sir Henry Goodere had served with the elder Lord Falkland years ago in Ireland, and both had been knighted by Essex there. Goodere, the father-in-law of Sir Francis Nethersole and related to Captain Rainsford, was the patron of Drayton and the friend of Donne. Lucius's mother, too, was a bluestocking and there were wits who admired her writing and valued her patronage. To be her son was a recommendation to them.

Henry Morison, and Cary's wife, Lettice, had even more connections with patrons and artists. Chief among the "noble families" in which "literature was a traditional interest or occupation, and the society of men of letters willingly cultivated . . . were those in which ran the blood of the Sidneys and Haringtons." The grandmother of Lettice and Henry Morison was a Harington, and their great-grandmother was Lucy Sidney. Lucy, Countess of Bedford, friend of Donne and Jonson, "who had made her country house at Twickenham a little court of literature," had been a cousin of Morison's mother. His uncle, Fynes Morison, had written of his travels and was known to Jonson. Another uncle, Sir Benjamin Rudyard, was himself a versifier, and a friend of both Jonson and Donne, as well as of John Owen, the epigrammatist, of the Earl of Pembroke, and of John Hoskins, who is said to have revised Sir Walter Raleigh's *History of the World.* Another cousin of Henry Morison's mother had been young Lord Harington, whom John Donne knew from boyhood and mourned in his "Obsequies"; still another, more distant, had been Sir John Harington of Kelston, highly renowned among Elizabethan wits.

English literary society of the early seventeenth century— the writers and their patrons—was closely knit. The shortest excursion into genealogical labyrinths shows that the major authors of the time found their most appreciative audience and their most generous support among a few of the gentry, often themselves dabblers in literature, who were either related to each other, or at the least friends and neighbors. Into this small world by no means all the educated and powerful entered; it was Cary's good fortune that, especially through the Morisons, he could. He was even received as one of Jonson's many "sons," "sealed of the tribe of Ben"—a privilege that gave him the chance to meet at the old Devil Tavern or at "the Dogg" most of the young wits of the town.

For Jonson himself Cary reserved special devotion. After Henry Morison's death he decided to make his "Elegie" on him the first of a series of "anniversary" poems to his memory. The third of these, written presumably in 1631, was sent to Jonson, with some lines written by Cary to the old dramatist himself, whom he calls his "noble father." The poem is better than the first "elegie," more compact, less strained in hyperbole, and although it emphasizes most Henry Morison's learning and Cary's admiration for Jonson, "our Metropolitane in Poetry," it preserves the vision of Morison as a pattern of the virtues, "a living Epick Poëme." The verses from Sir Lucius to Ben Jonson picture pleasantly a young man's awe of the Laureate and his appreciation of the old poet's kindness to his friends:

"That happines
You deale abroad, still you your-self possesse;
Though, given to others, it becomes their Due:
It, echo-like, reverberates to yow."

When Jonson died in August, 1637, "the greatest part of the nobilitie and gentry then in the town" followed him to his grave in Westminster Abbey. The new Viscount Falkland may have been with them; in any case he contributed to *Jonsonus Virbius,* a volume of memorial poems published in the next year. Indeed, he is said to have suggested the title. His contribution to the book was a long "Eglogue On the Death of Ben Johnson, Between Melybaeus and Hylas." "Jonson," says Hylas,

"When I whilome cities visited,
Hath made them seeme but houres which were full dayes."

Jonson's work, the verses declare, combined "wit, judgment, learning, art" and "industry." It was "the bayes of vertue, and the scourge of vice," conceding nothing to "the rich ignorant," since the poet would not "esteeme the beast" "for the trappings." He concentrated on "raising youth" to "noble actions." His comedies were "ethicke lectures," in which

> "the sham'd age
> Blusheth to meet her follies on the stage."

To Jonson flocked "all that had wit, or would be thought to have."

Cary modestly insisted that he was unfit to praise immortal Ben.

> "Digby, Carew, Killigrew, and Maine,
> Godolphin, Waller, that inspired traine,"

were the poets worthy to be heard. For all Cary's humility, another writer linked him with just this group, and his verses in *Jonsonus Virbius* are at least as good as most of the others in the volume. But their value is less for their manner than for their matter; as poetry they are tame, but their selection of qualities to be praised testifies to what young Lord Falkland most admired in Jonson. In the "Eglogue" as in his other work, Cary proved the justice of John Earle's verdict which "would not allow him to be a good poet, though a great witt; he writt not a smoth verse, but a greate deal of sense."

One couplet,

> "Not long before his death, our woods he meant
> To visit, and descend from Thames to Trent,"

suggests that Jonson may have planned a journey stopping to visit Falkland at Great Tew. He may at some time have been a guest there; certainly he kept in close touch with Lucius Cary, who expressed his allegiance in verses and letters and, more tangibly, in generous and sorely needed gifts in Jonson's straitened years.

The "inspired traine" of poets named by Falkland was

made up of his friends.[5] Tom Carew was a loyal follower of Jonson, and a courtier as well as a poet. The story ran that he once proved his tact and presence of mind by stumbling and dropping the candle, when he was escorting the King, in order that royal Charles might not see Henry Jermyn's arm about the Queen's neck. Carew was a rake, and some of his lyrics do not accord with the attitude toward love which Cary had found praiseworthy in Morison. But later Carew seemed to repent and some portents of piety may have been apparent even in his gayer days.

Henry Killigrew was another who combined wit with holiness. He became a minister, and his interest in divinity was more serious than Carew's. Falkland saw the first public appearance of his play, *Pallantus and Eudora*, at Blackfriars. Sitting near a noisy critic of the piece, he "suffered the unquiet, and impertinent Dislikes of this Auditor" as long as he could, but burst out at last when the character of Cleander was attacked for talking too well for a boy of seventeen. "Sir," said the Viscount, " 'tis not altogether so Monstrous and Impossible, for One of Seventeen Yeares to speak at such a Rate, when He that made him speak in that manner, and writ the whole play, was Himself no older." Cary's liking for the play, his recognition of Killigrew's precocity, and the playwright's taste for theology, all served to cement their friendship.

The playhouse was one of the chief charms of London, and *Pallantus and Eudora* cannot have been Falkland's only theatrical experience there. It is highly likely, for example, that he saw *The Shepherd's Paradise* acted at court in 1633, with two of his sisters in the cast. The author, Walter Montagu, was Lettice Cary's second cousin, and another of the group of wits whom her husband knew before 1638.

---

[5] The list of Falkland's friends in this chapter is made up from Athenae, Aubrey, Clarendon, Suckling's "Sessions of the Poets," together with Longueville, Marriott, and J. Tulloch, *Rational Theology and Christian Philosophy in England in the Seventeenth Century* (London, 1872), I, 95ff.

There were other dramatists, too. One was Aurelian Townsend, who may have helped Montagu write his masque; another was Jasper Mayne (included in the "inspired traine"); more famous was William Davenant. Mayne also turned eventually to the church. By 1639 he had some reputation both as poet and dramatist, but later he gave up poetry, except for such edifying lines as those in which he praised Lettice Cary and her husband, the young Viscount, whom he had known in London and at Great Tew. But he could not cure himself of his liking for bad practical jokes, and promised an old servant to leave him something which would make him drink after his master's death. He willed him a salt red herring. As for Davenant his first play was written about the time Cary came back from Ireland. In the next decade he steadily built up his fame as playwright and poet. He was no stricter in life than Carew, and his nose was eaten away by venereal disease. The wits loved to make ribald jests about his sacrifice to the charms of a "black handsome wench" from Axe Yard, and others retailed the legend that he was Shakespeare's son. In 1637 he succeeded Jonson as Poet Laureate.

His "great and intimate friend," and another of Falkland's, was Sir John Suckling. A familiar figure among Jonson's disciples, he was about Cary's age. He came home from abroad before 1630 "an extraordinary accomplished gentleman," famous for his repartee, and talking best when "most sett-upon and provoked." He, too, was far from the chaste ideal of the elegy on Morison. He gambled and loved with equal recklessness, and rejoiced in such exploits as the giving of a magnificent entertainment "for a great number of ladies of quality, all beauties and young . . . where were all the rarities that this part of the world could afford, and the last service of all was silke stockings and garters." He had much to teach a youth like Falkland about wit, about poetry, and, if his pupil would listen, about fashionable vice. He had his serious side, too, and wrote theological prose as well as profane verse. His friendship with Falkland prospered, and he praised the talents of the young lord. No doubt he visited at Great Tew, now and then, spicing the talk with his swift answers, priding himself on his "gracefull looke" and his curly beard, unashamed of his flaming nose. Even when the discussion ran on poetry or the place of reason in religion he was likely to keep his "brisk round eyes" alert for any pretty housemaid with a wanton look.

Sir Kenelm Digby was another whom Falkland admired. He was widely if superficially learned, and dabbled in astrology and alchemy, as well as in what passed for medicine. His "powder of sympathy" was notorious for its supposed power of healing without touching the wound, and sober men called him "errant mountebank" or "the very Pliny of our age for lying." He lied fluently, anyhow, for his volubility "surprised and delighted" as much as his "extraordinary person and presence." He was a giant, strong enough to lift a little man like Falkland, chair and all, with one hand. But he managed his bulk gracefully, and his "flowing courtesy and civility" admitted him to "the best places, and the best company." He breathed romance. Marie de Medicis was said to have fallen in love with him; he had been virtually a pirate; he had beaten the French and Venetian fleets at Scanderoon, and he had married Venetia Stanley. Her beauty was talked of everywhere. Jonson worshipped her as his "muse," but the scandal-mongers insisted she had been light in love. When she was younger, "a most beautifull desireable creature," living in the country, lovers, like "young eagles . . . espied her" and in the face of their passion she was, said the gossips, more generous than chaste. She was said to have been the "concubine" of the Earl of Dorset, but Digby married her vowing that "a handsome lusty man that was discreet might make a vertuose wife out of a brothell-house." To him she was probably faithful, but when she died in 1633 there was ugly talk of his having poisoned her. She would have been a strange companion for

Lettice Cary, but Lucius, at least in his early days in London, must have jumped at the chance to see the beautiful Venetia, and her husband's mind and talk were exciting. Digby, bred a Catholic, turned Protestant and then Catholic again. With him, as with so many other of Falkland's associates, theology was always a possible theme for debate.

Edmund Waller did not know Jonson but came to be a friend of Falkland. Brought up not far from the Carys' estate at Aldenham, he was in the early 1630's a sober citizen "nursed in parliaments," just beginning a career as poet. Slight and frail, with a small head, he was always very temperate, unlike the roistering Suckling and Carew. His life was not to be a noble one, but in the years before 1640 he had not revealed his cowardice. His political experience and his skill in verse were enough to interest Lucius Cary.

The last of the "inspired traine" was Sidney Godolphin. He was so small that Cary used to say that he got special pleasure from having Godolphin with him because he was then less conscious of his own shortness and felt "the properer man." "The very remarkableness" of Godolphin's "little person made the sharpness of his wit, and the composed quickness of his judgment and understanding . . . the more notable." He had been with the Earl of Leicester in Denmark, and had come back to wait for "some promotion in the court; where his excellent disposition and manners . . . made him very acceptable." Everyone liked him, but he loved to hide among his books. He seemed so indolent that his friends twitted him with laziness, and he hated physical discomfort. "A little rain or wind" was enough to keep him indoors, and when, at Great Tew, he rode out with his host and the other guests, he would "if the wind chanced to be in his face . . . (after a little pleasant murmuring) suddenly turn his horse, and go home" to books and a fire. He dabbled in poetry, but his real quality was moral. Falkland's warm affection for him was probably

based on his charm of manner and still more on his coura-
geous spirit, proved later, but even in his early years not quite
hidden by his little body and his fear of bad weather.

There were patrons as well as poets in Cary's circle. Endymion Porter wrote verses, but he was more useful to literature
in the help he gave to such men as Davenant and Dekker. He
had conducted delicate negotiations with Spain and knew the
inner workings of the court. He was, besides, a connoisseur,
and helped Charles I buy pictures. There were also writers
whose talents ranged beyond light verse. Thomas May, defeated by Davenant for the laureateship, was chiefly celebrated
as the translator of Lucan and of the Georgics. Later—his
enemies said it was because he was not made Laureate—he
turned against the King. From his classical studies he had
learned republican theories, but neither his political views nor
his accomplishments as a rake barred him from becoming at
least an acquaintance of Falkland. He was handsome, though
he had a defect in his speech, and he was learned. True, he
loved his bottle, and legend has it that he died, dead drunk,
choked by the strings of his cap which he had tied too tightly
under his chin. In his cups he spoke "slightingly of the Trinity," not disturbing the tolerant Falkland, but perhaps causing
a twinge or two to John Earle, one of the most frequent guests
at Great Tew and one of its owner's closest friends.

Earle had some critical sense, witness his remark on Falkland's verse, and his published "characters" show the nice
touch of a shrewd analyst of personality, as well as skill in
compact and deftly turned prose. He was an exceptionally
good classical scholar and helped Falkland in his study of
Greek. He felt that he was fully repaid, since, he said, he "got
more useful learning by his conversation at Tew . . . than he
had at Oxford." Unlike his host, he was careless in his dress,
but his untidy figure, familiar to everyone who visited Lord
and Lady Falkland, was always welcomed. His "discourse" was
"wary and cultivated," but none the less "pleasant and de-

lightful, so very innocent, and so very facetious, that no man's company was more desired and more loved." That the air of Great Tew was not too rarefied for laughter, would be proved, even if there were no other evidence, by Earle's intimacy there. Years later he was to be a bishop, and by 1639 he had a rectorship in the church, but there was nothing over-solemn in his piety or his learning.

Others, less concerned with wit than with law and politics, lent worldly lustre to the roster of Cary's friends. Sir John Vaughan, of Christ Church, Oxford, was in 1630 a barrister of the Inner Temple. He had sat in Parliament, and could tell Falkland enough of legal mysteries to whet his taste for more. That taste he tried to gratify, and he got himself admitted to Lincoln's Inn in 1638. Two years later, according to Clarendon, he was still "utterly ignorant" of law, but he must have picked up a smattering at least from Vaughan and that other lawyer who was his dearest friend after Morison's death, Clarendon himself. He was in the 1630's simply Edward Hyde, a young lawyer, admitted to Ben Jonson's company, but too sober-minded to feel at ease there. He met Falkland about the time of the challenge to Willoughby, and their intimacy grew with the years. Hyde was most at home in politics, and it was when Falkland entered Parliament that their relation became most important.

Two women Falkland admired especially, in the early years of his married life, and he wrote poems on each. One was Elizabeth, Countess of Huntingdon, who had married his wife's cousin. When she died in 1633 Cary wrote two sets of verses, an "Epitaph" and a "Funerall Elegy." [6] He praises the Countess's learning; explains that she was beautiful and virtuous, and dilates upon her wit. His tone, however, is tamely

---

[6] N. H. Bell, The Huntington Peerage (2d ed.; London, 1821), pp. 98, 118, 334. The shorter poem on Lady Huntington is in L. Carey [sic], Poems (ed. A. B. Grosart; n.p., 1871); the longer is in Egerton Mss. at the British Museum. I quote from a transcript kindly furnished me by Mr. Kurt Weber.

conventional, and suggests that his only inspiration was family feeling. The most vigorous lines come when the "Elegy" turns from the Countess herself to praise of the Church of England and ridicule of the Puritans.

The death of Margaret Feilding, wife of James, Marquis of Hamilton, in 1638, moved Cary to a far warmer tribute than he had paid Lady Huntingdon. The "Lady Marquesse Hamilton" was only twenty-five when she died, three years younger than Falkland, but she was already celebrated for her devout strictness of life and her friendship with the Queen. "No mist from knowledge her cleere soule debarres," Cary wrote, and declared that she hated "warre and strife," looked "downe on cloudes" and trod "uppon the starres." The poem also strikes a more intimate note:

> "To see her and to love her was the same:
> And if by chance, when shee did neere us stand,
> Her bright smoth palme but touch't my ruder hand
> That did both sences soe at once delight,
> The purest swans seem'd neither soft nor white."

The whole poem appeals directly to the senses more than most of Falkland's work. Obviously Lady Hamilton's physical beauty moved him as much as her moral quality. The sensuousness extends to his comments on some of the pleasures of country living. There are the "best of wheat and creame," "lillies loaded with the morning dew," "countrey sportes," "countrey layes," streams which run "purling on the peebles," and young goats in the fern. There is a heifer leaping "by a hornet stung," "darnell, cockle, and could poppie," and "rankest weedes, burrs, thornes and thistles." Falkland did not walk unseeing through his Oxfordshire fields.

The most superficial sketching of a few of Cary's friends shows how rich and varied were the resources on which he drew for companionship, intellectual stimulus, and vicarious experience, during his early manhood. Poets, courtiers, noble ladies, rakes, travellers, lawyers, men of different ages, points of view, and attainments, godless and godly, Protestant and Catholic, all appealed to his tolerant and versatile interest. Some of them became intimates; all were at least acquaintances, and there must have been distinction of personality in a young man who could attract friends of so many kinds. Some of them he knew before his marriage, others perhaps not until after his father's death; some were brought into touch with him through Jonson and others through Hyde. Some he saw only in London, but to them he wrote when he was in the country, and others followed him out of the city to be his guests at Coventry, where he lived for a time before 1633, or at Burford, at Aldenham, nearer town, or at the best loved of his residences, Great Tew.

Wherever his friends were he was happy. With Suckling and others of the wits he went to Eton where, in the rooms of John Hales, still another close friend, there was a great debate as to whether Shakespeare, whom Hales admired passionately, outshone the poets of antiquity. Falkland and "all the Persons of Quality that had Wit and Learning, and interested themselves in the Quarrel" found a verdict for the English poet. Such an occasion Falkland loved, as he did any chance for good talk, whether it was with Hyde or Vaughan about law, about religion with his mother and brother, or about poetry with any one of the versifiers he knew.

Much as he loved the city, with the plays, books, and friends he found there, he could not stay indefinitely, postponing decisions about the future. He had at last to make up his mind to go back to Oxfordshire. This was partly because the King had made it clear that loyal country gentlemen should live on their estates and not in town.[7] On them rested

---

[7] June 20, 1632, a proclamation ordered "the Gentry to keep their Residence at their Mansions in the Country . . . forbidding them to make their habitations in London, and places adjoining"; Rushworth, II, (187). A list, dated in the same month of those whom the King permitted, in spite of the proclamation, to stay in London or other towns, includes "Sir Lucius Cary to dwell in Coventry, by his father the Lord Viscount's motion"; CSP, Do-

much of the responsibility for local government, and it was no time to have the machinery weakened. Falkland seems to have had no office which demanded his presence at court, and, furthermore, he could hardly afford to keep up an establishment in London. He could support his wife, his mother, and his brothers and sisters, more cheaply elsewhere. It was a wrench to leave the city, but he still loved his books, and peaceful study in his library was hardly less attractive than the gaieties of courtiers and playwrights.

He had to sell the house at Burford, where he was born, to pay some of his father's debts, and within a few years he turned over Aldenham to his mother. But Great Tew was left. The windows of his quiet house there looked down on one of the loveliest of English villages. The garden, the laurels, the church a stone's throw from his door, blended into a theatrically perfect setting for a retired scholar. Oxford was only a few miles away, with books in plenty, and learned men. Once out of London Falkland's "severe course of study . . . was very delightful to him," and life ran smoothly at Great Tew. "While others studied the Heraldry of Horses, of Doggs, or at the best their owne," he read on graver themes; when "Hawking and Hunting Gentlemen" sat sulkily indoors, he was always busy, and used to say, "I pity unlearned gentlemen on a rainy day!" If there were noisy riots in London, the discontented in Oxfordshire were less vociferous; if the plague slew its thousands in the city, Great Tew was safer; if the town distracted the mind from the abstract and the absolute by the pressure of immediate symptoms of conflict, Falkland's country village lived about as calmly as it had for generations. There one could think and write verse without too drastic

mestic, 1631–1633, p. 369. Aubrey, I, 150, speaks of Cary's living at Coventry. Two of his sons, born 1637 and 1639, were baptized at Aldenham; another, born 1632, was baptized at Great Tew; a fourth, 1634, at Burford; (F. Harrison), *The Devon Carys*, II, 458–459; *Complete Peerage*, V, 241.

reminders that the world was changing in spite of bookish precepts and scholars' dreams.

There were friends at Great Tew, as there had been in London—some more often seen there than in town. One was the brother of Captain Rainsford. Another, who lived near by at Caswell was Sir Francis Wenman, a close friend of both Falkland and Hyde. The latter described him as the type of country gentlemen, though one "esteemed in court." His honest wisdom endeared him to Falkland, with whom he was in such "entire friendship and confidence . . . that he had great authority in the society of all his friends and acquaintance." Sharp witted and alert to current affairs, he was indolent—perhaps because of his bad health—and preferred to be a commentator on the political drama rather than an actor in it. He foresaw the Civil War, and his prophesies must have sometimes struck a sombre note, even when the talk was gayest.

At Wenman's house often lived George Sandys, whom Falkland valued hardly less than Ben Jonson. He was a famous traveller, had finished his translation of Ovid's *Metamorphoses* in Virginia, and was long active in the affairs of that colony. Probably he helped Falkland to get an office there for one of his brothers-in-law, three of whom tried their fortunes in the New World. Certainly Sandys and Cary knew each other well, and for the time when the former lived with Wenman, they were near neighbors. Three of the Viscount's poems were in honor of Sandys, and most of a fourth, ostensibly praising Grotius.

There was no lack of good company, then, at Great Tew, and however unworldly Falkland's interests were, his house was no ivory tower. With Sandys, Wenman, and Hyde, as well as with the friends who came out from London or rode over from Oxford, there must have been as much discussion of current affairs as of history and doctrine. However detached the physical circumstances of Cary's life were, he had every chance to keep himself well informed about what went on in the nation.

Much had happened since he left Dublin. 1629 was a critical year. In the stormy dissolution of the Parliament by the King, when the House of Commons greeted the royal order to adjourn with cries of "No, no!" and the Speaker was held in his seat by violence, "the opposition showed a new temper, and a readiness to appeal to force." [8] King Charles and the Parliament were virtually at each other's throats. The interests of a newly powerful middle class were in danger from the King's insistence on his prerogative; economic and social grievances, neatly labelled as abuses of "liberty," were tinder which religious and political emotions kindled easily to a blaze. The Puritans, the growing body of extreme Protestants, hated both the Catholics and many elements in the national church. Even in the Anglican fold there was little harmony. The Arminians, the "high church" party led by William Laud, who was made archbishop in 1633, were outraging some of their more moderate brethren. Laud's very strength and moral earnestness held seeds of tragedy for the nation, the real temper of which he did not understand. At Oxford there were "great Disorders" when two young divines dared to contest Arminian tenets. In London, a commission, including Lucius Cary's father, had been set up to carry out repairs on St. Paul's Cathedral and practically to enforce donations to pay for the work. Puritans who saw in the great church only "a rotten relic," muttered about "superstition" and "idolatry." There were trials of obstreperous zealots, and unruly members of the last Parliament including Cary's friend, John Selden, had a chance in jail to reflect on the folly of opposing the King. There was the unsavory trial of Lord Audley, who brought obloquy on his class, by assisting while a servant raped his wife and by his own even less mentionable sexual crimes.

---

[8] I. D. Jones, *The English Revolution* (London, 1931), p. 26.

There appeared a succession of devices for fattening the King's purse. The work of government was carried on by proclamations and the decisions of loyal judges. Viscount Wentworth whom the elder Falkland hated, was chosen to succeed him as Deputy in Ireland, and Henry Cary's "secret Malice" was "bubbled . . . abroad" in critical gossip. A prince was born, and good subjects rejoiced.

Storm clouds were gathering, but so long as there was no actual war young landowners like Lucius Cary got on very well without looking at the threatening sky. "Never, in spite of all that had occurred, had civil war appeared farther off than in the spring of 1633. Never did there seem to be a fairer prospect of overcoming the irritation that had prevailed four years before."

Even if Cary got glimpses now and then of dangers ahead, he managed to keep his confidence in the monarchy. If he smarted when he remembered Fleet Prison, he chose not to show it or at least not to blame Charles I. In 1631 he included in some verses to Jonson flattering lines on the King, and in 1632 he wrote a poem celebrating that "great prince's" happy recovery from smallpox.[9] "Father" and "master" were the proper epithets for a sovereign whom all servants of virtue hoped to "have everlastingly their own." For a youthful Cary to praise the King was as natural as to love a soldier's life; with such instinctive likings Lucius's reasoned doubts and principles had always to contend. But the 1632 poem, outspoken as is its praise of Charles, rings hollow. Its adulation is in the most general terms and it gives no clue as to just why the King's survival seemed a boon. If Cary knew or felt why, he did not reveal it in his neat phrases, which seem to express

---

[9] The poem on the King's recovery is in Ashmole Mss. 38, #85, p. 74, at the Bodleian. Charles had smallpox in Dec., 1632 (Rushworth, II, 139), so that the poem was probably written late in that year or early in 1633. Since the preceding poem in the ms. refers to the King's smallpox, it seems probable that the "Recouerye" which occasioned Cary's lines was from that disease.

neither emotion nor thought. The poem was the work of a man who took allegiance to Charles for granted, as one of the traditional attitudes to which he had been bred. Those attitudes prevailed even when, a few years later, the royal impositions of "ship-money" provoked some other Englishmen to open defiance and many to passive resistance. Perhaps Cary questioned the justice of the tax—certainly he did later—but he paid his share. The habit of deference to the King was fixed. Early doubts, even mild rebelliousness, could not dissipate the loyalty in which he had been reared.[10]

No doubt most of his friends agreed with him. For those who did not his tolerance was beyond reproach. "Towards his friend's infirmities no man was more indulgent." More and more with every year that passed, he came to be not simply the host of Great Tew but the actual centre of a group of men who turned to his house as to "a college situated in a purer air."

Lettice deserves her share of the credit. She had faults, no doubt, for all her piety, and may have been an expensive luxury for her husband. Like his mother she was recklessly generous.

> "She
> As Costly was in *Alms* and *Piety*,
> As *City Madams* are in *Luxury*,
> And made more *Visits* to the *Poor*, then those
> Do to the *Rich*, when they've *new Coach & Cloaths*."

Aubrey tells, with malicious pleasure, how she boasted of her ability to get from her husband anything she wanted, even

---

[10] CSP, Domestic, 1636–1637, pp. 210, 230-231, 277, 432; Id., 1637–1638, p. 88; Gardiner, History, VIII, 258; W. J. Monk, History of Burford (London, 1891), p. 125. Gardiner, Longueville (p. 96), and Marriott (pp. 128-129), point out that Cary paid in Oxfordshire but not in Hertfordshire. They fail to notice that his Hertfordshire estate, Aldenham, was probably now his mother's, or, at least, the subject of legal dispute. It seems obvious that Cary did not pay ship-money in Hertfordshire because his liability for it was not proved. If he refused to pay because of scruples about the justice of the tax, why should he have paid in Oxfordshire?

permission to rent a farm for less than its value, by tears, "kisses, and secret embraces." But if Lucius Cary's business sense was overruled by affection, it was a generous defect, and even Aubrey does not suggest that Lettice used her power except in the interest of charity to others. Moreover, she performed miracles as a housekeeper. Somehow she contrived so that guests might come as they liked, always sure that rooms would be ready for them, the library open, and the table spread. Except that everyone dined and supped together, no one need ever be bothered by anyone else. Falkland himself never knew who was in the house until he met them at the table, where he would forget his books and plunge into "facetiousness of wit . . . and pleasantness of discourse, which made the gravity of the argument itself (whatever it was) very delectable." His wife may have had her bad moments on days when scholars rode over from Oxford, and arrived just as a coach full of guests from London rolled up with servants to be cared for, horses to be stabled, and a carefree company seeking beds and food, but her domestic magic was a match for such occasions. The historical record of Great Tew gives no hint that turmoil in kitchen and pantry ever disturbed the host or his friends.

When Falkland left Great Tew in 1639, he was a very different person from the impetuous boy who had challenged Willoughby. He had ripened into a scholar. He knew most classic authors, and had studied especially "the most allowed and authentic ecclesiastical writers." His memory was exceptional, but he had tact enough to use it without seeming affected or pedantic. Better still, his personality enriched those who knew him. For them he was a "noble friend," one who was "prodigal" of his "great soul." His "disposition and nature was so gentle and obliging," so marked by "kindness and generosity, that all mankind could not but admire and love him." His mind and manners were "most accomplished," his "affability . . . was transcendent." "His conversation . . . was the most cheerful and pleasant that can be imagined"—so pleasant that no one minded his bad voice. "If any thing, though never so little unhandsomely, had been spoken or done where he was, he was the greatest sufferer in the company, and much more out of countenance then he that made the offence. . . . He that was so tender of another mans *Civility* . . . had a great regard to his owne" and "to do an ill or an uncivill thing . . . was an arrant Coward." There was "nothing so . . . handsome in all *Seneca's Lawes* of *Benefits*, that he knew not how to do, and to out-do for his Friend." But he never sacrificed his personal standards to be agreeable, and one measure of his character is the way in which his guests made his scruples their own. "He had so chaste a tongue and ear, that there was never known a profane or loose word to fall from him, nor in truth in his company." Yet even if they had to leash their tongues when they were with him, the wits were well paid by the "great gayety" and "flowing delightfulness" of his talk. Without assurance as to that "gayety," without the comforting knowledge that he made friends of some of the more ribald, the picture of Falkland at Great Tew might be cloying with too much "sweetness and light." But a man who could hold his own with Carew, Suckling, and Jonson, was no prude, and a man who liked both Kenelm Digby and John Earle was no mere type of bloodless excellence.

"Quick-silver if fixed, is incomparable," wrote David Lloyd, contrasting Cary's youthful rashnesses with his later distinction as "a knowing Statesman, a learned Scholar, and a stout man." To the "fixing" of his character, many things contributed: his mother's example, his wife's piety, and chiefly his friends. With him they loved to "examine and refine those grosser propositions which laziness and consent made current in vulgar conversation." They were masters who could teach him how, even in scholarly isolation, to avoid sterile intellectuality. They were his pupils, too, increasingly as the years passed, for more and more he concentrated on basic problems of importance for every thoughtful man in his troubled time. The only real leadership he ever achieved, was leadership among his friends, but in making them not only friends but disciples he did more than most men could in politics or war. There remains to be told the tale of how from 1633 to 1639 he turned the full vigor of his mind to the championship of religious tolerance, the supremacy of reason, and the right to intellectual freedom. In that tale is the clue to the persistence of his reputation as the noblest of Charles I's cavaliers.

V

"THINKING FOOLS"

The Scholar at Great Tew, 1631–1639

DURING Falkland's bookish retirement in Oxfordshire, Sir John Suckling wrote his "Sessions of the Poets," a potpourri of comment on contemporary wits. For many of them there was a flick of mockery, but the lines on Lucius Cary were unspiced with satire:

> "He was of late so gone with divinity,
> That he had almost forgot his poetry,
> Though to say the truth (and Apollo did know it)
> He might have been both his priest and his poet."

Falkland was indeed by 1637 "gone with divinity." He had progressed from being simply a verse-maker and the companion of court wits to become a hard student, concentrating on the problem of religious authority and especially on the place of reason in Christian thought. His work carried his fame beyond the circle of his devoted friends, and, in 1638, a Fellow of Cambridge University, Robert Cresswell, wrote a poem praising his championship of reason. In return Falkland sent him a book, and Cresswell seized the chance to recommend to his Lordship one of the young scholars of Trinity College, a precocious poet named Abraham Cowley. When Cary joined the King's troops in 1639, Cowley wrote verses extolling him as a "great *Prince of Knowledge*" and possessor of "a *Monopoly of Wit*." The poet's admiration, like Cresswell's sprang from reverence for Falkland's scholarly conquests. Cowley was fatally complacent in his susceptibility to poetic fashions, but he was steadfast in his worship of reason. He celebrated Falkland as a high priest at the same altar, a high priest by virtue of his solid attainment in theology.

The shift from poetry to "divinity" appears in Falkland's own verse. The elegy on Morison, except for Biblical references and an assertion of belief in the Scriptures, is unconcerned with religion, and in it Donne is alluded to only as a poet. But when, not long afterwards, Falkland devoted another elegy to Donne, it was the divine that he celebrated. Donne, according to his admirer, excelled chiefly in his command of his rebel passions and in his insistence on a rational testing of faith.

> "Experience makes us see, that many a one
> Owes to his countrey his religion;
> And in another, would as strongly grow,
> Had but his nurse and mother taught him so:
> Not he! The ballast on his judgement hung:
> Nor did his preconceit do either wrong:
> He labour'd to exclude what ever sinne
> By time or carelesnesse had entred in;
> Winnow'd the chaffe from wheat, but yet was loath
> A too hot zeale should force him burne them both;
> Nor would allow of that so ignorant gall,
> Which to save blotting often would blot all;
> Nor did those barbarous opinions owne,
> To think the organs sinne, and faction, none."

The emphasis on religion as necessarily determined by "judgement" became central in Falkland's thinking. So did his distrust of those Protestants who, he thought, advocated schism. That would weaken the English ecclesiastical system, which might need correction in details but not drastic alteration by those who were so pedantically blind that they would condone destroying what was good rather than put up with organ music in church. The true believer was he who could rise above passion and use his reason to sift the sound wheat of doctrine from the chaff.

Falkland returns to the attack on the Puritans in the longer of his two poems to Lady Huntingdon, calling them:

> "that Companye,
> Who having first set their conclusions downe,
> Seeke promises in Scripture, whose grave frowne
> Hopes to confute; to whom Virginity
> With Almes and fasting, appeares Popery;
> Who to be indiscreet, count to be stout;
> With whom the factions are alone devout;
> Thinke all in state of grace, and void of sinne;
> Hate Hooker perfectly, and honour Prynn;
> Preach oftner than say grace; whose schollers doe
> Beleeve to heare's more pious then to doe,
> As though from kings, those most deserv'd applause
> That read their statutes, then that keepe their lawes;
> To whom the want of Charity seemes noe losse,
> Soe they have confident faith, and hate Christ's crosse
> Worse then his Crucifiers, and soe proud be growne,
> To give his spouse lesse honour then their owne;
> Who, when first towards divinity they come,
> Have for their journey Sole viaticum,
> To rule the people, and their fame advance,
> Good Lungs, not learning, and a Concordance."

This echoes what good Anglicans commonly said of the extreme Protestant zealots of the time and reflects the prejudices of the young nobleman trained to identify loyalty and churchmanship. For Falkland the national church was "Christ's spouse." To it the Countess of Huntingdon had been loyal, and of her he writes:

"THINKING FOOLS"

"Thy end was to live well, not confute
And damne all that deny; not to dispute
Hourely such Questions, wert thou proudly glad,
As made Divines giddy and Laymen Mad,
But, modestly assured, for thee Christ dyed,
Didst not confine it to some few beside."

Here is a positive plea for Christian harmony as more important than minor differences of creed, coupled with scorn for useless theologizing. The Puritans' narrow dogmatism, he felt, excluded Lady Huntingdon's generosity of mind.

As early as 1634, then, Cary had come to distrust the narrowness of the "sects." The very search for truth, it seemed to him, demanded greater tolerance than theirs. "In religion he thought too careful and too curious an inquiry could not be made . . . by men who were furthest from being of one mind . . . for the . . . support of their several opinions, in which they most contradicted each other. . . . In all those controversies, he had so dispassioned a consideration, such a candour in his nature, and so profound a charity in his conscience, that in those points, in which he was in his own judgment most clear, he never thought the worse, or in any degree declined the familiarity, of those who were of another mind." Catholics, like Digby, were welcome as friends; so, probably, was Toby Matthew, notorious for his attachment to Rome; and with his mother, of course, Falkland could talk of religious differences without heat.

Talk of them he did, with her and others, and he read and thought of them more and more every year, candidly confessing his change of interests. To Sandys he wrote:

"Thy pen next, having clear'd thy Maker's will,
Supples our hearts to love, and to fulfill;
And moves such pittie, that her power layes
That envie, which thy eloquence doth raise.

Even I (no yeelding matter) who till then
Am chiefe of sinners, and the worst of men . . .
Suffer a rape by Vertue, whilst thy lines
Destroy my old, and build my new designes."

Then comes a reference to the scattering of "those mists . . . which my passions bred." What they were, or what possible excuse Falkland had for calling himself "chiefe of sinners, and the worst of men," remains a mystery. Probably he was simply indulging in the mild exhibitionism common to those who believe they have renounced evil. But it is certain that he had crowded out some of his lighter interests, and that he sincerely felt that he "who lookes down on vice, looks down on Fate." By 1638 he spoke of his "dying Muse"—proof that he did not hope to go farther with poetry—and treated with contempt

"Those looser poets whose lacivious pen
Ascribing crimes to Gods, taught them to men."

He had no use for

"Those who make wit their curse, who spend their brain,
Their time, and art in looser verse, to gain
Damnation and a mistres, till they see
How constant that is, how inconstant she."

For Falkland the "blessed way" had come to be not that of Tom Carew, Suckling, and the wits whom he had met with Ben Jonson, but that of the graver scholars whom he entertained at Great Tew. To follow it meant to read deeply in church history and theology, and as he read he became more and more intent on the hunt for a secure basis for faith.

Today, a young man with his way to make and no wish to make it in the ministry or in education, who gave up several years to such study, might seem to be retreating from life. In many quarters he would be condemned for cutting himself off from reality in order to pursue a futile academic hobby.

A generation or two after Cary there were to be many English intellectuals so sceptical about all except material values as to regard such men as Falkland and his friends as "thinking Fools." But in the 1630's Christian doctrine and polity were matters of direct concern for most active-minded men. A statesman who acted without knowing something of what the Puritans, the Arminians and other Anglicans, and the Catholics, believed, and why, would act foolishly. Questions about beliefs and modes of worship, were woven into politics. Men who had no god but their pocket-books had to recognize the link between the monarchy and the national church. The bishops, and what the bishops held to be law, were often as important to them as civil officers and courts. Even the scientists and the philosophers gave a large place in their thought to current ideas about God, his worshippers, and the nature of Christian morality, however isolated their laboratories might be and however unreligious their attitude. Spiritual beliefs powerfully affected men's actions, and the practices of the Church and its enemies were forces in everyday life. Order and morality were linked with Christian faith; laws, taxes, worldly ambitions, all were affected by ecclesiastical rule. There was, by the standards of his day, nothing strange in Falkland's interest in religious history and dogma. What was unusual was the intensity of his concern, and the length of time he gave to the uninterrupted study of "divinity."

The explanation was that he felt, besides the normal curiosity of any intelligent young man about matters which it was useful to understand, a special need to inquire into the bases of faith and worship—a need arising from the circumstances of his life. For him the study of the Church Fathers and the varieties of doctrine was no escape from reality, but a coming to grips with problems of great personal moment. In no other way could he hope to make order out of the warring intellectual and emotional elements which underlay his whole relation to the world.

In the winter of 1633–34, in London, he had seen much of his mother, and had learned something of her happiness in her faith. He knew her faults, but he admired her. He was very like her, after all. He had inherited her taste for books; he shared something of her zeal for giving away more than she could afford, and had his full portion of her contempt for the merely expedient or useful when principles were at stake. His impetuous courage reflected the nature that had defied a "very absolute" husband, the Lords of the Council, and the Chief Justice himself. His mother had taught him "knowledge, love, and esteem of all moral virtue," based on Christian precept. She had told her children that "when they loved anything . . . they were to love God more than it. . . . They must love Him and honour Him more than their father: He gave them their father, He sent them every good thing, and made it for them; the king was his servant, and He made all kings and gave them their kingdoms." Thus Lucius Cary got a "great . . . sense of good and ill"—a sense stimulated by Henry Morison's virtues and by Ben Jonson's robust insistence on an exalted moral code. Naturally Lady Elizabeth Cary's influence over her eldest son remained strong, even after she turned to Rome. She hoped that he would become a Catholic too, and her confidence that only in her church could spiritual security be found, and her ability, strong in her faith, to contend triumphantly against a sea of troubles, were impressive enough to give weight to her pleas. They rested, probably, on the idea that there must be a single divinely ordained Christian church, to which all believers owed loyalty. She was instinctively, as Bishop Neile saw, a lover of authority.

For her generation belief in universal truth embodied in an institution was far easier than for her son's, exposed as it was to the disintegrating force of growing individualism. "In politics, in thought, in religion, in art there was everywhere a dissolution of accepted things" before the advances of science and new economic and social theories. Men were being forced to seek out new patterns for their acts and aspirations, and hence came "the emergence of the individual to consciousness of himself," often at the expense of the creeds and organizations which his parents had contentedly accepted.[1] Falkland's mother was ready to subjugate both will and reason in order to win salvation through the power of her church. If faith demanded that she believe in what she could not rationally explain—such as the angelical apparition she thought she saw at her daughter's death-bed—she must obey. Some things she knew, without being able to give proofs, and it was easy for her to receive whatever the church endorsed as truth.

Her son and his fellows had outgrown her state of mind. They lived in a "strange crepuscular period between the reign of superstition and the reign of reason." [2] Old assumptions of exclusive truth were breaking up. The physical world was being scrutinized and defined in opposition to traditional schemes, and the effort was more and more to rest all thinking on what could be objectively demonstrated in physical or mathematical terms. It was only natural, therefore, that some

---

[1] J. Buchan, Oliver Cromwell (London, 1934), p. 21; anonymous review of M. Bishop's Pascal in London Times Literary Supplement, April 3, 1937.

[2] L. Powys, "The Quincuncical Doctor" in Saturday Review of Literature (N. Y., June 4, 1932). Related to the greater emphasis on the power of reason in Falkland's day was the conviction that men knew how to reason then better than of yore. He wrote that the "first Ages" were not "so carefull and subtile in their Logick, as these more learned times both Arminians and Calvinists, Dominicans and Jesuites, Papists and Protestants, seeming to me to argue much more consequently to their owne Principles . . . and every way more rationally then the Ancient Doctors used to do"; L. Cary, "Reply" in Discourse of Infallibility (London, 1660), p. 148. Keats's comment in Letters (ed. M. B. Forman; 2d ed.; N. Y., 1935), pp. 144-145, is relevant: "In his [Milton's] time englishmen were just emancipated from a great superstition—and Men had got hold of certain points and resting places in reasoning which were too newly born to be doubted, and too much opposed by the Mass of Europe not to be thought etherial and authentically divine. . . . Protestantism was considered under the immediate eye of heaven, and its own remaining Dogmas and superstitions, then . . . constituted those resting places and seeming sure points of Reasoning."

men tried to strip off from religion all that could not somehow be vouched for by similar tests. Their attack was not only on the miraculous or the legends that ran counter to the experience of reasonable men, but also on anything that depended solely on the authority of a church. Was there any church or any single way of life that was universally valid? Could there be? However much he talked with his mother, Falkland remained in doubt.

How could he believe her right unless much that he had learned at Trinity College was wrong? How could he follow her without betraying his father's memory? To Sir Henry Cary, Lady Elizabeth's Catholicism had seemed a crime, and in his gallant efforts to serve the King in Ireland, Papists had been his foes. Lucius Cary loved him less than his mother, but could not idly dismiss his boyish reverence. Even more intimately moving was Lucius's affection for his own wife. She was sure in her faith and as serenely dependent on it as the Dowager Lady Falkland, but the older woman was a Catholic and the younger as ardently a Protestant. One Cary loved as a mother; the other, as a wife who was more than a wife because she was the sister of his dearest friend, untimely lost, and because she was very like his mother. She would have regarded his turning Catholic as treachery to the truth. So it would have seemed, probably, to her dead brother, and certainly to Cary's father. Beset by such tangled loyalties all he could tell his mother was that he could not decide finally on the choice of a religion until he was forty. He confessed that "he knew nothing but what the Church told him," but added that even this only "seemed to him to be" so.

He could not evade the issue by dismissing it as unimportant. To say it did not matter how one worshipped might have been a way out for some men, but he had in his wife and his mother proofs that faith might bring greater security and integrity than doubters knew. As one of his wife's eulogists put it:

"'Tis true, Sh'had many scruples . . . they're such
As neither *Gods*, nor *Kings* Prerogative touch.
'Mongst all her holy Doubtings, you'l find none
Startling at *Gods Decrees*, or *Three in One*.
Such Mysteries her Faith had conquer'd."

Her assurance, extending even to the divine right of kings, was
something for a restlessly uncertain husband to envy.

"*Her Soul lay well for His;* and made as fit
A Match, as when *Discretion* meets with *Wit*.
His *Knowledge* rectifi'd Her *Zeal*, and then
Her *Faith* His *Reason* qualifi'd agen.
 Thus Two Elixirs mingled safely pass,
 Whereas each single often breaks the Glass."

That was the root of the matter. Lettice's faith made Lucius
Cary long also to believe, and it helped to keep his unanswered
questions from making him a complete sceptic. He was forced
to wonder whether he might not gain from religious confidence like hers, and his highly developed moral sense pointed
in the same direction. The virtues that he admired in his
mother and his wife, and had praised in Henry Morison, were
the virtues which were ostensibly fostered by Christian
churches. Even men without allegiance to particular com-
munions had to admit that morality and religion went hand
in hand. John Selden said: "They that cry down Moral-honesty,
cry down that which is a great part of Religion, my Duty towards God, and my Duty towards man. . . . Morality must
not be without Religion. . . . He that has not Religion to
govern his Morality, is not a Dram better than my Mastiff-
Dogg . . . he is a very good Moral-Mastiff, but if you hurt him,
he will fly in your Face, and tear out your Throat." Moral
honesty ranked so high in Falkland's scale of values that he
could not treat religion with indifference.

Sure as to the benefits of a fixed faith, but still helpless to decide upon one, he was thrown back on analysis and study in an effort somehow to prove what way of belief could satisfy him. In the meantime it was natural to be an Anglican, rather than a Presbyterian or a Catholic, since loyalty to the King, and patriotism, construed as support of the established order, involved respect for the existing national church. Puritans, whether Presbyterians or members of some one of the minor sects, were, in Falkland's opinion, upstarts, and the baser of them threatened the safety of his class. He could not identify himself with them, nor, in view of his wife's Protestantism, with the Catholics. He could call himself an Anglican, and still be open-minded and patient in his search for some surcease from doubt. There was at the moment no better way.[3]

His mother's principles were as exalted as his, and her moral enthusiasm as hot, but her religious certainty ruled out tolerance. So she kidnapped her children from Great Tew lest they be made Protestants by Lettice Cary or by William Chillingworth. Clarendon has it that her folly in this lessened Falkland's "charity" for Catholics and that he afterwards "quite declined" "any correspondence with them." This must be exaggeration. No doubt his mother's rashness whetted his eagerness to test once and for all the Catholics' assumption of exclusive truth, but his tolerance seems to have remained unshaken. He resolutely upheld the right of every man to think as he chose. Even a child's conscience must not be forced. He refused to take his brothers and sisters into his house, though he wanted to spare his mother the cost of caring for them, until he was sure that they came to him of their own free will. However much he disagreed with his mother, he was always kind to her in her poverty, helping her whenever her pride and consideration for him allowed her to confess her

---

[3] Cf. Falkland's, "In all decency and Majestie of ceremonies, the Kings Chappell seems to me to equall the Queens, and our Cathedrall Churches, much to surpasse" Catholic "cock-lofts" ("Reply" in *Discourse*, pp. 177-178).

plight. Moreover, when his brothers and sisters deserted Protestantism, he did not try to prevent it, and seems even to have done his best to aid one of the girls to become a nun.

Nor did he avoid those whose whole turn of mind, apart from differences in creed, was quite foreign to his. He achieved friendship with John Selden, for example, probably the most learned Englishman of the century and a thoroughgoing intellectual aristocrat, sure that none but scholars were worth listening to. Deeply versed in law, an erudite antiquarian, and a great linguist, he had no sympathy for religious feeling. His whole temper was sceptical and ironic. When D'Ewes said he was "much more learned than pious" he was understating; he was not pious at all. Spiritual aspiration was for him irrational emotionalism. Religious zealots were fools, and, if given their heads, enemies to society. Men chose their religions on subjective grounds of no general validity, and the various sects reflected their ambitions, selfishness, and cravings for recognition, not any real thirst for truth.

Selden was, to be sure, tolerant in religion, but tolerant only because he regarded creeds as unimportant. Churches were inevitably fallible, and the Bible was a man-made document. Inspired by God it might be, but it was known only in a form garbled by human errors and prejudices, so that it was idle to look to it for clear authority. Such views ran directly counter to the Dowager Lady Falkland's and Lettice Cary's. Their faith must have seemed to Selden devotion to nonsense, and Falkland's quest for certainty probably appeared futile except in so far as it involved a healthy readiness to challenge the bases of religious loyalties. The great scholar's "icy scepticism" might make the devout wince, but it was tonic for a young man hopefully determined to believe, but not until his reason as well as his emotions could be appeased.[4]

---

[4] W. K. Jordan, *The Development of Religious Toleration in England* . . . *1603–1640* (Camb., 1936), p. 483.

What really mattered for Selden was the state. What good government demanded was right; all that interfered, wrong. The test was utility, and if anything worked well, abstract principles could be forgotten. But even political standards were unstable. Selden had twice been jailed for siding with the Parliament against the King, and had been officially censured because one of his books annoyed the bishops. But another, in 1636, was loudly praised by the King's adherents. Each was, by its author's standards, sound. What determined their reception was not truth but whose ox was gored. What folly to talk as if abstract conceptions had anything to do with practical affairs! Why not admit that the world is mad and support any government which can keep it running without too much interference from the most stupid of mankind? The same scepticism, not to say cynicism, Selden extended to the whole range of human behavior.

His talk was famous, spiced with wit and seasoned everywhere with his dryly humorous contempt for folly. Many of his remarks will carry the weight of proverbial truths as long as institutions are imperfect and men and women silly. Corrosives for smug pretense, his sayings were useful when poets' visions and the exuberant speculations of theologians outran the limits of discreet worldliness. They must have stimulated Falkland, though his reverence for nobility of character implied a belief, not shared by Selden, in human goodness, and though the lawyer's readiness to trim his sails when expediency bade was opposed to the young Viscount's resolve to follow his "private sense" at all costs. Falkland was not the man to agree with Selden's dictum: " 'Tis not seasonable to call a Man Traitor that has an Army at his Heels. One with an Army is a Gallant man." Even Hyde, who respected Selden, found him too complaisant about abuses in the state, but Selden's defense was that "Wise men say nothing in dangerous times" or that "In a troubled State we must do as in foul Weather upon the Thames, not think to cut directly through; so, the Boat may be quickly full of water; but rise and fall as the Waves do, give as much as conveniently we can."

Conveniently! Convenience and expediency were sovereign values for Selden, perhaps partly because he was physically "a most tender man." The Falkland whom Jonson had praised aimed higher. But he could not close his ears to Selden's acid commentaries, and no doubt they intensified the scepticism forced upon him by his experience of religious disagreement in his own family. Certainly many of his friend's aphorisms might touch him nearly. Wits were good, but wise men better. "Wit is upon the sudden turn, Wisdom is in bringing about ends." Universities needed lectureships upon "Discretion." "Verse proves nothing but the quantity of Syllables, they are not meant for Logick." Even scholarship did not escape. "No man is the wiser for his Learning, it may administer Matter to work in, or Objects to work upon, but Wit and Wisdom are born with a Man." And as to the divine right of kings, "The Text [render unto Caesar the things that are Caesars] makes . . . against Kings . . . for it says plainly that some things are not Caesars."

The salt in such talk keeps its savor. Selden pointed his maxims with anecdotes of mastiff dogs and country wenches; he said cryptic things like "Syllables govern the world"; and tuned every sentence to the tangible data of a materially ordered universe. For Falkland the sting was sharpest when his friend spoke of religion and the churches. "The Clergy would have us believe them against our own Reason," and "They talk (but blasphemously enough) that the Holy Ghost is President of their General-Councils, when the truth is, the odd man is still the Holy-Ghost." What would the elder Lady Falkland and her pious daughter-in-law say to that? What would they answer to Selden's: "Is there not enough to meddle with upon the Stage, or in Love, or at the Table, but Religion?" or to his declaration that neither church nor Scripture but the state, was "Judge of Religion"? What of his final chilly splash: "Disputes in Religion will never be ended, because there wants a Measure by which the Business would be decided"? What answer could Falkland find, even though it was to seeking just such a "Measure" that he had dedicated his studious hours?

Much like Selden in some basic attitudes was another acquaintance of Falkland's, Thomas Hobbes. In 1629 he had published a translation of Thucydides, and Cary must have known him first simply as a man of letters and the friend of his friends, Jonson, Godolphin, and Mayne. But the mind which was later to produce the *Leviathan*, and in its drastic materialism to supply one of the most effective intellectual ferments of the century, was even in its earlier development something for idealists to reckon with. Hobbes had learned much from Francis Bacon, and that alone gave him enough to talk about. Moreover, he must have been already maturing convictions about politics, and gathering material for championing the sanctity of absolute monarchy. He was, finally, in love with geometry, and made himself a trying guest by working problems in bed, drawing his diagrams on his thigh and on the sheets.

Like Selden he had no sympathy for religious feeling, and was realistic in his view of human frailty. He slammed the door on spiritual heartburnings and poets' dreams, and opened it only to admit what could be expressed and understood in terms of a mechanical conception of the world. If Falkland was ever in danger of straying too far into metaphysics, or letting his feelings betray him into religious emotionalism, he had only to turn to Hobbes—or to Selden—to be brought sharply to account.

On the other hand he had in his circle others who, though not the intellectual equals of Selden and Hobbes, knew how to plead for what they denied. Hyde characteristically says nothing in his list of Falkland's friends about the profane poets, Carew and Suckling, and nothing about Hobbes, whose later views outraged him. He concentrates on the divines who came to Great Tew in force. There were George Eglionby, friend of Hobbes, and later Dean of Canterbury; Charles Gataker, a chaplain in the household; and Thomas Triplet, who tutored one of the Cary children. Then there was a handful of clerics whose abilities were to earn them bishoprics. Later Falkland had harsh things to say of bishops, and remarked that he never knew one "that a paire of lawne sleeves had not altered from himselfe, but only bishop Juxon." Juxon, apparently, was not an intimate, but Barlow, Sheldon, Morley, and Hammond were, in the days when they were still not "altered" from themselves.

Thomas Barlow became Bishop of Lincoln in 1675. When Falkland knew him he was metaphysical reader to the university at Oxford, and more staunch in orthodox Anglicanism than he dared to remain when the Puritans threatened him with loss of his place. George Morley hated Catholics, and disliked High-Church Anglicans. He was famous as a debater, and for his "temper and prudence" in speech. He was a close friend of Edmund Waller. That poet, sitting one day in talk with Falkland, Chillingworth, and others, heard a commotion in the street below his windows, and, going down, found the bystanders gleefully celebrating the arrest for debt of one of "Jonson's sons." The victim was Morley. Waller promptly paid his bills on condition that he would come and stay with him. From then on Morley was often at Waller's house in Buckinghamshire, and his host said that he learned from him to appreciate the classic poets. He probably also learned something of wit. Morley, asked about the tenets of the High-Church party: "What do the Arminians hold?" replied dryly: "All the best bishoprics and deaneries in England"— a shrewd saying that his delighted friends kept alive. Eventually he became Bishop of Worcester, but it was said that he was first "known to the world as a friend of the lord Falkland's: and that was enough to raise a man's character." As for Gilbert Sheldon, he was Warden of All Souls', Oxford, and the very model of a perfect ecclesiastical politician. With worldly eyes he saw religion as "an engine of government, and a matter of policy." He was clear headed and able, and a good conversationalist, though perhaps a thought too glib. Sir Francis Wenman met him at Great Tew, listened, and looked him over—then uttered his verdict: "This man was born and bred to be Archbishop of Canterbury!" He was right. More shrewd than Morley, but less devout and less honest in his faith, Sheldon achieved the highest office in the English Church.

Henry Hammond did not live long enough to get a bishopric, but he earned one by his scholarly and pious writings, one of which was a defense of Falkland's arguments against Catholic infallibility. He seems to have been more spiritually minded than either Morley or Sheldon, but his pious biographers have left him veiled in a haze of saintliness.

There were other clerics at Great Tew on occasion—Hyde has it that "all men of eminent parts and faculties in Oxford" came there. Earle, of course, was a divine as well as a wit. Hugh Cressy, later to turn Catholic and write against Cary's views, had known the Viscount in Ireland, had been generously treated by him, and no doubt visited him afterwards now and then. He is said to have been for a time Falkland's chaplain. But two men of the church, John Hales and William Chillingworth, held a special place among his associates. Their ideas were like his, and they worked with him in forming them.

Hales had been bred for the ministry but he chose to live on a fellowship at Eton, in voluntary retirement among his books. He had a good library and an exceptional memory— better than "any man I ever knew," said Hyde, "my lord Falkland only excepted." Like Lucius Cary, Hales was very small. His voice was weak, and no doubt part of his taste for

solitude came from his dislike of trying to make himself
heard in public. He loved his friends, though, and for their
sake would "sometimes, once in a year, resort to London, only
to enjoy their cheerful conversation." He may even have ventured as far from home as Great Tew, since he shared both
Falkland's admiration for Shakespeare and some of his views
about religion. Hales had been a spectator at the disputatious
Synod of Dort in 1618, and had been revolted by it. Were
angry debates and unchristian abuse necessary to godliness?
Was holiness impossible except for those who would ignore
the impartial search for truth in order to worst those who
disagreed? For Hales better than dogma and victory in debate seemed the harmony which Christians might have
through tolerance. Shyly he said little of his convictions, lest
they do harm to others, but about 1636 he wrote a little treatise on "Schism and Schismatics." It attracted the attention
of Archbishop Laud, who saw what the effect might be upon
his crusade for the exclusive dominance of one rigidly doc-
trinated church. But he was too powerful really to fear Hales,
and wise enough to see that a retired scholar might be encouraged, outwardly at least, so long as he did not air his
views too widely. Hales did not, and was left alone to earn
the title "ever memorable," by his sweetness of temper and
the later influence of what he wrote. He contributed vastly
to the spreading of rational and tolerant attitudes among the
moderates of the national church, but his modest hatred of
self-assertion made him less immediately a leader than William Chillingworth or Falkland himself.

Chillingworth was one of Falkland's closest friends, and
had on his theological ideas probably more effect than anyone else. Less attractive as a man than Hales, his intellectual
vigor was greater, and his book, *The Religion of Protestants*,
remains a cardinal document in the history of English Protestantism. He had been a Catholic for a time, led to Rome
by a conviction that if God wished truth to prevail he must

have supplied a sure guide in the form of an infallible church. He then deserted Catholicism because his reason balked at accepting any single institution as incapable of error. He fell back on the Bible as the one ultimate authority, but, seeing the inconsistencies in Holy Writ and the difficulty of making a complete and harmonious interpretation of it, he cheerfully surrendered all that did not seem so clearly stated as to be acceptable to any reader. In other words he limited to a few essentials what Christians must believe in order to be members of the true church of Christ, lumping together all else, about which dispute waged, as material of no fundamental importance. About it Christians might differ as their own judgments demanded, without losing their claim to be considered followers of Christ. Thus Chillingworth became a force for religious tolerance by insisting that harmony was to be had not by setting up a creed every detail of which all believers must accept, but by reducing all except a few major tenets to the level of "inessentials." There need be agreement only on the few basic Christian doctrines which scepticism had not yet dangerously shaken.

He wrote his book largely in Falkland's library, and "the benefit he had by my Lord's Company, and rational Discourse, was very great." His host showed him books he had never heard of, and gave him a place to live and work. Both men worshipped reason, and both saw that the battleground between Catholic and Protestant was an arena in which they must fight for what they reverenced. They were constantly together and it used to be said at Oxford that if the Great Turk were to be converted "by natural reason," Tew was the place, and Chillingworth and Cary the scholars, to win him over. The two little men—Chillingworth was as small as Falkland, Hales, and Godolphin—were personally unlike. About Chillingworth's writings and what we know of his life there is a coldness, a calculated and bloodless intellectualism, a drastic scepticism, that carry him farther in analysis and conclusion than Cary was willing to go. His efforts to convert Falkland's brothers and sisters, and his probable service of Laud as a spy among the Catholics, whose confidence he had won when he was of their faith, gave good reason for the elder Lady Falkland to hate him. Lettice, on the other hand, adored him for his Protestant zeal. Apparently he actually had few definite convictions about any church, but he was not above proselytizing for the Anglicans in order to please a bishop or a hostess. Hyde's account of him—and Hyde knew him well—glows with praise, but there is distrust between the lines. He was "confident of nothing, and a sceptic . . . in the greatest mysteries of faith"; he had too much "levity" in changing creeds. Hyde, sure in his Anglicanism, had reason to dread Chillingworth's ideas, which, logically carried out, would leave little need for any established church; and it may be that Hyde's generosity and warm appreciation of moral loftiness were repelled by Chillingworth's cold detachment. "If a man will begin with certainties, he shall end in doubts" was a saying the age was proving true for Hyde and his friends; and such men as Hales and Falkland and, ostensibly, Chillingworth, wanted "to begin with doubts" in order to "end in certainties." But Chillingworth's mind leaned naturally to doubts. He is at his best when his criticism is most destructive; he is weakest when the positive side of his argument is reached. Hobbes admired his talents, but remarked, "By God, he is like some lusty fighters that will give a damnable back-blow now and then on their owne party." Chillingworth's sweeping back-blows were wounding to any religious attitude founded on worship and faith.

The interests of such friends as Chillingworth made them Falkland's allies in his study of theology, and as Great Tew became a place of resort for scholars, a "university bound in a lesser volume" where books, discussion, and strong personalities gave visitors more than they brought, the gatherings there began to take a definite intellectual color. The house became the centre of a "school," with Falkland as one of its leading spirits.

By 1639 he had written a sheaf of verses and had shone as a wit among wits, and had also proved himself one whose ideas must be reckoned with wherever there was debate about reason in religion or the definition on rational principles of a truly Christian church. The details of his theological writing and the relation of his views to what other men in his time and before had thought and said, deserve thorough study, but for the realization of his character and of the part his rationalism played in his career, as well as of the large intellectual conflicts illustrated in his life, no more is necessary than a glimpse of the outlines of his position.[5]

He concentrated on the application of his convictions about reason to the problem of whether the Catholic church could rightly claim to be infallible. It was a weighty question in a day when Rome was commonly supposed to menace national institutions; it particularly concerned Falkland because his affection for his Catholic mother and her differences with his father had dramatized it in intimately personal terms. Moreover it had far-reaching implications, involving fundamental queries as to whether any one organization may pretend to the exclusive possession of religious truth, or, failing that, as to whether there is any single authority to which believers may confidently appeal.

For a time he could only read and ponder, and get what

---

[5] Mr. Kurt Weber's forthcoming study of Falkland will, it is to be hoped, go thoroughly into Cary's theological writings, and the sources and relations of his thought. For Falkland's reverence for reason, cf. his: "I professe my self not onely to be an Anti-Trinitarian, but a Turk, whensoever more reason appeares to me for that, then for the Contrary"; "That every man should yeeld to that discourse which seemeth fairest to him, I confesse, it is alwaies, not onelie safe and fit, but also necessarie"; "I conceive it the best way to follow my own Reason, since I know I have no will to cozen my self"; "Those who trust their Reason least, yet trust it in this, that some other instead of it is to be trusted, and so chuse who they are to trust" ("Reply" in Discourse, pp. 241, 242-243, 260).

he might from his learned friends. Gradually his ideas took shape, and in 1635 he committed some of them to paper. In November of that year, Walter Montagu wrote to his father, the Earl of Manchester, justifying his having become a Catholic. Someone showed the letter to Lucius Cary. It interested him because he had, he said, "been sometimes in some degrees moved with the same Inducements" which had decided Montagu. Therefore, modestly describing himself as a "Lay man, a young man, and an Ignorant man," he wrote a reply which was "dispersed in many Copies" and printed in 1641.

Montagu relies on the argument that if Luther began Protestantism, then Protestantism cannot have been the original faith of Christ. At once Falkland, like Chillingworth, counters with the assertion that the Bible is the one safe authority, and the Bible in its "plaine places" which no reasonable man can misinterpret. The Church of Rome, suppressing heresies and censoring books, might easily have hidden any truth, so that no one could hope to discover "whether any thought like *Luther*" before him. But even if Montagu were right, his argument might prove that Protestants were in error, but it would not support the Church of Rome any more than the Greek Church. Falkland insists that whether the Pope is infallible is the question which "must determine all the rest." He argues that the Church of Rome can be shown to have deviated from its first tenets, so that it cannot be held to be the continuing "visible" repository of pristine truth. Neither Protestant nor Catholic can claim a church that has "been alwaies visible," but, Cary says, "the difference is this . . . we are most troubled to shew our Church in the Latter, and more corrupt Ages, and they theirs in the first and purest. . . . We can least find ours at night, and they theirs at Noone."

He agrees with Montagu that if God could not keep the truth intact before men's eyes, God would be less than God, but he denies that this is an argument that one church must always have been the exclusive possessor of the light. His position is that a church can only be believed right if her doctrine—by the test of Scripture—is proved correct. Whoever regulates his life by the Bible, then, "may mistake Error for Truth" but "shall never mistake Hell for Heaven in the end." This is the central thesis, reiterated throughout. God gives man the Bible and reason; reason justifies acceptance of the Bible as God's word; if man follows his reason, as best he can, in interpreting the sacred pages, he cannot be damned. All that is necessary to Christianity is clear in the Scriptures, and differences on minor points do not matter. Therefore the true continuing and "visible" church comprises all who try to live according to Holy Writ, and no one institution is needed or can be found, to supersede by its decrees what reason can derive from God's word. Nor can there be doubt about the authority of Scripture, since its writers command the reverence of all followers of Christ. That they were the writers is proved by "the generall Tradition and Testimony of the first Christians." [6]

---

[6] Cf. also passages from Falkland's "Reply" in *Discourse*. He defines the "true Church" as "the Commpany of true believers, in points any way materiall (or rather the truest)" (p. 214); "I cannot see why we may not in some points joyn with the one, and with others in other, and besides find some Truths which ly . . . well in the mid-way betweene the Parties . . . nay in some points differ wholly from both: Which Liberty, if it were generally allowed, and generally practised, if particular interests were trod wholly under foot, especially by the greatest, and if such spirits as those of *Cassander* and *Melancton* were more common, no considerable things would in a short time be left, but all would flow againe in the same Chanell, whereas this opinion, that allwaies one part erres not, is both prejudiciall to Truth, and the best Unity, which is, that of Charity" (pp. 138-139); "[I] am confident, that all who receive the Scripture for the onely rule, and believe what is there plain to be onely necessarie, would if they truely beleeved what they professe, and were not lead aside either by prejudice, or private ends, or some Popish relicks of holding what they have long been taught . . . soon agree in as much as is necessarie, and in concluding no necessity of agreeing in more, there being no doubt, but it would soone appear plainly what is plaine" (p. 235); God "hath made every man (who pleaseth) Infallible, in respect of his journys end, though not of all Innes by the way, certaine to find Heaven though he

To the discussion Falkland brought much information about ecclesiastical history, and especially about the variations in Catholic teaching through the centuries and the differences among the Church Fathers. The details are unimportant. The essential was that Montagu, probably like the Dowager Viscountess, accepted what he conceived to be an infallible church as an authority above reason. Falkland, on the other hand, put reason higher, and, believing that there was intelligible proof for the authority of the Bible and none for the authority of a single church, defined the duty of a Christian as the following of Scriptural precept in so far as he could understand it.

At about the same time as the answer to Montagu, Falkland wrote another shorter letter to Francis Morison, his brother-in-law, who was also flirting with Rome. For a Morison, Sir Henry's brother, to listen to the Papists, in spite of Lettice's Protestant piety, was more than Cary could quietly endure, and the sharpness of his remonstrance is not surprising. Apparently he had talked theology with his brother-in-law, but Francis was not convinced, and wrote what Lucius said was not a letter but a "Declamation." To it he replied that it was silly to be moved by the authority of a Church Father, "living 400 years after Christ," to accept a church against whose tenets other Fathers of equal claim to credence

---

may misse many Truthes in Divine matters. . . . Unlesse God should damne a man for weaknesse of understanding, (which were as strange, as if he should damne him for a weak sight, or a feeble arme) . . . every man is Infallible in his way to Heaven, so he lay no blocks in it himself, (at least is undoubtedly secur'd of any danger of Hell)" (pp. 150-151); God "requires onely . . . a reasonable service . . . also . . . a reasonable Faith" (p. 193); the way of salvation "is seeking the Truth impartially, and obeying diligently what is found sincerely, and who treads this way, though he misse of Truth, shall not misse of his favour who is the Father of it" (p. 262); "To beleeve, that they should be so punisht who do their endeavours, is to lay their damnation to Gods charge" (p. 263); "That the Scripture cannot prove everything in foro contentioso I beleeve, but all necessarie Truths, I beleeve it can; for onely those, which it can, are such" (pp. 197-198); the authority of Scripture depends on "Universall Tradition" (p. 255).

had written. Again it came back to whether Roman infallibility could be rationally proved. It was nonsense for Francis Morison to turn Catholic "for the convenience of an Infallible Guide" when no one could know Rome "Infallibly to be Infallible, nor Infallibly what Definitions are hers, when those are yet more hard to be understood, than to be known, and those who have the convenience of so infallible a Director neither agree by what Notes she is to be known, nor what Doctrines she teaches, and cannot but confess, that there are infinite Questions which concern the Duty of our lives, of which she is wholly silent, and concerning which they are in the same miserable estate, in which we are who have none." That there are many Catholics is no argument—"almost all the world hath been Idolaters, and most Christians have been Arrians." And what of the "unreasonablenesses" in "so many of" Catholic "doctrines, as Transubstantiation, &c?" "If God (as we say) requires our Assent to nothing, but what is apparent to be his Will, then there is no necessity of a Guide, since those who would deny apparent Doctrines, would as well resist an apparent Guide." Only those who obstinately refuse truth are heretics; who is obstinate is for God to decide; therefore allow each man his own opinion until God brings in the verdict. On such a plane of tolerance there is neither need nor place for a church asserting that it alone possesses divine verity. The Catholic was such a church, and, said Falkland, kept "her children from Scripture, as a mother would keep her children from Ratsbane." That was, for a rationalist of his stamp, to keep wouldbe Christians from the source of light.

His heaviest assault on Roman "infallibility" came, however, in a "Discourse," and a much longer "Reply" written to refute a Catholic's objection to it. Neither goes beyond the main positions of the letters to Montagu and Morison, but the details are discussed at greater length. Falkland insists that it is idle to talk of the "infallibility" of any authority unless that "infallibility" can be demonstrated. But even if it be granted that there is one unchallengeable source of truth, the Catholics must prove that their church is that source and that although the doctrines of others may be tainted with error their own never can be. To prove that any authority is infallible is difficult; to prove that any single institution is such an authority, is harder still. Falkland declares that any dogma, however confidently proclaimed as incontestable, depends at last upon the individual's understanding of it. He can grasp it only with his reason; if he does his best but fails to comprehend, he is not to be condemned. But then why should he be damned if he mistakes the meaning of Holy Writ? Why is it less allowable to interpret it by reason, than to use reason to find the sense of ecclesiastical decrees? When both Bible and Church "seem equally clear, and yet contradictory, shall not I as soon believe Scripture, which is without doubt of as great authority?"

Linked with the main argument is a bitter attack on religious persecution as used by the Church of Rome. "I do not believe all to be damned that they damne, but I conceive all to be killed that they kill," and "It should be to take ill care of Christianity, to hold it up by Turkish meanes," are but two of Falkland's comments. He exposes the cruel folly of persecution by pointing out that it is, and must always be, unreasonable to punish anyone for hunting for the truth, even if he falls into error, since only through individual search can truth be found either in the Bible or the laws of a church. Cary's "Discourse" and "Reply" are, therefore, not only arguments against Rome but pleas against limitations on freedom of thought and, especially, against religious persecution.[7]

[7] Falkland may have written other anti-Catholic treatises, in addition to those mentioned. Clarendon, *History*, III, 181, says "he writ two large discourses against the principal positions of that religion. . . . The Church is deprived of great jewels in the concealment of them, and that they are not published to the world." When this was written the *Discourse* had been printed.

He spent long hours preparing his attacks on the notion of Roman infallibility and translating in part, at least, the *Du Vrai Emploi des Pères*, by Jean Daillé, whose acquaintance, Falkland thought, "was worth a Voyage to Paris." Daillé's book was serviceable to both Cary and Chillingworth for its critique of the doctrines of the Fathers and its argument against their being too implicitly followed, and Falkland's translating it was a normal product of his interest in the history of Catholicism. Prose was his mistress now, not poetry, and in her service his achievement was modest. His style is not distinguished, nor did he always manage well the arrangement of his arguments. According to legend he used to wonder as he wrote whether this or that word would be clear to his readers, and to settle it would hunt up one of his wife's chambermaids, "(not the waiting-woman, because it was possible she might be conversant in romances)," read her the doubtful passage, and let her decide whether the sense was plain or not. The chambermaids may have helped to keep the diction simple, but it is a pity that they, or the waiting-woman, did not warn him about the loose structure of his work and the breathless complication of some of his more sprawling sentences. His learned admirers, however, recognized current rhetorical fashions in his prose, and accepted as wit some things that now seem cumbrous. It is fair to remember, too, that he did not believe in "Eloquence" for sober tracts, since "the eloquent wander into figures, which are so many, and have gotten such footing in language (whilst in the search of significancie proprietie is lost) that those, who use them, are obliged to those who will please to understand, because all they say may beare two sences."

But his style deserves praise, because it escapes the twin evils of most theological controversy of the time. He does not overload his text with pedantic references; and maintains an undogmatic and persuasive tone, in harmony with his theme. He was no dogmatist, and he pleads for moderation in dispute, urging his opponents to attack his main arguments, not trivial details, and to attack "with that temper which is fit to be used by men that are not so passionate, as to have the definition of reasonable Creatures in vaine." He emphasizes his own open-mindedness, protesting that he will yield to the Catholics if they "can prove that Scripture may be a certainer teacher of truth to them, then to us, so that they may conclude the Infallibility of the Church out of it, and we nothing," "if they can prove the Churches Infallibility to be a sufficient Guide for him, that doubts which is the Church, and cannot examine that (for want of learning) by her chiefe marke, which is conformity with the Ancients," or "if indeed any can prove by any infallible way, the Infallibility of the Church of Rome, and the necessity under paine of damnation for all men to beleeve it." [8] But Falkland never found proof sufficient to swerve him from his confidence in reason and the Bible as the sole pilots for doctrine and life.

The daily routine of Great Tew was bound up with his intellectual conclusions. The discussions with scholars there were not mere recreation; they were, he believed, a means by which, on his principles, truth might be approached. He

---

[8] "I have ever thought that there should bee as little bitterness in a Treatise of Controversie, as in a Love-letter, and that the contrary way was both void of Christian charitie, and humane wisdome, as serving onely . . . to fright away the game; and make their Adversarie unwilling to receive Instruction from him, from whom they have received Injuries; and making themselves unabler to discover Truth . . . raising besides a great suspition of ignorance in him that useth it; since it is a very true Rule. . . . Confidence of knowledge conduceth much to meeknesse" (p. 52); "I was never more ready to part with my clothes when they were torn, then with my opinions when they were confuted, and appeared to me to be so." (p. 54) Falkland argues against the man who is unwilling to "find that to be truth, which is contrary to what he now thinks, and so to hazard either the affection of deare Friends, or the favour of great Friends, or the feare of some other humane Inconvenience, as want of present meanes, Improbability to get more, or of that disparagement so terrible to flesh and blood, of descending to confesse that they have so long erred" (p. 151); an ingenuous man may not "hold an opinion, because he hath turned to it, nor . . . stay, onely because he went." (p. 298) ("Reply" in Discourse).

longed for "a society of men, whose opinions must be certainely true, and who would . . . labour to discusse and define all arising doubts, so that" he "might be excusably at ease, and have no part left . . . but that of obedience." He could find no such society, and the next best thing was constantly to consult other scholars in order to learn from them and test his own opinions against theirs.

More Catholics, he felt, would doubt, if they were not too lazy or too impatient to inquire, and he was sure that it was the duty of both Catholic and Protestant to doubt until rational certainty could be had. But it is patent that all the time he really wanted to be able simply to believe, to find some answer to fretting queries and rest secure in it. He "was wont to say that the great conveniency there seemed to be (according to human understanding) of an infallible guide, and the great aptness every one had to wish there were such a thing" helped to make converts for Rome, and he admitted "that indeed it would be most reasonable to believe that if God" had "any care or providence over mankind" he must have "provided such a guide." For him an "infallible guide" meant one adapted to, and interpreted by, what he understood as "reason." Others in his day contented themselves with assurance that whatever the Bible said, fully intelligible or not, must be accepted as revelation, beyond all cavilling; still others gave the same reverence to what a church, through the mouths of its priests, declared as truth; and philosophers might satisfy themselves with theories about innate ideas or the all-sufficient efficacy of knowledge of the physical world. But for Falkland nothing could be received as authority unless it could be justified by what seemed to him the principles of reason. Therefore he stuck at finding authority in the Catholic church, which taught things that were "more against reason than" belief in an unerring guide "was according to it."

His attitude was that of a group of moderate Anglicans,

who contributed much to the progress of religious toleration, and helped to free English thought from stifling dogmatisms. In this group his high position came from no striking orginality nor exceptional clarity of mind. In both, Hales and Chillingworth surpassed him. Hales's pages have a warmth and rich wisdom lacking in his, and Chillingworth's *Religion of Protestants* is far more trenchant in its inquiry than anything Falkland wrote. It was his personality—his gentleness and charm, his moral earnestness, and his unfailing open-mindedness—that attracted scholars to his house, and gave special currency to what he said. Of course the timeliness of his onslaught on Catholic infallibility, in a day when Protestants were frightened by frequent conversions to Rome, enhanced his reputation, but he shone chiefly as an inspiration to others who wrote better and thought more profoundly than he. It was thus that he played his part in developing ideas fundamental to much that is noblest in English Protestantism.

But rational principles were hard taskmasters and there were dangers in the attempt to rest everything on them. It might give sanction to the vagaries of the deluded or vicious, if they pled that they followed their understanding of the right. Moreover it meant limiting the place of revelation in religion. To be sure, both Falkland and Chillingworth held that a few central truths must be agreed to because God stated them in the Bible, but they found authority in Holy Writ only in so far as it was consonant with reason and only because they thought there were rational grounds for considering it divine. Essentially this left it only such sanctity as reason itself had. The ultimate test became subjective and was as fallible as the thinker who applied it. The whole tendency of Cary's teaching was, however imperfectly he saw its implications, toward making reason, not faith, the final arbiter.

It did not help much to say: "When I speak . . . of finding the Truth by Reason, I intend not to exclude the Grace of God, which I doubt not (for as much as is necessarie to Sal-

vation) is readie to concurre to our Instruction. . . . Yet . . .
I mean not, that it infuseth a knowledge without reason, but
workes by it, as by its Minister, and dispels those Mists of
Passions, which doe wrap up Truth from our Understandings.
For if you speake of its instructing any other way" you "leave
visible Arguments to flie to invisible." This is only lip-service
to the idea that God's grace supplies the truth to man; it
leaves "visible arguments" as the only real criteria. It was
a starvation diet for those who asked of religion something
that transcended reason and logic, and were happy only with
what seemed to them to be truths comprehensible solely by
the mysterious agency of faith. Such individuals may be the
victims of delusion, but there have been many of them in
every age, and Falkland's time had its full share. For them
the result of his reasoning was the destruction of what they
lived by.

He himself may have had moments of uneasiness. He is reported to have said that "there were few truths so clear that
it was not more hard to prove them, than to find something
to object against them; and to one that would deny more
than he, he should not be able to prove plainly—in such a
degree as he seemed to require to have things proved to him—
what he did yet think to be so." In other words rationalism
ran easily into scepticism, and doubt was always waylaying
belief.[9]

Study was exhausting. "I take no pleasure," Cary wrote,
"in tumbling hard and unpleasant Books, and making myself
giddy with disputing obscure Questions." To accept, rather
than to question, if one "excusably" could, "must needs be a

---

[9] Cf. Falkland's "I see whom to fly, but not whom to follow," and his:
"Having ever marked Error and Confidence to keep so much company, that I
seldome find the first, but I mistrust the second, makes me loath to affirme
any thing over-dogmatically out of these objections" ("Reply" in Discourse,
pp. 138, 92). I use "scepticism" not in any narrowly technical philosophical
sense but to mean simply readiness to question anything and everything, and
unwillingness to assert or believe anything without definite proof.

lesse difficult, and so a more agreeable way, then to endure endlesse Volumes of Commenters . . . harsh Greek . . . harder Latin . . . and be pained by distinguishing between different sences, and various Lections." Only a fool would prefer such labors to more pleasant ones (he had once been a maker of verses!); only a fool would rather "imploy his understanding then submit it" if—here was the crux—there was any way to be content with unresolved doubts. Falkland's emotions were those of many of his time, realized or not—the emotions of a man still hungry for finalities, for absolutes, but no longer able, in the face of new ideas and contrasted creeds, to subjugate his intellect enough to make the old absolutes possible to accept.

He had, however, some satisfactions from his work. For one thing it was grateful to the "severe nature" which was only partly masked by his "cheerful conversation." For another, it supplied him with a half solution to some of his problems. He unearthed, to be sure, no proof of the infallibility of any church, to whose decision he could refer all his perplexities. Like Hawthorne's Zenobia he found the "effort to establish the one true system" was "of all the varieties of mock-life . . . the very emptiest mockery." But at least he need no longer feel that either his Catholic mother or his Protestant wife was doomed to perdition for her views, since he had come to think that only the essentials of Christianity were required for salvation. All conscientious believers might be in the odor of sanctity if they followed Christ's teaching as they understood it, even if they disagreed about trifles in worship or creed. He had learned how to be tolerant and sure of God's tolerance; he thought he knew how to keep the fundamentals of faith without betraying his "private sense."

Perhaps his enemies recognized, as he did not, that the object of his faith was after all only that "private sense," and that he was mistaken in supposing he had discovered a higher court of appeal. They may have suspected how readily his theories about the sacredness of "reason" might lead to scepticism rather than to certainty. In any case, they felt themselves threatened by the reverberations from Great Tew, and inveighed against Falkland's arguments. Francis Cheynell, an ardent Puritan, hated those who trusted "their own private spirit, which they call Right Reason." "Every man," he said, "is apt to think himself infallible, and that his *Private Iudgement* ought to be the *Publike Standard*. . . . Every one desires to give a Toleration or a Dispensation to himselfe, that he may be allowed to maintain such opinions and goe on in such courses as are generally condemned by the judgement of Learned and Pious men." This was aimed at Chillingworth, but would have served as well for Falkland. Cheynell continues: "Naturall Reason being helped by a supernaturall Revelation in the Word, is not able to discerne saving truths, so as to beleeve them after a saving manner, without the speciall assistance of the holy Ghost, such assistance as is vouchsafed to none but the Elect of God." Cheynell differed from Cary here in his emphasis on the need of believing "after a saving manner." Both agreed that reason might disclose truth, but the Viscount stopped there, sure that straight thinking was enough, whereas the divine held that enthusiastic and heartfelt faith, transcending the capacity of mere intellect, was required for righteousness and was possible only with the "assistance of the holy Ghost." For Cheynell, faith, supernaturally inspired, was paramount; Falkland's comment on God's grace had rested everything on the potency of the mind.

As for the Catholics they pointed out that to follow Cary was to make any church unnecessary, even the Anglican, which he and his colleagues professed to support. This criticism was shrewd, since if truth is always to be determined by each man's following his own best judgment in everything except the few basic doctrines which must be taken on the authority of the Bible, there is small need for church councils and little excuse for priests except as leaders of the public worship of independent individuals.

Finally the stricter Anglicans shuddered at the rumors from Oxfordshire. Archbishop Laud himself, toiling to make the national church strong with the strength of complete uniformity in creed and polity, worried when he heard that Falkland's views smacked of such perilous heresies as questioning the doctrine of the Trinity and denying the divinity of Christ. A young Viscount could afford to be contemptuous of fanatics like Cheynell, but he could not safely risk Laud's displeasure, and Falkland wrote a defense of his basic orthodoxy in order to set right the Archbishop's exaggerated ideas of his nonconformity. Apparently this sufficed to keep him out of official hot water, but Laud had been right in being uneasy. Cary might manage to save himself from scepticism about all Christian teaching by his confidence in Scripture, but his insistence on reason was none the less dangerous for traditional orthodoxy and the power of established churches. An Anglican historian later calmly remarked that the Church of England suffered no loss when Lucius Cary died.

Falkland may have had hints now and then even from his friends that he was precariously diluting the content of Christian thought. John Earle, for example, could warn him. He had no use for "the scepticke in religion," and spoke his mind about him. "He finds reason," said Earle, "in all opinions, truth in none: indeed the least reason perplexes him, and the best will not satisfie him. . . . He finds doubts and scruples better then resolues them, and is alwayes too hard for himselfe. . . . He hammers much in generall vpon our opinions vncertainety, and the possibility of erring makes him not venture on what is true. . . . He puts his foot into Heresies tenderly, as a Cat in the water, and pulls it out againe, and still something vnanswer'd delayes him. . . . You may sooner picke all Religions out of him then one. . . . He hates authority as the Tyrant of reason, and you cannot anger him worse then with a Fathers *dixit,* and yet that many are not perswaded with reason, shall authorize his doubt. . . . His whole life is a question, and his saluation a greater, which death onely concludes, and then he is resolu'd." This was not written of Falkland, but, stripped of its witty exaggeration it might have been, or at least might have applied to those who carried his teaching to the logical extreme, since it indicated adroitly some of the dangerous consequences of his scholarly method.

In order to be sure of what could rationally be believed everything had to be examined and questioned. The difficulty was to know where to stop. Was it quite sure that the Bible could be proved a source of divine revelation? Was it sure that God's justice, benevolence, and omnipotence could be demonstrated? Could anyone "make it appeare by the light of Reason, that there shall be a *Resurrection* . . . ; that there are three persons and one God: that the Word was made flesh; that God was made man; that Christ was born of a Virgin; that God justifies many thousands of the ungodly by the obedience and satisfaction of one man"? Could it be proved reasonable that a just God permitted evil in the world? Falkland and his friends found the assurances they needed in the Bible, but what was to become of them if their habits of rigid intellectual scrutiny carried them beyond, or if other men, as reasonable as they, decided that Holy Writ was human rather than divine? What could become of the infallibility of reason, on which they rested their whole case, if it were shown that most men reason erroneously if at all, and that what passes for reason is usually the working out of prejudice, greed, or fear? [10]

---

[10] Professor Laski suggests that economic motives may have aided tolerance. This raises an interesting question as to the degree to which the rationalism of such men as Falkland was influenced by the economic ideas of the period. In the case of Falkland and most of his friends any *direct* influence of economic interest is hard to trace. H. J. Laski, *The Rise of Liberalism* (N. Y., 1936), pp. 141ff.

Was there even any positive test as to what was or was not reason? To read the seventeenth-century "rationalists" is to grow thirsty for a definition. Reason seemed to involve proceeding logically from premises, and it was linked with "common sense . . . the Judgement of all men." It relied on the "Law of Nature," the ineluctable principles back of the physical universe and man's life in it.[11] But it was not easy to be sure about "the Judgement of all men" or the "Law of Nature." Murder was wrong, perhaps, because most men agreed it was, but for one man war was wholesale murder and for another it was a necessary element in national welfare, justifiable by an allegedly natural principle. Some men who tried to worship reason, arrived at scorn for religious faith, or upheld ethical codes and political theories that to others, quite as sure of their own clear thinking, seemed hostile to all that was conceivably good.

At the root of the problem lay the fact that all efforts to follow reason were dependent on the premises that were taken to be rational. Where material objects or mathematical data were concerned, it was possible, certainly, to agree on these premises; but in religion, in ethics, in politics, in any sphere in which emotion and prejudice might enter, was agreement to be had?[12] If not, what hope was there for in-

---

[11] F. Cheynell, *Rise, Growth and Danger of Socinianisme* (London, 1643), p. 41: "Why doe the *Socinians* so often challenge us to be tryed by reason, by common sense, by the Judgement of all men, but because they conceive, Reason by her own light can discover" etc. But mere agreement of many was not enough to make a thing rational; "For multitude, I find not what that proves" (L. Cary, "Reply" in *Discourse*, p. 179). Elsewhere Cary points out that unity of assent is not necessary to prove reasonableness (*Id.*, pp. 247-248; also pp. 209-210). Cf. Laski, *op. cit.*, pp. 52ff. He speaks (p. 54) of the theory that nature supplies "rational principles as clear and immutable as those of mathematics and physics" and says that Grotius's state was to be guided in its practise "by that rule of reason which he takes to be nature's law."

[12] P. Meissner, "Die Rationalistische Grundlage der Englischen Kultur des 17 Jahrhunderts" in *Anglia*, LV (Halle, 1931), p. 326, gives one example of the way in which, with different premises, rational thought might come to

tellectual harmony; what hope that reason could ever go beyond conclusions dictated in advance by the individually determined assumptions from which it started? Unless he could guard against such queries the rationalist was defenseless against paralyzing scepticism. Clever Catholics now and then encouraged sceptical attitudes in order that men might be brought to a pitch of hopeless uncertainty and so driven at last to submerge themselves in blind faith in Rome.

Falkland himself was wise enough to see how hard it is to think straight. Prejudices, he knew, were hard to escape. "The Authority of . . . Teachers, the Flexibility of the Taught" were sources of error, and so was "Interest it selfe (which consists of two Parts, Feares, and Hopes)." Had he searched himself deeply enough he might have been startled to see how much of his own assurance of the sanctity of reason and the necessity of tolerance, might be traced to his emotional needs. Like all thinkers who want to be rational, he was, however unconsciously, the victim of those needs. They dictated the axioms he accepted and colored his very definition of what was reasonable. He reverenced historical evidence, for example, and the testimony of books, perhaps because he had the tastes of a scholar and very little experience of practical affairs. He could swallow ideas which would have gagged hardheaded men whose encounters with society seemed to teach that passion often overrules reason and that money and power are more worshipped than truth. Even Falkland's ardor for freedom of opinion may well have been rooted in his personal necessities. He may have groped for rational principles to support tolerance chiefly because he had suffered in a discordant family setting and yearned for harmony. The yearning had been best satisfied by friendship.

different conclusions. Falkland seems to have seen that in religion even the premises are generally not capable of absolute proof. He says "the Pillars" of Christianity "are not absolute Demonstrations (of which it may be scarce any thing is in nature capable but lines and numbers)" ("Reply" in *Discourse*, p. 245).

"Freindshipp may rule with greater power than love," he thought, and his eagerness to have friends must have directed his severest thinking toward regarding agreement with others as a good in itself. No wonder he hated "that passion and uncharitableness which he saw produced by difference of opinion in matters of religion." No wonder he tried to make Great Tew attractive; no wonder he sought to multiply and deepen his sympathetic relationships with other men.

But by 1639 he had not faced what close examination of himself might have revealed, nor inquired where the "rational religion" he advocated might lead at last. The deeper problems lay in ambush for other men. Championship of reason, a sceptical attitude toward all that could not be rationally endorsed, and confidence that faith and unity were to be had by logical thinking, were to breed graver doubts than he had squarely met. But already he had gone too far to be a dogmatist even about his dearest theories, and remained "rather an inquirer . . . than an absolute defender of anything."

This saved his tolerance but brought penalties. If nothing is quite certain, is anything much worth caring about? Falkland's promise to his mother that he would postpone choosing a church, was the easier to keep because any choice was hard to make without more certainty than he could rest on his temperate convictions. And, since doubts were always at hand, there was a strong temptation to conservatism. If it is hard to be sure that any action is right, it is easier not to act at all; if new doctrines cannot be securely proved, it is always possible to get on passively with old ones. If there are queries about what to think, it is restful to fall back upon what need not be thought about at all; and the most sceptical minds may relapse into reliance on instinctive feelings, and conventional beliefs.[13]

---

[13] On the ease with which rationalism, by requiring examination of everything to be sure it is reasonable, may run into scepticism, no elaborate discussion is needed. It has been said, "The possession of truth involves the

That may be one reason why, in 1639, Falkland deserted his books. He may have suspected that longer study would only weaken his assurance that every man is "Infallible in his way to Heaven, so he lay no blocks in it himself." He may have wondered whether further poring over histories would do more than increase his sceptical awareness of all chances for doubt. In any case he did not wait to make the test, and when the King called loyal noblemen to volunteer in his service against the Scots, he left his library to gather dust and let physical activity put perplexity to sleep. Hard riding, danger, and excitement, were the more attractive just because of the rigors of his search for wisdom. An instinctive loyalty to the monarchy and an instinctive dislike for Puritans and rebels, combined to make him slip easily from scholarly questionings to the simple verities of war. Given the emotions, it was possible to rationalize them into principles. No doubt, if Falkland bothered his head about it at all, he found ways to make marching with Charles I against the Scots seem like a logical step in his crusade for truth.

Abraham Cowley, in the first flush of his enthusiasm for his new friend, was too admiring to be critical. He wrote:

---

wrestling for truth, and skepticism is this very struggle"; W. Mitchell, "The Meaning of Skepticism" in Arena, XL (Boston; July, 1908), p. 309. Laski, op. cit., p. 138, writes of the "new philosophy" which presented a "universe the laws of which man discovers by the research of reason," as leading to "scepticism." G. Santayana, Reason in Religion (N. Y., 1905), p. 121, says: "It would be easy to write, in a satirical vein, the history of Protestant dogma. . . . It consisted in a gradual and inevitable descent into a pious scepticism"; Protestantism's "true essence is not constituted by the Christian dogmas that at a given moment it chances to retain, but by the spirit in which it constantly challenges the others." Falkland, at least at this time, was not a blind worshipper of the past, and said: "I count it by no meanes reasonable . . . like sheep (without more examination) to walk in the steps of those, who have gone before us" ("Reply" in Discourse, p. 172). But his scepticism seems, none the less, to have made him conservative, as his later life shows. That scepticism may easily lead to inaction seems to me to need no proof. Cf. T. V. Smith, Creative Sceptics (N. Y., 1934), p. 65, on Descartes.

"Great is thy *Charge*, O *North*; be wise and just,
England commits her *Falkland* to thy trust;
Return him safe: *Learning* would rather choose
Her *Bodley*, or her *Vatican* to loose.
All things that are but *writ* or *printed* there,
In his unbounded Breast *engraven* are.

· · · · ·

He is too good for *War*, and ought to be
As far from *Danger*, as from *Fear* he's free.
Those *Men* alone (and those are useful too)
Whose *Valour* is the onely *Art* they know,
Were for sad *War* and bloody *Battels* born;
Let *Them* the *State Defend*, and *He Adorn*."

Brave words, and sincere; there were plenty at Great Tew
to say "Amen." But Cowley does not ask why his friend, this
living library, who was "fitter to live in *republica Platonis*,
than in *faece Romuli*", gave up adorning the state in order to
defend it. He says only:

"This great *Prince* of *Knowledge* is by Fate
Thrust into th' noise and business of a State."

Was it Fate? Probably the King's summons put no com-
pulsion upon Falkland, as the holder of a Scottish peerage.[14]
In any case, in 1630 he had been bold enough to defy the
law, and presumably might have been as independent in
1639. Was he forced to take up arms by intellectual conviction or by disillusion? Was it Fate, or his need for relief from

---

[14] Cf. Marriott, p. 134: "Whether the summons addressed to the English
nobility would technically extend to a Scotch peer, residing in England, is not
clear." See, however, Gardiner, *History*, VIII, 384-385. Clarendon's account
(*History*, III, 187), although not specific on the point, suggests that Falkland
joined the King's forces in 1639 not because he was required to but because,
as in 1630, he hoped for success as a military leader.

the goadings of the mind he had trained to question more easily than to believe? Had Sir John Suckling persuaded him that his "great soul" was "like a spider, working all inwards, and sending forth nothing but, like the cloistered schoolmen's divinity, threads fine and unprofitable"? Falkland's study had brought him to principles that were admirable, but he may have been frightened by a glimpse of the course he had charted stretching on to chilly regions where thought might wither apart from feeling and doubt taint all that feeds the will.

Whatever his motives, he decided to enter "the noise and business of a State." Never again did he taste fully the academic peace of Great Tew. He elected to try whether, "great in his Gown," he might be "greater in his Buffe." He was to match the wisdom and learning he had toiled patiently with his friends to win, against the selfish ardors of politics and the blind hatreds of battlefields. It was an adventure that appealed to his gallantry, and he was too bold a gambler to stop to read the odds.

VI

"THE NOISE AND BUSINESS OF A STATE"

Falkland in War and Parliament, January, 1639–March, 1641

LATE in January, 1639, Charles I ordered "most of the Nobility" to join him in arms against the Scots. The dispute had been simmering for years. Ten months earlier, Archibald Armstrong, the King's jester, had learned to his cost how serious it was. He was probably Scottish himself and shared his countrymen's hatred of English clerics; in any case he saw fit to jeer at Archbishop Laud. In his cups he called him rogue, monk, and traitor, and, excited by the news of the northerners' stubborn refusal of the new service book which the English wanted to impose upon them, he waylaid Laud one morning to cry: "Who's fool now? Doth not your Grace hear the News from Stirling about the Liturgy?" The archbishop went fuming to the Council, which voted that "the Kings Fool . . . shall have his Coat pulled over his head, and be discharged of the Kings Service, and banished the Court." Armstrong was lucky to have the punishment no worse.

Many Englishmen would have sympathized with him and not with Laud. Some good Calvinists held that the Scottish church was nearer than the English to the way of Christ. Others, caring little for creed or ritual, resented the political power of the bishops. The archbishop was the villain of the piece. He had insisted that the Scots accept the liturgy he had ordered for them, and had no scruples about enlisting the authority of the crown. A stool thrown in the church of St. Giles at Edinburgh, whizzed uncomfortably close to an episcopal ear, and began an ugly riot. There were others, and sober citizens held defiant meetings. It was easy to build up Scottish resistance against tyrannical meddling from "foreign" Canterbury.

Charles might have eased the tension had he been content to compromise on the religious question and to let the Scots follow what they thought were the proper legal forms for making changes in their church. But he had swallowed the doctrine "No Bishop, no King," and since 1633 had relied on Laud and his church as bulwarks of the throne. By supporting the English bishops' dictation to the Scottish church, he staked his own authority on their success, and made enemies at home as well as in the north. Against him ranged many who were discontented with him, with his government, or with the bishops. What might have been a minor quarrel became a major one, and Scotland's resistance looked suspiciously like rebellion against the King.

In appealing to the nobility Charles wrote: "The late Disorders in Our Realm of Scotland, began upon pretence of Religion" but appear "to have been raised by Factious spirits, and fomented by some few ill and traiterously affected particular Persons, whose aim hath been by troubling the Peace of that our kingdom, to work their own private ends, and indeed to shake off all Monarchial Government." By harping on this note and on the danger of an invasion of England he could work up English patriotism, but he did nothing to silence awkward queries as to whether there need have been any danger at all had he been less docile before Laud.

As the King stated them, the issues back of the first "Bishops' War" were grave, and his putting of the case committed him to a test of his power to rule a united people. He roused feelings which were to be expressed later in more serious conflict. But on the surface the English campaign was rich in material for Archie Armstrong. Charles I had too little money to act effectively, and he did not dare to call a Parliament to get more. Many of the nobles, on whose loyalty he depended, were half-hearted, feeling that victory might strengthen his ability to govern without respect for their rights. Some of the courtiers, to be sure, were his devoted servants, but many of them knew nothing of war. The Earl of Arundel, as general-in-chief, had a motive for valor, since he leaned toward Rome and hated Scottish Protestants, but this could not make up for his having "nothing martial about him but his . . . looks." The cavalry was led by the Earl of Holland, not because he was a tried leader but because he was "very handsome . . . of a lovely and winning presence and gentle conversation," and had taken pains to endear himself to the Queen. He "continued to flourish above any man in the Court whilst the weather was fair," but in 1639 the skies were full of storm clouds, and it was a grave error to suppose that beauty and good manners could make "the most incompetent of men" worthy of high command. Holland's appointment displaced the Earl of Essex, a better soldier and a sturdier character, who had to serve as second to Arundel.

With such officers leading badly drilled troops, Charles could hope for little more than to disguise his plight under an impressive show. "He more intended the pomp of his preparations than the strength of them." He needed loyal gentlemen because they could bring with them troops that he could not pay for himself, and because they could give his forces a veneer of brilliance. To Sir Edmund Verney, for example, he prescribed exactly how he and his men should be equipped—Sir Edmund "as a curassier in russett armes, with guilded studds or nayles," and his servants "horst in white armes . . . in good equipage." Ten years without a Parliament, in fancied independence of the nation, had made it fatally easy for the courtiers, perhaps even for the King, to think that a royal expedition against unruly subjects was little more serious than a court masque, and might be carried off by the same theatrical devices. Sir John Suckling caught the spirit of the affair, and at his own expense "raysed a troope of 100 very handsome young proper men, whom he clad in white doubletts and scarlett breeches, and scarlet coates, hatts, and . . . feathers, well horsed, and armed. . . . 'Twas one of the finest sights in those dayes."

Earnest citizens whispered solemnly about the state of the nation; the courtiers preferred to smile.[1] They were in no mood for a war of life and death, and their apathy crippled the King. He had a shrewd sense of how much was at stake; they cared little about the journey to the north except for the chance it gave them to exhibit the elegance of their retinues or to win royal favors by their display of loyalty. Charles I's "progress" to York late in March, was less a military expedition than a parade. Clarendon thought it would have been better had there been fewer gentlemen and more soldiers, but "the soldiers were the least part of the army and least consulted with."

The date for the rallying of the nobility at York was, appropriately, All Fools' Day. The news was not cheering. The King had "beene . . . betrayd." Edinburgh, Dumbarton, and Aberdeen fell into the enemy's hands. The crown and sceptre of Scotland were taken by the rebels. Royal proclamations did no good, and even the English nobles showed signs of unruliness. They would not take an oath promising to fight in the King's cause "to the utmost hazard of their life and fortunes." When this was changed to read, "to the utmost

---

[1] "While one part of the town is in whisper and serious, the other part smiles"; letter in J. Suckling, Works (ed. A. H. Thompson; London, 1910), p. 330.

of my power and hazard of my life," two Lords still refused to sign.

All the straws showed the wind was in the wrong quarter. Charles I's own courage was beyond reproach, and many brave men did their best, but the campaign miserably petered out. The Scots had no wish to fight unnecessarily, or to cross the border, lest they alienate their English friends. The English were not strong enough to attack. The war degenerated into a strange contest in which each side tried to stare the other out of countenance. Holland, on a blazing hot day, rode from the royal camp near Berwick to Kelso, followed by three hundred horsemen and three thousand foot soldiers, plodding listlessly through the heat and dust. At Kelso his sweating cavalry came face to face with the Scots. They were "well-timbered men, tall and active," and their garb bore no relation to court styles. They wore "blue woollen waistcoats and blue bonnets . . . bases of plaid and stockings of the same . . . a mantle of plaid cast over the left shoulder and under the right arme." Each had a pair of dirks; some were armed with swords and shields and some with muskets, but most with bows and arrows. They looked savage, and the din of their bagpipes was terrifying. Holland gazed at them, and they at him, and then without firing a shot he led his weary troops back over the hot roads to Berwick. It was much the same when the Scottish army pitched its tents on Dunse Law, a dozen miles from the King. He watched them calmly through his telescope, and said, "Come, let us go to supper; the number is not considerable." It was once more a matter of watching, not fighting. The war had become a farce.

The Scots were well drilled, fed, and officered. The English at Berwick had poor shelter, the water of the Tweed was too salt to drink, beer was expensive, and smallpox began to spread. All Holland's careful dressing and all his courtly arts were wasted in such a setting, and neither he nor Arundel cared to try conclusions with the barbarians they despised.

Those barbarians, with their hideous music and their out-
landish costumes, were startlingly calm in the face of the gay
uniforms of the King's followers. But they were pleased with
the magnificence of Suckling's coach, and captured it, with
£300 and a heap of gay clothes. Whether hard looks or hard
blows were to decide the war, the Scots and not the English
seemed masters of the situation. There was, as Suckling said,
"a calm greater than the storm, and if you will believe the
soldier, worse. Good arms and horses are already cheap, and
there is nothing risen in value but a Scotchman." There was
but one way out, and on June 18 a treaty was patched up.
The Scots promised to disband their force, and the English
agreed that the Scottish parliament and assembly should decide what was to be done in church and state. It was a compact "in which nobody meant what others believed he did."
It could not possibly be construed as a royal victory, and it
took unscrupulous casuistry to make it seem other than a
defeat.

In this ridiculous mock war there can have been little to
please Falkland. The outcries of the poets who shuddered at
his risking his life in battle, could have been spared, and his
wife, who loved him "more then all the things of this world,"
need not have worried when "he went from his *Library* to the
Camp; from his *Book* and *Pen*, to his *Sword and Spear*." He
was in no danger, except perhaps from the stray bullets fired
by the King's own drunken soldiers, which now and then
ripped through the canvas of the officers' tents at Berwick.
His "*Sword and Spear*" were useless against disease and bad
weather, the only enemies within reach. The whole affair began in a rebuff. He had been promised command of a troop
of horse, but did not get it. He was famous as a scholar, not
as a warrior; and those who had heard the stories which had
made Laud question his orthodoxy, may have distrusted his
zeal in the bishops' cause. His homely face and short figure
did not suggest the dashing cavalier, and, most important

of all, he was neither very rich nor a master of court intrigue. At the very outset he had to swallow his pride or go home again. In 1630 he had faced the same decision and had been ruled by pride; now he meekly set out as a volunteer with Essex when he marched north to Berwick in the early spring of 1639. There were other volunteers but "not many of quality," and none of them had much to do except to put up with the monotony of an inactive camp.

Falkland did, however, see something of the King and his officers. Early in May he was at Newcastle with Arundel and Essex. With them and "divers other gentlemen, Lords sonnes and knights," he rode over to Durham to dine with Bishop Morton. He, like Cary, was famous for his writings against the Catholics, but it was no time to talk theology. Where courtiers gathered there was apt to be more mirth than sobriety. "Wee have noe neede of foolinge," wrote one of the more staid followers of Charles, "Wee have an enough of that. . . . If the wisest were not a little guilty of it, wee might bee happier then now wee are likly to be."

After the bishop's dinner his guests went to the royal headquarters at Durham and "spake with the king," before returning to Newcastle. Then, and at other times during the campaign, Falkland may have had glimpses not only of his royal master but of some old friends. Lord Barrymore had a troop of thirteen hundred men. He had married Alice Boyle, daughter of the Earl of Cork whom Falkland had known in Ireland. The Earl's son, Viscount Dungarvan, was also with the King's army. His wife, Elizabeth Clifford, was another friend of Falkland's, and her father, Baron Clifford, was in command of a company. Charles's Commissary-general, Henry Wilmot, was the son of one of the Irish Lords with whom Falkland's father had worked during his Deputyship in Dublin, and must have often seen Lucius Cary there. Suckling, of course, was apt to be on hand wherever courtiers gathered.

Three weeks later Falkland visited the King at Durham

once more, bringing him a message from the Earl of Holland. But otherwise life was dull. There was no chance to show that a little man with a great heart might ride and swing a sword as fiercely as the stoutest trooper. Suckling wrote from the camp: "You may . . . imagine us walking up and down the banks of Tweed like the Tower lions in their cages, leaving the people to think what we would do if we were let loose." Nor was there anything to look forward to. "Our people are not together" wrote one of the King's officers, "and are most unready and undisciplined. . . . The tales they told at London, that the Scots would . . . run away at our approach . . . are every day disproved . . . for they are 40,000 strong . . . and may go where they please, and do what they list. I think that no man who loves the honour of his prince and safety of his country, but must be sensible of the loss and danger of both by this fatal business, wherein all men are losers, but the King most."

If Falkland had entered the "fatal business" because he wanted adventure and a chance to prove his warlike mettle, he had been cheated of his hopes. His case was worse if he had expected to find in the field anything to content him intellectually. He had advocated tolerance, but the whole attempt against the Scots was rooted in intolerance. He had insisted that controversies must be managed without heat, and here was an effort to settle a controversy by force. He had, no doubt, drugged his scepticism by falling back on the ideal of loyalty to a sovereign, an ideal to which his father had trained him; and had contrived to convince himself that Charles's cause was just by persuading himself that the monarchy might be rationally supported as the one proper government for England and was threatened by danger from the north. But it cannot have been easy to believe all this, and it must have been hard always to justify the ways of the world about him. He was temperamentally serious; most of his companions were not. He was conscientiously loyal, and too many of them were loyal only because they lived by the King's favor. And what was a worshipper of reason to think when the Earl of Holland and the Earl of Newcastle squabbled about the order in which their companies should march? Charles, "very melancholic" and aware "that he had lost reputation at home and abroad," was ungracious to his officers. He mustered them out without the "obliging circumstances" which might have made them readier to serve him again. Essex, Falkland's commander, had done as well as anyone could in such a blundering business, but "was discharged in the crowd, without ordinary ceremony." This "wrought very much upon his rough proud nature," and must have offended Falkland's sense of justice.

By the summer when the Scottish fiasco was over, Lady Elizabeth Cary was sick, and in early October she died. The last link that bound Falkland to his boyhood was broken. For him the loss of a friend was worse than the loss of a parent, but his mother had been both mother and friend. Her death relieved him of a heavy responsibility, since his brothers and sisters were provided for and he had now only his wife and children to consider, but he paid for his freedom a heavy price in loneliness for the woman whose influence, for better or worse, had most directly shaped his character.

He was left to face once again the problem of what he was to make of himself. Should he try to pick up the broken threads at Great Tew, and go on poring over books? Could he hope, now that troubled times were upon England, to find friends who still had leisure enough to talk theology or philosophy with him? Could he any longer be content in scholarly isolation? Perhaps further study might lead only to more doubts. His mother had written an answer to his letter to Montagu, and he had been quick to admit that her criticisms had weight. He said that her argument did not satisfy him, but confessed that he could not refute it without going further and denying more than he had yet done. Spying out truth by the light of reason had involved constant questioning and denial, and they might all too easily lead to despair. Could he run the risk? Could he, young as he was, and loving action as much as study, happily hide from life in a pallid existence bounded by books?

But, if he was not to be a scholar, what was he to be? He had got nowhere as a soldier, and Essex's faithfulness had been rewarded by a slight. He could succeed as a courtier only by forgetting his nobility enough to intrigue and bicker for sordid ends. He had seen enough in the past few months to realize that neither courtiers nor soldiers had much use for the values he cherished most. The problem was how to make those values and the talents he was ready to devote to serving them, count somehow for his troubled country.

He had often thought of passions and prejudices as mists which veiled the light of reason and virtue. That light had seemed to shine clear at Great Tew when his friends had echoed his assurance that men might be saved by clear thinking. Once out of Oxfordshire, however, he had found mists everywhere. They were almost as dense in the camp at Berwick as the actual fog that rolled in from the sea. The gay officers and unhappy troops had shown passion and prejudice enough, but the light of reason had been far to seek. Was there nowhere that it could burn bright; could he hope for nothing better than pale shadows through the mist or the dull glare of his own light reflected bleakly from a cloud too thick to pierce?

He may have decided independently that the best opportunity for a rational man was in politics; it may have been that Edward Hyde or some other politically minded friend persuaded him that his duty lay there. In any case, in December, 1639, when the King at last called a Parliament, driven to it by his need for funds, Falkland was elected from Newport, in the Isle of Wight. No one was very sanguine about what he and his colleagues could do. Thomas Wentworth,

Henry Cary's successor as Lord Deputy in Ireland, was now one of Charles's chief advisers, and both he and his royal master looked on the calling of Parliament as an experiment. It might grant the subsidies they needed to subjugate the Scots; if not, it could be quickly dissolved. This was as obvious to the King's enemies as to his friends.

The elections went quietly, and the Parliament met on April 13, 1640. Even Edward Hyde, though he was a staunch supporter of King and church, was satisfied with its character. "It could never be hoped," he wrote, "that more sober and dispassioned men would ever meet together . . . or fewer who brought ill purposes with them." Some members, of course, hated Laud; some feared Wentworth's power; and there were men of property who were resentful because they had been forced to contribute heavily to the King's revenues; but there were few who wanted to redress grievances by making a direct attack on the monarchy itself.

Two months earlier, Falkland's youngest son, born while he was in Scotland, had died, and his house at Aldenham was shadowed by the loss. It was an anodyne for grief to plunge into the work of the House of Commons, meeting each morning at eight for a four hours' session. In the first two weeks of sitting, Parliament usually did little that mattered, but now everyone knew that the King might dissolve it before it had fairly begun, and the most serious issues were taken up at once. Lord John Finch, the new Lord Keeper, suspected as the judge most to blame for the impositions of ship-money, lost no time in asking the House to postpone everything else until they had granted Charles the funds he needed, but John Pym, who cared more for correcting evils in the state than for pleasing the King, swiftly took command and answered Finch's plea. In "a set discourse of above two hours" he summed up the complaints of the people against the government of the last decade. Perhaps he did not see how crucial the occasion was; there was little in his words to show any realization "that he was virtually proposing a revolution" in the far-reaching implications of his attack on abuses of power.[2] His summing up was admirable, and cries of "A good oration!" testified to his hearers' approval. He crystallized the spirit of the Commons, and they made no move to supply money to the King, devoting themselves instead to a discussion of the nation's grievances. As Harbottle Grimstone said, the Scottish danger was "at the Back Door," but violations of the laws protecting the subjects' property and liberties, were perils already upon their backs.

Pym listed three broad grounds for complaint: "Grievances . . . against the Liberties and Privileges of Parliament," "Innovations in Matters of Religion," and "Grievances against the Propriety of . . . Goods." On all three there was much talk, and much work in committees. Papists were said to have been granted favors, the imprisonment of members of Parliament was denounced, and Falkland's friend, Edmund Waller, accented the idea that property rights were "the Mother of Courage and the Nurse of Industry." According to him, they made the nation "valiant in War, and industrious in Peace." The debates were "managed . . . with wonderful order and sobriety," but the King was irritated. He could not pay his bills with Parliamentary criticism. He got some comfort from the House of Lords, which voted to propose to the Commons that talk about grievances be put off till his purse was filled, but the members of the lower house resented the vote and claimed that their privileges were infringed by it. It hardened them in their determination to put an end to what they regarded as the evil practices of the last ten years, before they granted a penny to the monarch whose government had permitted these wrongs to exist.

Falkland sat silent. He was a novice in Parliament. So, indeed, were three-quarters of the other members of the House,

---

[2] G. Davies, *The Early Stuarts*, 1603–1660 (Oxford, 1937) p. 90.

but many of them were business men or lawyers who presumably knew more than he about government. To be sure,
he had seen something of the workings of the royal authority
while he was in the army, but little that he learned then had
much direct bearing on what he was called upon to think
about in Parliament. He had seen enough, however, to make
him cynical about Finch's valiant attempt to make the inglorious Scottish expedition sound like a proof of the King's
mercy toward rebellious subjects instead of a demonstration
of his helplessness in war. The one topic, of all those which
the Commons debated, upon which Falkland could qualify
as an expert was "Innovations in Matters of Religion." He
had reason to know the narrowness and exclusiveness of
Laud's policy, and disliked the Presbyterians and the extreme
Protestant sects because he thought they were equally hostile to freedom of conscience. But there was much to learn
about issues of the moment before he could intelligently join
in discussions of church policy, and the Short Parliament
passed without a speech from him.

He had many friends in the House. Sir John Vaughan was
there from Wales; Richard Boyle, Viscount Dungarvan had
a seat; Sir John Suckling and Thomas May came from Sus-
sex; from among the Carys' neighbors in Oxfordshire were
Sir Francis Wenman, representing the University, and William Lenthall, to whom Falkland had sold his house at Burford. Lettice Cary's uncle, Sir Benjamin Rudyard sat for
Wilton. Then there was Sidney Godolphin, coming faithfully to the House each day, though he hated the trip to
Westminster when the bleak streets were swept with rain
and fog. He and Rudyard were familiar with the work of the
Commons; so was Waller. But the closest of Falkland's
friends in Parliament, and the man who from 1640 until his
death was his chief intimate, was Edward Hyde. Like Lucius
Cary, he was making his debut in the House, but unlike Cary
he had lived close to politics for years.

A little too solemn, determined to get ahead but eager to do so honestly, Hyde's hard work was beginning to win him a name among lawyers. For all his occasional pompousness he had a strain of dry humor, and he was blessed with a shrewd eye for character. He thought that a young man with his way to make could improve himself by knowing wise men, and he made friends accordingly, among them the lord of Great Tew. When Hyde visited there he can have played little part in most of the more learned discussions, since his devotion to the Church of England pretty well closed his mind to speculations about religious authority. But he liked the company of scholars and prospective bishops. He admired Falkland's earnestness, and came under the spell of his charm, the more easily since he recognized beneath his friend's affability a seriousness as deep as his own.

Parliament gave scope for Hyde's talents. He saw in legal precedents and the constitution as he interpreted it the remedy for all ills; he was sure that constitutional monarchy was the one proper government. This made him an ardent enemy of extra-legal devices, even if sanctioned by the sovereign, and joined him with the critics of the bishops and the court in so far as they attacked practices not vouched for by constitutional usage. He made his maiden speech against the Earl Marshal's Court, ridiculing its recent pretensions to power and pointing out some of its more absurd performances. The sharpness of his assault endeared him to those who were most concerned with the "grievances" of the nation, and his adroit stopping short of too direct censure of any individual conciliated the courtiers. The Earl Marshal himself, Lord Arundel, saw that Hyde was too clever to ignore, and later made what excuses he could for the court over which he presided and thanked its critic for the civility of his speech, professing an affection he certainly did not feel.

Here was an auspicious beginning for a political career. As Hyde said himself, "the first part he had acted upon that stage, brought him much applause; and he was ever afterwards heard with great benignity." Furthermore he soon "showed that he could add to a brilliant maiden speech an astonishing skill in the tactics of debate," and did his best to keep the Commons from jumping too swiftly to a downright refusal of all the King's pleas for funds.[3]

From such a man Falkland could learn much, and his experience in his first Parliament was richly satisfying. There was much said about loyalty to Charles. Sir Benjamin Rudyard proclaimed: "If it were for my Life, I would desire nothing more, than that we proceed with Moderation, that so we may have many happy Parliaments." Cary loved moderation, and temperate and frank discussion were, he thought, ways to wisdom. He was instinctively loyal to the ideal of monarchy. Thus the Short Parliament seemed to him to represent the noblest aspect of government. There were loyal Englishmen apparently trying to rise above passion and prejudice; there were earnest individuals who seemed to be as eager as he was for harmony and temperateness in debate. Pym, already marked as the real leader of the Commons, was both firm and moderate. It was a far cry to this from the quarrels and futility of the Scottish expedition. Could it be that Falkland had at last found his place in a sphere ruled by reason? He must have heard with electric excitement Pym's declaration that the "powers of Parliament are to the body politic as the rational faculties of the soul to a man." [4] If this were true, devotion to reason might be put to practical use in the House, if nowhere else. Thus far Cary's essays toward truth had been largely doubtings or denials, and he had reduced to smaller and

---

[3] Sir H. Craik, *The Life of Edward Hyde, Earl of Clarendon* (London, 1911), I, 77.

[4] Rushworth (III, 1131-1132) gives Pym's words as: "A Parliament is that to the Commonwealth, which the Soul is to the Body." Gardiner, *History*, IX, 102, note on pp. 105, 106, relying on "something better than 'a later amplification' " of the speech, gives the sentence as I have quoted it.

smaller areas what a sensible man could believe and act upon. That was negative; the work of the Commons was positive. Falkland persuaded himself that it was "really impossible that" Parliaments "could ever produce mischieve or inconvenience to the kingdom, or that the kingdom could be tolerably happy in the intermission of them."

But Charles and Wentworth, now Earl of Strafford, did not want instruction from the "rational faculties" of the body politic. Even if Parliament was Reason, the King—as Will, or Passion?—could defy it. Hyde saw how dangerous such defiance would be for Charles himself, and, since he admired Laud and had realized, with one of his flashes of insight, that what the archbishop most needed was "a true friend" to tell him "seasonably . . . of his infirmities," went to him to urge that the King be persuaded to allow Parliament to continue in session. Laud, "sad, and full of thoughts," listened patiently, but confessed that "he had not so good an opinion of" the Houses' "affections to the king or the church, as to persuade their longer sitting, if the king were inclined to dissolve them." Charles was so inclined, and on the morning of May 5 the Lords of the Privy Council had to crawl sleepily out of bed in time for a meeting at six. It was held thus early to prevent Parliament's petitioning the King to make terms with Scotland. Reason or no, this he was not prepared to do, and at the Council meeting he announced that he was about to dissolve the Houses. All but two of the counsellors agreed, and the Short Parliament ended after three weeks of life. It had focussed the opposition to government by King and court alone, and had reinforced Falkland's belief that rulers must never exceed their legal powers. To do so, he thought, was to be like "a Mayor of a Town" who "should command the People to make his Hay," "commanding more then his Magistracy authorizeth" and so becoming "no Magistrate."

To dissolve the Parliament was political folly. Charles had scraped together a little money, but he could not go far without Parliamentary grants, and having dismissed an assembly which was swayed neither by the malcontents nor by the sycophants of the established order, he made inevitable the creation of a less docile one. He misread the temper of the people whom Parliament represented, and failed to see that his course must transform many of its loyal members into downright opponents of his authority. The unruly had reason to be glad at the turn of affairs, since nothing could do more to build up resentment against Charles and his advisers. The real losers were the moderates like Falkland, who hoped that errors might be corrected and abuses reformed coolly and without acrimony, and that prudent planning might safeguard the future. As feeling ran higher, the chance for harmony lessened; as controversy warmed, passions veiled clear thinking. Falkland was too inexpert politically, no doubt, to see all that the ending of Parliament implied, but "from the unhappy and unseasonable dissolution of that convention, he harboured, it may be, some jealousy and prejudice of the Court, towards which he was not before immoderately inclined; his father having wasted a full fortune there." Memories of his father's failure, his own loss of his Irish company, his imprisonment, his disappointment in Holland and the similar one in the army of 1639, were quite sufficient grounds for doubt about the ways of the court. Nor had his encounter with Laud led him to think well of him, and though Hyde constantly defended the archbishop, Falkland was not convinced. But he was sure of the virtue of Parliament.

Inevitably he longed to serve again in the House of Commons, and to try further how the "rational faculties" of the state might overrule the courtiers and bishops and restore order to the government. His chance came soon, for Charles's plans went awry. He marched again against the Scots, but mutinies chequered his progress. The English soldiers defaced churches as a tribute to Laud, and in London the archbishop, though his house was guarded by cannon, was threatened by mobs. The Scots gave up staring and began to fight, and at Newburn the royal troops fled before them. Even Wentworth had to admit that there was "a general disaffection to the king's service." London City refused to lend the King money, and Spain, France, and Rome, were equally hard-hearted. The Scots had to be left in possession of Northumberland and Durham, until the dispute should be settled. There was no way to settle it except with a Parliament.

More than half of the members of the Short Parliament were re-elected to the new one, Falkland among them. The elections showed a clear prejudice against courtiers. "The richest and most populous part of the country (with the exception of Somerset), . . . the heart of England, in wealth, population, and progressive quality," "declared against the king." [5] Whether Falkland realized it or not, the task of a moderate man and a lover of reason was bound to be harder now than it had been in April. Then prejudice and selfishness had at least been masked with a show of zeal for peace and thoughtful debate; now feeling had reached a pitch where "Truth," which Cary thought was "in the *still voice*," was likely to be lost in "the *loud wind*" of impatient defiance. Even Charles saw that the new Parliament would be subject to "affections and appetite, which were not likely to be contained with any modest bounds." Pym told Hyde "that they must now be of another temper than they were, . . . that they had now an opportunity to make their country happy, by removing all grievances and pulling up the causes of them by the roots, if all men would do their duties." Hyde saw that this meant that "the warmest and boldest counsels and overtures would find a much better reception than those of a more temperate allay."

Warmth and boldness were commonly enemies to reason, but for the moment Falkland, like most of his colleagues, was

---

[5] R. N. Kershaw, quoted in G. Davies, *op. cit.*, p. 96.

so impressed with the rottenness of the state that drastic action seemed the only sane course. Sitting beside Hyde, neatly dressed as always, his coarse straight hair straggling untidily as he moved excitedly during the debates, his wide-set eyes alert and his honest homely face intent on following every turn of the discussions, he threw himself eagerly into the struggle of the Commons to bring order out of what he thought was chaos.[6] For months he worked with Hyde, hand and glove with Pym and the most radical of the House, because for months the ostensible goal was only the correction of abuses of the law, and the punishment of those who had misled the King.

The Parliament opened on November 3, 1640, with what seemed to Hyde ill omens. "It had a sad and melancholic aspect." Charles did not ride in state to the opening, but came privately in his barge on the river, as though ashamed of the part he played. He had cause for foreboding. As early as November 11, Pym, with an adroit theatrical sense, had the doors locked and proceeded to air charges against Thomas Wentworth, Earl of Strafford, for his "tyrannical carriage" in Ireland and for his raising of troops to invade Scotland. A proposal to impeach him was approved, and a committee promptly decided to accuse him of high treason. Falkland at once had a thorny problem to face. His father had hated Strafford, and he himself liked neither the man nor what he believed to be his purposes in government. Could he then vote against him sure that he was not blinded by his own feeling? Even if he could, was it rational to bring an accusation of treason before all the facts had been examined and their interpretation discussed?

In any case he could no longer be silent. He had listened and watched; he had formed a conception of the true function

---

[6] T. Lewis, *Lives of the Friends and Contemporaries of Lord Chancellor Clarendon* (London, 1852), I, 198-206, gives an interesting list of many of Falkland's activities in the Long Parliament.

of Parliament; he had been outraged by the throttling of the last "convention"; and now he was ready to speak out. Waller, Godolphin, Rudyard, and Selden, were friends on whose sympathy he could count; the new speaker was Lenthall, whom he at least knew; John Hampden was well spoken of; Pym's speech in the Short Parliament had been for him a rallying cry; he could try his weak and unpleasant voice in the unfamiliar art of political speaking believing still that most of his hearers were as dispassionate as he in the search for truth. Appropriately his maiden effort in the House was a plea for more deliberate procedure. He thought there were good grounds for accusing Wentworth, but he could not know, and he urged that it would "suit better with the gravity of their proceedings . . . to digest" the evidence before taking action.

He was true to his principles, but Pym, true to his, was ready with an answer. Unless something were done quickly Wentworth would have the Parliament dissolved, "or take some other desperate course to preserve himself, though with the hazard of the kingdom's ruin," whereas if he were charged with treason he could be kept in safe custody until the facts were weighed. Here spoke the politician, with his eyes on the immediate practical necessities, impatient of counsels which might make action useless. The dilemma involved was often to recur, and Falkland, after this first taste of an unpleasant reality, was to have the lesson many times repeated. His scholarly desire to do nothing until all the data could be taken into account was often directly opposed to what was politically expedient. The one way, at the moment, to satisfy reason, was to allow the end to justify the means, granting the premise that Strafford was an evil force and that, therefore, however hastily or even unjustly, he must be made powerless. Some such compromise with his conscience Falkland must have made, for during the long campaign leading at last to Wentworth's execution, he served on at least two committees and labored hard enough to earn the Houses' thanks. But he did not lose sight of principle, and though he worked against the Earl, he tried hard to make sure that justice, as he understood it, was not quite forgotten. When the Commons protested because the Lords gave Strafford an extension of time to prepare his defense, Falkland took the other side and praised the upper house for its effort to be fair. Nor did he forget to be humane. The guilty man should be punished, but to penalize his children would be wanton cruelty. They "proceeded as well from his inocent wife as his owne guilty person; 'tis better they should be spared in there estates for the inocents sake, then punished for the guilty." [7]

Other ministers than Strafford were attacked. Windebank, the Secretary of State, supposed to have been lenient toward Catholics and certainly one of those to whom Falkland's mother had looked for help, fled to France. Even wits were in danger when they meddled with the plans of Parliament. Both Davenant and Suckling had to scurry out of London to avoid charges of having plotted to get control of the army for Charles.

The Long Parliament in its first year not only accused and punished or drove out those whom it regarded as the principal enemies of the state, but did its best to provide machinery for its protection in future. Parliaments were to be held every three years, and not dissolved except with their own consent. This alone was a death-blow for arbitrary monarchy. Falkland approved, but once again felt that hasty action was dangerous, and succeeded in having the matter referred to a "Grand Committee of the house" for discussion before it was

---

[7] That Falkland favored the Bill of Attainder against Strafford as well as the impeachment is indicated by Ralph Verney's note of his remark, Apr. 19, 1641: "In equity lord Straford deserves to dye" and of what he said on Apr. 15; R. Verney, *Verney Papers. Notes of Proceedings in the Long Parliament* (ed. J. Bruce; London, 1845), pp. 53, 49. J. Buchan, *Oliver Cromwell* (London, 1934), p. 108, agrees. Richard Baxter, *Reliquiae Baxterianae* (ed. M. Sylvester; London, 1696), p. 19, suggests that Falkland may none the less have wished to save Strafford from the death penalty.

voted. The Star Chamber was abolished, and the Court of High Commission. Ship-money was declared illegal. Thus within twelve months Parliament captured more power than it had ever had, and corrected the grievances most complained about. Inevitably feeling ran high, but even when political tempers were hottest, Lucius Cary tried hard to champion reasoned moderation. It was a task that called for vigilance and a ready tongue. He had both, and not only prevailed now and then on the side of what seemed to him to be wisdom, but won for himself a place of influence and respect.

Much of this was because of his speech on Monday, December 7, on the question of ship-money and, especially, the iniquities of Lord Finch.[8] In the past English kings had required ports and coastal counties to furnish ships and men for the navy. Charles had gone further, and had demanded funds to equip and man his fleet, even from inland counties. Thereby he in effect imposed a tax without the sanction of Parliament. His judges, Finch a leader among them, defended him on the ground that his course was "necessary" for the national defense in times of peril. Inevitably a Parliament, jealous of its privileges saw the levying of ship-money as a major grievance, and looked on Finch with intense disfavor. Falkland's attack on him and on the "tax" he had upheld spoke the mind of most of the Commons.

"I Rejoice very much to see this Day," he began, "and the want hath not lain in my Affections, but my Lungs, if to all that hath been past I have not been as loud with my Voice as any Man in the House; yet truly my Opinion is we have yet done nothing if we do no more." Here was a man after Pym's own heart—a Viscount and a courtier's son as zealous

---

[8] The speech was printed as The Lord Favlkland His Learned Speech in Parliament, in the House of Commons, Touching the Judges and the late Lord Keeper. Printee [sic] in the Yeare, 1641. My quotations from the speech, except as noted, are from the text in Rushworth, IV, 86–88.

as the most rebellious commoner in the good work of the Parliament!

Falkland felt that he needed some introduction and, in a few sentences confessed to slight knowledge of the law and dilated on the purity of his motives. "I hope it will be believed," he said, "that only publick Interest hath extorted this from me." He was sure that all who knew him knew that his "natural Disposition" was "to decline from Severity" and even more "from Cruelty." His opinion, he felt, need not be grounded on legal knowledge, since he was "confident that History alone is sufficient to shew this Judgment," which had declared ship-money to be legal, "contrary to our Laws, and Logick alone sufficient to prove it destructive to our Property, which every free and noble Person values more than his Profession." Here the premises of his thinking are plain. Precedent, "history," was a measure of law, and to be free and noble was to defend the rights of property. Both these propositions involved large assumptions, but they were commonly made by men who had lands and goods and believed themselves the heirs of a beneficent tradition of law. The very "Constitution of this Commonwealth hath established . . . the Security of our Goods, and the Security of those Laws which would secure us and our Goods," Falkland declared, and since the Commons represented men of property his hearers were not likely to ask whether his theory that the aim of government was to protect "goods," was broad enough to care for all the needs of all classes in the nation.

The judges were the defenders of law, but instead of guarding their sheep had become "Wolves to worry them." They had, on the ship-money question "delivered an opinion, and a judgement, the first in an extrajudiciall manner, and both upon an extrajudiciall matter, that is such as came not within their cognizance, they being *Iudges of Law*, and not of *necessity*, that is being *Iudges* and neither *Philosophers*, nor *Poli-*

ticians." When necessity "is absolute, and evident, the law of the Land seaseth, and that of generall reason and equitie, by which particular Lawes at first were framed, returnes to her Throane and government, when *salus populi* becomes not only *suprema,* but *sola lex.*"[9] Behind the laws of the land there was, in Falkland's opinion, a supreme law of reason. If the laws of the land were inadequate for a case of "necessity," then the higher law, dictated by the interests of the people, became the one authority.

This theory had important consequences. As Sir John Marriott has pointed out, Falkland was, whether he realized it in such terms or not, striking against the principle that the executive might appeal to a rule beyond those made for the welfare of the nation. He maintained that an appeal from the established laws must be to a law of reason which made the people's safety the first consideration. Therefore judges who stepped beyond specifically legal limits and claimed "necessity" as an excuse, must be judged according to whether the nation's best interests were served. If they were not, the magistrates were guilty of evil. Applied to Strafford, similar reasoning might justify the conclusion that, even if he could not be proved guilty by the "particular" laws to which he appealed, his accusers might plead "necessity" and fall back on higher authority, insisting that he was a danger to the state, so that legal technicalities did not matter, since he stood condemned before the supreme tribunal of reason. Selden, for one, was too reverent a lawyer to believe Strafford a traitor, but Falkland, impatient of what seemed to him legal details, declared: "How many haires breadths make a tall man, & how many makes a little man, noe man can well say; yet we know a tall man when we see him from a low man; soe 'tis in this, how

---

[9] The last two quotations follow the text in *The Lord Favlkland His Learned Speech,* which seems to be here more clearly phrased than that in Rushworth. At best, the passage is not easy to follow.

many illegal acts make a treason is not certainly well [known], but wee well know it when we see."

Had not Falkland's scepticism been blunted by his admiration for Parliament, he might have detected dangers to his own position in his doctrine. He was fundamentally conservative and held that an essential test of right and wrong in the state was conformity to the legal structure which supposedly had been built to protect Englishmen's liberties and property. By suggesting that if the specific laws were ignored, or proved insufficient, there must be invoked a higher test, that of the welfare of the people, he gave himself an excuse for proceeding against Wentworth and a platform on which to denounce Finch, but raised the awkward question of who was to decide what popular welfare required. Surely not the idle vagabonds against whom John Randol had inveighed years ago in Burford Church. Surely not those who had no property and hated the government which allowed them to be poor. Surely not the fanatic followers of new sects, threatening both the church and the established order of society. Surely not the courtiers, evil-livers, bad soldiers, and idle wits. Yet any of these might turn Falkland's argument against him, saying that they knew the needs of the nation better than he. He might have answered, had he seen the problem, by asserting the authority of Parliament. It represented the people, by which of course he meant those Englishmen who shared his interests and allegiances, and no other agency of government did. Therefore its judgments expressed the "united consent," which alone "gives force" to law, and defined what English rights and liberties were. This solution would have comforted him, but could not content anyone who, for whatever cause, distrusted the infallible virtue of the House of Commons.

The rest of his speech against Finch reveals other elements in his attitude. By their acts the judges had "allowed to the King" to take from the people "what he would, when he would, and how he would," and had transformed them "from the State of free Subjects . . . unto that of Villains," depriving them of their chance to express their love for the sovereign, and win his for them, by "Legal and Voluntary" grants of Parliament. The King, "a most excellent Prince, hath been most infinitely abused by his Judges," Falkland said. They had subverted the most fundamental of all laws and had introduced the most arbitrary of all forms of government. Finch was particularly at fault. He "gave away with his Breath what our Ancestors had purchased for us by . . . an Expence of their Time, their Care, their Treasure, and their Blood." He "strove to root up those Liberties" which others had only pruned back. His attempt was "to make our Grievances immortal and our Slavery irreparable"; he gave a power to the crown in which Parliament had no share.

On the next day Falkland spoke again, and proposed that there be drawn up "a thorough charge" against the Lord Keeper, "which the Howse allowed well." Cary and Hyde were made members of a committee to examine the judges as to whether their decision on ship-money was influenced by solicitations or threats from anyone. Two weeks later Finch appeared to defend himself before the House, but its members resolved, with only a few dissenting votes, that he was guilty of high treason. A resolution that Falkland should carry to the Lords a message accusing him, was passed unanimously. Cary executed the commission on the 22nd, but Finch was discovered to have fled during the preceding night. In January Falkland was delegated to present the detailed charges to the upper house, and at his request Hyde was appointed to assist him. His speech before the Lords went over the same ground he had covered in the Commons, and underlined some fundamentals in his creed.

Finch's offense was against "the Excellent Constitution of this Kingdom," and he had usurped rights which belonged to Parliament, the "Fountain of Justice," the streams of which were the laws. The judges were the "Conduit-Pipes." Finch's acts destroyed the nation's "Liberties," and "included the Destruction of . . . Propriety," which meant "the Destruction of . . . Industry." Thereby the gates were opened "to the terriblest of all Invasions, that of Want and Poverty." Law was the people's "Guard"; Finch had made it "the Ground of Illegality."

Surely this was treason, Falkland argued—"a Treason as well against the King as against the Kingdom; for whatsoever is against the Whole, is undoubtedly against the Head." It was criminal to take "from his Majesty the ground of his Rule, the Laws" and "the principal Honour of his Rule, the Ruling over Free-men, a Power as much Nobler than that over Villains, as that is than that over Beasts." Finch had "endeavoured to take from his Majesty the principal Support of his Rule, the Hearts and Affections of those over whom he rules (a better and surer Wall to the King, than the Sea is to the Kingdom.)" If the King and the people regarded each other with "mutual Distrust and . . . Disaffection" there was "Danger even of the Destruction of both." Falkland bolstered his case with a direct appeal to the Lords' material interests. Their "great share in Possessions" gave them a "Concernment in Propriety"; and the "care and pains used by" their "Noble Ancestors in the founding and asserting of . . . Common Liberties" made the "just Defence of them" the "proper and peculiar Inheritance" of the nobility. The Lords were impressed and ordered Finch into custody whenever he could be caught.

Falkland was plainly hostile to government by the King alone. He believed in the "mixt monarchy" which Hobbes laughed at. According to that philosopher, such men as Cary and Hyde "thought the Government of *England* was not an absolute, but a mixt Monarchy; and that if the King should clearly subdue this Parliament, . . . his Power would be what he pleased, and theirs as little as he pleased, which they counted Tyranny." For Hobbes the chance that King, Lords, and Commons, would disagree, was enough to make such a theory impractical; that chance, he believed, was something Parliament "never thought of." Perhaps not, but for its first months it did not have to. The Commons and the Lords worked together smoothly enough, and the King was gratifyingly meek in acceding to their votes. There was some excuse for an idealist like Falkland to hope that clear thinking might bring harmony even in the three branches of a government.[10] By that hope he steered his course, starting from the idea that a sound political structure is a means by which reason may be made effective among men—at least men of property. His attack on the impositions of ship-money, which a few years earlier he had paid apparently without protest, was more than an attack on an unjust tax. It was a denunciation of a departure from what now seemed to him a basic principle of government.

Hyde's attitude may have been less lofty. He respected the law because he had been brought up as a student of it, and had thought about little that transcended it. So long as Parliament worked simply to reform what had gone wrong, keeping within the limits of what could be legally justified, he collaborated; but when it outran strict law and threatened the established position of the King and church or what seemed to him to be constitutional precedent, he resisted. Much as he loved Falkland, "his dear sweetheart," he felt that he was misled "by the authority of those he believed understood the laws perfectly, of which himself was utterly ignorant," and thought that Falkland's readiness to hold Finch and Strafford guilty of treason, proved the point. But at the same time Hyde recognized that the Lord Keeper and Wentworth must

---

[10] Cf. K. Feiling, *England under the Tudors and Stuarts* (London, n.d.), p. 146: "The unanimity for six decisive months of this purely aristocratic Parliament is the real indictment of Charles, Strafford, and Laud. Falkland ... joined hands with Pym's associates, to pass the Acts against Star Chamber and High Commission, to secure triennial Parliaments and abolish ship-money, to suppress Laudianism and to impeach Strafford."

be removed, so that the House had been in session for months
before any question arose on which he and Falkland completely disagreed.

For them both, as for their colleagues, religious questions
were of prime concern—for Hyde because he supported the
church as an integral part of the governmental structure, and
for Falkland because years of study had brought him to certain convictions about the nature of a true church and the extent to which an institution might control the beliefs and
worship of free men. In the House sat some who saw a complete ecclesiastical reorganization as necessary for English
Protestantism, and others who hated Anglicanism because its
ministers had supported obnoxious acts of the King. Others
disliked Laud personally; still others were loyal to the Church
of England itself but feared the Arminians and thought their
High-Church principles were destructive of older and better
standards. Everywhere there was suspicion of the Papists, and
hatred of them. Few men in the House of Commons could
think of religious questions without emotion, and prejudices
of all sorts, personal, local, and social, were sure to be expressed in any debate about the national church. Inevitably in
the very first weeks of the session it began to be warmly discussed.[11]

Archbishop Laud, passionately devoted to a crusade for
religious uniformity, had carried matters with a high hand.
He was either unaware of the hostility provoked by his insistence on his own brand of Arminian piety and on the forms
which for him represented beauty and order, or cared nothing
for his enemies in the intensity of his personal devotion to a
single ritual and faith. In spite of those who thought of him

---

[11] Mr. Jones points out that the reformers in Parliament were united by
their Protestantism, and that dread of Catholicism brought temporary "harmony between the radicalism of the Puritan middle class and the conservatism
of nobles like Digby, lawyers such as Hyde, and devout and cultured landowners of the type of Falkland." I. D. Jones, The English Revolution (London, 1931), p. 60.

as a secret ally of Rome, he had climbed to great power. His influence with Charles I was vast, and in a day when the royal counsellors were being blamed for everything that was censurable, he could not hope to escape. On December 18, the Commons accused him of high treason. Probably Falkland concurred. He had no love for Laud, and was radically opposed to the idea that any man or even any church might pose as an infallible authority. He was loyal to the Church of England, and, no doubt, believed like nearly everyone else that a strong national church was necessary for a strong nation, but he thought that it should comprise all who could be called Christian, in the broadest sense. For him intolerant rejection of believers, because of differences about ceremonies or minor points of doctrine, meant weakness not strength. But to denounce Laud, or to admit grave misdeeds by other bishops, was not to renounce either Anglicanism or the episcopal form of government. The extremists wanted such a renunciation, but Falkland quickly became a leader of those who hoped to reform the church without destroying it, and believed that a reformed Anglican system might be a refuge for tolerance and truth, exiled by both Papist and Puritan.

Four days after the session began, his wife's uncle, Rudyard, told the House that religion must be its main interest. Pym followed suit, and criticized the existing church. The tables were soon loaded with complaints against Laud and his agents. On December 11 there came from London, with more than fifteen thousand signatures, the famous "Root and Branch Petition." It demanded the abolition of the whole system of church government, "with all its Dependencies, Roots and Branches" and all "Laws in their behalf." The signers called themselves "humble Suppliants," but they were far from humble in asking that, once the old structure was razed, the new be "rightly placed amongst" them. In other words a scheme of their devising was to replace episcopacy. They asked not for reform but for revolution.

To this Falkland could never agree. As he saw it, the petitioners wanted to substitute for one church, wrongly claiming infallibility, another making the same claim with no better right. He had no use for pretensions to infallibility, but the Anglicans might be taught to abandon theirs, and he had no confidence that the Puritans could be, in view of their apparent confidence in the sanctity of even their narrowest tenets. This alone would have been enough to determine his attitude, and there was another argument which, confessed or not, carried weight with him and with many of the other members of the House. Presbyterianism was associated in their minds, however unjustly, with rebellion against government and with restless strivings of the lower classes toward greater power. Fear of Puritans was almost as potent as fear of Papists, and was quite as effective as cool reason or study of precedent in rousing from the Parliament a body of defenders for the Church of England. Even the most radical in the House dared not move too fast. Scotland, to be sure, with an army in the northern counties, could probably be counted on to champion Presbyterianism against Anglicanism, but how far English voters would go in the same direction was as yet uncertain. One group took a middle ground and expressed itself in the "Ministers' Petition and Remonstrance," which came to the Commons on January 23, 1641. It voiced the desires of the Anglican reformers, who by no means agreed with those who favored a complete change in the established church. The petition came from "several Ministers in behalf of themselves and many others [of] their Brethren of the Church of England, praying a Redress of certain Irregularities in the Government of the Church," and carried with it a list of "those supposed Irregularities." Among these were the holding of secular offices by the clergy, the "sole acting of Bishops in Ordinations and Censures, and the great Revenues and little use of Deans and Chapters."

This was read on Saturday. On Monday the King sum-

moned both houses of Parliament to his presence at Whitehall. As in the previous year, he was annoyed because the legislators talked of the nation's wrongs and voted him no money
for use against his enemies. He made this clear, and went on
to state explicitly his position on larger issues. He said: "There
are some Men, that more maliciously than ignorantly, will put
no Difference between Reformation and Alteration of Government." So far as the church went, that was just the difference between the Root and Branch Petition and the Ministers' Petition. That Charles had religion in mind appeared in
his next sentence: "Hence it cometh, That *Divine Service* is
irreverently interrupted, and Petitions in an ill Way given in,
neither disputed nor denied." He thought he had a remedy,
declaring that he would agree to "the reformation of all Innovations both in Church and Commonwealth" and professing
to want "to reduce all Things to the best and purest Time, as
they were in the Time of Queen *Elizabeth*." Beyond this he
would not go, and directly criticized the petitions. They were
"against the present established Government"; they contained
"great Threatnings against the Bishops." He was willing to
reduce the bishops' power, if it exceeded what was proper
"according to the Wisdom of former Times"; he was even
ready to strip them of any temporal authority they held which
was "inconvenient to the State" and "not . . . necessary for the
government of the Church, and upholding Episcopal Jurisdiction." But on one point there could be no compromise. He
would never consent to deprive the bishops of their votes in
Parliament, for, he said, "in all the Time of my Predecessors
since the Conquest, and before, they have enjoyed it, and I am
bound to maintain them in it, as one of the Fundamental
Constitutions of this Kingdom."

Wisely or not, Charles in this speech laid out a clear line of
battle. Anyone who thereafter voted against the bishops' sitting in Parliament would do so against the King's wish; loyal
members of the houses knew now how far they might go. The

royal will was proclaimed; if Parliament went beyond, it must do so with open eyes. But unfortunately Charles was more explicit about what he would not agree to than about what he would. Many of his hearers got small comfort from his talk. "It filled most of us," said one, "with sad apprehensions of future evils, in case his Majesty should be irremovably fixed to uphold the bishops in their wealth, pride, and tyranny."

The Commons showed its mood by proceeding to examine suspiciously the appeal which had been made to English Catholics for funds to be used against Scotland, and on January 28 it was decided to examine Walter Montagu and Sir Kenelm Digby. A committee was appointed to prepare the questions to be asked them. John Hampden was one of its members; Falkland another. Montagu was his connection by marriage, and Digby his friend. That he was chosen to help in investigating them, testifies to his reputation for staunch Protestantism, proof against friendship and loyalty to a Catholic mother. For Hampden he had great respect, and his service with the committee gave him a chance to see more of one of the noblest champions of the Houses against the King.

This was only an interlude, however, in the course of the attack upon the bishops. On February 1, Harbottle Grimstone, who had spoken vigorously against Laud, had a brief brush with Selden, who took the occasion to say plainly, "Parliaments are not *Jure Divino*." No one said they were, in so many words, but Selden read the omens and saw how easily some members of the Commons might convince themselves that Parliament's authority was divinely infallible. As a sceptic, and a hard-headed historian, he had small use for pretensions to "divine right," least of all for those which ran counter to his conception of a properly regulated monarchy.

The real battle came on February 8 and 9, when the House took up the Root and Branch Petition and the Ministers' Petition. It called forth Falkland's most vigorous speech. Lord

George Digby, a kinsman of Sir Kenelm's, perverse and unreliable but a handsome darling of the court, had taken up the cudgels against the Root and Branch Petition. He was scornful of his social inferiors, and in his denunciation of the Petition, left little doubt of his contempt for its signers. He detested "irregular and tumultuous Assemblies," and pled that the evil deeds of the bishops could not excuse the abolition of their whole order. To replace them by Presbyterian leaders, he thought, would be to threaten monarchy itself. That struck a responsive note with those who had taken Charles's speech to heart. It carried weight in the House just because it appealed frankly to certain men's prejudices and loyalties, and Digby did not weaken his effect by going deeply into the fundamental rights and wrongs of episcopal government. But Falkland, fresh from his study, dug deeper.

He began with a fervent assault on the bishops, which must have warmed the hearts of their extremest enemies. The kingdom had long suffered "Oppressions, both in Religion and Liberty" and "a great, if not a principal Cause" had "been some Bishops and their Adherents." "Some" was an important word. Throughout his address Falkland strove to set against the faults of Laud and his party, the ideal of a better church led by better bishops. But for the "some" he had no mercy. They had destroyed "Unity, under pretence of *Uniformity*"; "had brought in *Superstition* and *Scandal*, under the Titles of *Reverence* and *Decency*"; had "defiled" the church by "adorning" the churches; and had "slackned the strictness of that Union which was formed between us, and those of our Religion beyond the Sea." They had been careful about their tithes, but careless of "the weightier Works of the Law"; they had been less hard on downright foes of the church than on those who stayed away from its services because of minor scruples. "*Masses* have been said in Security, a *Conventicle*" of Puritans "hath been a Crime." To conform to ceremonies had been made more important than to be a

Christian. Preaching had been discouraged, and the bishops had fostered ignorance, perhaps "to introduce the better that Religion which accounts it the *Mother of Devotion*." Intolerant, arrogant, asserting their own divine right, they had worked for "the demolishing of *Puritanism* and *Propriety*" and the "Building of the Prerogative at *Pauls*. . . . Their Work was to try how much of a *Papist* might be brought in without *Popery*; and to destroy as much as they could of the *Gospel*, without bringing themselves into danger of being destroyed by the *Law*." Some of them aimed at an English "*Popery*," "a blind dependance of the People upon the Clergy." They had endangered "Liberties," too, by supporting usurpations of authority by the King's agents. "A little of their freedom of Speech at *White Hall*, might have saved us a great deal of the use we have now of it in the *Parliament House*." By keeping the clergy, and ecclesiastical cases, out of the jurisdiction of civil courts, and by influencing judges, they brushed aside all checks on "their Arbitrary Power," and conquered "the *Common-Law* of the Land." They turned "their Brethren out of their *Freeholds*, for not doing that which *no Law of Man* required of them to do; and which (in their Opinions) the *Law of God* required them not to do." Scottish troubles and Strafford's misdeeds were alike abetted by them.

But with this much pressed home against evil bishops, Falkland turned to insist that there were good bishops too, and that the faults of some should not bring destruction upon all. "I wish we may distinguish," he said, "between those who have been carried away with the *stream*, and those who have been the *stream* that carried them, . . . between the more and less Guilty," and, especially, "between the *Guilty* and the *Innocent*." Throughout the ages, bishops had done much good, and even in 1641 there were some who were blameless. A few had proved their "Moderation and Humility," had opposed popery and Arminianism, had preached faithfully, and had lived untouched by guilt or malice. This being so, Falkland said, "Let us give but good Men good Rules; we shall have both good Governors and good Times."

The proper way was to take from the bishops all that had bred mischief. "Temporal Title, Power and Employment" might go if need be—the bishops could be shorn of their lordship or even, in spite of the King, of their seats in Parliament. Their revenues might be cut, provided they were left enough so that they could be scholars serving "in some good Degree to the Dignity of *Learning*." The laws which lent themselves to ill purposes could be changed. As for ritual, Falkland suggested: "Let no *Ceremonies* which any number counts *unlawful*, and no Man counts *necessary*, against the Rules of Policy, and Saint *Paul*, be imposed." Given wise regulations made by Parliament, there need be no fear of episcopal tyranny or laxness in duty. Since all dangers could thus be taken care of, there was no possible reason "to abolish, upon a few Days Debate, an Order which hath lasted (as appears by Story) in most Churches these Sixteen Hundred Years ... from Christ to *Calvin*." It would be folly "in an Instant" to "change the whole Face of the Church like the Scene of a Mask."

Bishops had no divine right, but they need not be harmful; their existence was not required by any law, but none forbade it. The simple question was whether they could be useful. But—and here spoke conservatism—"all great Mutations in Government are dangerous ... since ... all the Dangers and Inconveniences they may bring are not to be foreseen." "No wise man will undergo great Danger but for great Necessity." Therefore, Falkland declared, "My Opinion is, That we should not root up this Ancient Tree, as dead as it appears, till we have tryed whether by this, or the like lopping of the Branches, the Sap which was unable to feed the Whole, may not serve to make what is left both grow and flourish. ... If we may ... take away both the Inconveniencies of Bishops, and the Inconveniences of no Bishops, that is an almost universal Mutation; this Course can only be opposed by those who love Mutation for Mutation sake."

All this led up to the proposal that the Commons have considered and debated the abuses and grievances charged against the bishops in the Ministers' Petition. If discussion proved that what was wrong could be made right without doing away with episcopacy altogether, it would be idle to take up the Root and Branch Petition at all, but, said Falkland, perhaps committing himself dangerously, if Parliament decided that reform could be had only by eliminating bishops, "Let us not commit the *London* Petition, but let us grant it."

Carefully listened to, the speech was an admirable statement of the moderate reforming position. Its conservative emphasis was marked, and the reluctance of the sceptical mind to assume that the untried can be less open to doubt than the existing scheme, was written large. But the purport of what Falkland said was positive. He was reiterating his wish for religious unity through tolerant acceptance of differences in ceremonial and doctrine, insisting on agreement only in the essentials of Christianity. He pictured a truly liberal church in which there would be no blind "dependance" on a presumably infallible clerical organization and the individual would be free to be a Christian as his own conscience bade. Episcopal government would be kept not because it was indispensable but because it was sanctioned in tradition and because diligent bishops might advance learning. To reform abuses Falkland was willing to go as far as was needed— farther than the King—but he saw no reason to be more drastic than was clearly required.

Like most temperate utterances in active controversies, his speech was distorted to suit the wishes of violent partisans. His attack was directed against some of the bishops only, but it was easy to remember his sharp phrases and forget the rest. By slurring over the word "some," his remarks could be twisted into an argument for Presbyterianism against episcopacy, and this was done.[12] In Gardiner's words, "it was with the sure instinct of a true debater, that Nathaniel Fiennes . . . replied to Digby and not to Falkland. That ecstatic vision of a Liberal Church, where no ceremonies were enforced which were unpalatable to any considerable number . . . had no hold on the actual world." Few men in the House of Commons were prepared to forget their immediate prejudices and the rooted habit of conceiving a national church in terms of a single exclusive system. Hatred of Catholics, love for Presbyterianism, and dislike for bishops or the King, were more urgent motives than academic dreams of a liberal and comprehensive church. Falkland had talked too much like a scholar; most of his audience thought like men of the world. He yearned for moderation and tolerance grounded in reason; they for political success, fatter purses, or the victory of their dogmas. Some of them had seen Laud driving through London. He had fifty mounted retainers, and ushers cried before him, "Roome, roome, for my Lords Grace; Gentlemen be uncovered, my Lords Grace is coming!" Children playing in the streets were tumbled head over heels out of the way, and costermongers had their goods, baskets and all, tossed into the Thames lest they block the smooth progress of the archbishop's coach. One glimpse of such a scene stirred hotter feelings than a dozen speeches as carefully balanced as Falkland's. Laud in his pomp was easily made a symbol for all bishops; why waste time with speculations as to what bishops might be, when it was all too clear what the greatest of them was?

---

[12] Wood (Athenae, II, 568) comments on this speech and quotes Heylin, Laud's contemporary biographer, who called it "a bitter speech against the bishops, upon which account it is much used and quoted by the presbyterians." D. Lloyd, State-Worthies. Or, The States-Men and Favourites of England (2d ed.; London, 1679), p. 940, calls the speech "the bitterest Invective against the Governours and government of the Church, that ever was penned in English."

Nor were the friends of episcopacy any better able to be dispassionate. Sir John Strangways spoke for many of them when he said: "If we make a parity in the Church we must come to a parity in the Commonwealth. The bishops are one of the three estates of the kingdom, and have voice in Parliament." Men of breeding and property naturally inclined to defend the bishops less because of sixteen hundred years of tradition or abstract definitions of authority, than because bishops were of their own class and could be trusted to vote against encroachments by the rabble. To Strangways it no doubt seemed a proof of his case when he was hotly answered by a man whose clothes seemed to have been made by a bad country tailor, whose linen was none too clean, whose hat had no band, whose face was "swoln and reddish," voice harsh, and utterance quite undisciplined by graceful court fashion. Oliver Cromwell appeared to Strangways, as to Sir Philip Warwick, a portent of evil days for gentlemen who identified manners and stylish dress with virtue.

The "great and tedious Debates" of February 8 and 9, ended at last with a compromise suggested by Sir John Colepeper and by Falkland. Most of the Root and Branch Petition, as well as the Ministers' Petition, was referred to a committee, but the question of the episcopal system itself was kept for the House to discuss later. This merely postponed the crisis, but it kept the extremists in check for the moment, and Falkland's worshipful attitude toward parliaments probably made him sure that the governmental structure of the church would be safe when it was finally soberly debated. Pym himself was said to feel that it "was not the intention of the House to abolish either Episcopacy or the Book of Common Prayer, but to reform both wherein offence was given to the people." If so, he and Falkland were agreed.

On March 10 the committee to which the petitions had been referred, reported to the House, which resolved that the legislative and judicial power of the bishops in the House of

Lords was "prejudicial to the commonwealth," and, on the
11th, resolved further "that no judicial functions of any kind
should be exercised by the clergy." On March 30, the so-called
Bishops' Bill, ejecting the bishops from the upper house and
the Privy Council, was read for the first time, and on May 1
it passed. During the debates Hyde spoke against it. To him
it meant "changing the whole frame and constitution of the
kingdom, and of the Parliament itself."

As he sat down, his neighbor, Falkland, jumped up and began to speak. The drowsiest members of the House opened
their eyes at his first words, for, after months in which he and
Hyde had sat together and had never voted on opposite sides,
he was at last taking issue with his friend. Hyde was amazed,
and his enemies—Cromwell among them—were delighted. A
split in the ranks of the moderates meant new hope for the
extremists. The whole House buzzed with excitement.

Falkland's argument was simple. He believed the change
proposed in the bill was needed to save the church, and he
saw nothing in the constitution to forbid it. Not all pious men
who were fit to be bishops were good legislators; "they may
doe more good in their callings which requires a whole man."
If they held land they had a voice in choosing representatives
in Parliament, and in any case there were many of them who
would not admit that the bishops could speak for them.

Falkland took his seat while the House "could not contain
from a kind of rejoicing" and Hyde sat too startled to conceal
his feeling. Falkland had come a long way since the Short
Parliament. In it he had satisfied himself that in parliaments
lay the only hope for decent government. That opinion he
clung to, and his opposition to Hyde in 1641 was one result.
Good Englishmen in the Commons had decided after careful
thought that the bishops should be deprived of power in the
state, and he trusted his colleagues enough to accept their verdict. He conceived of the duty of the clergy as the advance-
ment of learning and religious instruction, and was ready to

admit that temporal power might be a clog, not an aid. His clerical friends at Great Tew had read deeply and talked well about what really mattered in religion, not about palaces, great revenues, and the temptations and cares of public administration. Falkland was prepared to assert his opinion even though it meant defying Charles I and taking issue with Hyde. He was no longer dependent on the man who had brought him up in politics. He had made himself heard in the House, and his influence there was real. The time had come to stand alone, if need be, rather than to compromise with his beliefs.

He might have been less bold had he seen as clearly as Hyde the possible political consequences of his vote. That cool-headed lawyer was beginning to realize that many members of Parliament wanted for it not only the place he thought it was constitutionally entitled to, but vastly enlarged powers which would weaken the King and warp the entire traditional framework of the state. He knew better than Falkland what really lay in the minds of some who admitted to no more than a desire to reform the church. For them the real goal was its destruction and replacement by a Presbyterian system. Robert Baillie, a shrewd Scot, had written home from London that the "utter abolition" of bishops was "the onlie aime of the most godlie" and would be achieved by "the axe of prayer." But it was, he thought, to be helped also by Falkland, who declaimed "most acutelie, as we could have wished, against the corruptions of Bishops." What if he did defend limited episcopacy? He, with others, was taking the roof off a rotten structure, and Baillie's friends were sure that this would make the walls and the very foundations more vulnerable, "let Selden and . . . others gnash their teeth as they will."

Falkland understood too little of such men as Baillie. A lover of moderation is always likely to look upon compromise as the best way out of controversy, and Falkland was no exception to the rule. Open discussion, consideration for the views of others, and readiness to yield any save fundamental points, were, he thought, the securest approaches to truth. Hampden had assured him that if the Bishops' Bill passed, there would be no more attacks on the church. Was it not then better to sacrifice an inessential, by stripping the bishops of temporal power, than to run the risk of more radical change? For anyone who would accept his premises, his position was wholly reasonable; what he failed to see was that others, starting from different conceptions of what the church was and could be, might logically come to opposite conclusions. Nor did he yet comprehend how far Parliament was swayed by forces less admirable but more potent than reason. His moderation, whether he knew it or not, was caught between extreme opinions. Some of those were weighted by fear, some by fervent faiths which his intellectual temper made it hard for him to understand, and others by the covetousness of business men and courtiers. There were the jealousies of rival social classes to reckon with, and the petty scheming of selfish men. His faith in the wisdom of Parliament made him too uncritical of its members, and he was so sure of the theoretical rightness of his ideas that he worried too little about their political utility. He voted as he believed, but in so doing he gave aid and comfort to those whose beliefs were sharply hostile to his. He was a philosopher in a Parliament in which the prizes were to go to politicians, and the only reward reserved for him was ultimate disillusion.[13]

---

[13] "Nothing can be more fatal in politics than a preponderance of the philosophical, or in philosophy than a preponderance of the political spirit"; W. E. H. Lecky, *History of the Rise and Influence of the Spirit of Rationalism in Europe* (Rev. ed.; N. Y., 1868), II, 132.

VII

"THE VALLEY OF THE SHADOW"

Falkland in Parliament, the Privy Council, and the Secretaryship of State, March, 1641–September, 1642

ON THE night of November 22, 1641, the House of Commons sat until four in the morning. In the half-darkness weary members yielded to jaded nerves. "I thought," wrote Philip Warwick, "wee had all sat in the valley of the shadow of death" and "had catcht at each others locks, and sheathed our swords in each others bowels." Men forgot the dignity of the place, and wildly waved their hats. Voices rose feverishly, and at the climax sword-blades flickered in the candlelight and thudded ominously as tense hands drove their points into the floor.

During the long session, from noon on the 22nd until nearly dawn of the 23rd, Falkland suffered more than defeat on a specific issue. As the debates grew hotter and the strain heightened before the final tumult, every hour robbed him of part of his old confident reverence for Parliament. It was small comfort to score a petty victory over Cromwell, whose intensely partisan assurance of the divinely ordained necessity for radical action had warped his political judgment, so that he had assured Falkland that the debate would be "a very sorry one." Actually it had been longer and more violent than any either man had seen in the House. As they met, leaving the session, hollow-eyed, hoarse, and lax with fatigue, Falk-

181

land could not resist asking whether there had not been a debate. "I will take your word another time," Cromwell answered, and then, tired as he was, blazed out in a passionate whisper that if his party had not won he, and many other honest men, would have sold all they had in England and left it forever. Hyde commented acidly, years later: "So near was the poor kingdom at that time to its deliverance!"

Falkland on November 23, 1641, had no way of knowing what Cromwell was to become, but he must have caught from his comment on the night's work an indelible impression of how fiercely devoted were the advocates of a new order for the nation and of how little hope their fanaticism left for cooler counsels. They had faith and emotion that commanded action. Men of Falkland's stripe, eager not to act until it was proved wise, and fearful lest emotion interfere with clear thinking, had too little fire with which to fight.[1] Parliament was growing less inclined to listen to them. The taut restraint of Cromwell's whisper, the angry shouts that still rang in his ears, and the remembered flash of naked swords, were enough to burn deep into Falkland's mind the ugly fact that in the House of Commons other gods were usurping the place of intellect.

The debate on the 22nd and 23rd centred on one of the dearest ambitions of the King's enemies in the House, the passing of a long statement of the evils from which the nation suffered. This, the Grand Remonstrance, "one of the most important documents in English constitutional history," was a sweeping attack on the abuses of power charged against the King and bishops.[2] It was also a defense of the Parliament's work in relieving some of the country's woes. It ended with proposals which were essentially a platform for reorganizing

---

[1] "Moderation . . . was a mood rather than a faith . . . and . . . could not have the compelling power of the extremer creeds." J. Buchan, *Oliver Cromwell* (London, 1934), p. 33.

[2] G. Davies, *The Early Stuarts* (Oxford, 1937), p. 118.

the national church. "We hold it requisite," the Remonstrance reads, "that there should be throughout the whole Realm a Conformity to that Order which the Laws enjoin according to the Word of God . . . We desire to unburthen the Consciences of Men of needless and superstitious Ceremonies, suppress Innovations, and take away the Monuments of Idolatry."

The words were innocent. What they meant must depend on those who interpreted them. The Remonstrance asked for a synod of "the most Grave, Pious, Learned and Judicious Divines of this Island; assisted with some from Foreign Parts, professing the same Religion with us; who may consider . . . and represent the Results of their Consultations unto the Parliament, to be there allowed of and confirmed, and receive the Stamp of Authority, thereby to find Passage and Obedience throughout the kingdom." But who was to decide what divines were grave and learned enough to dictate what should become the law for English Protestants? The Anglican bishops had few friends in the House of Commons, but who else was there to plead for the existing ecclesiastical order? Foreign Protestants would by and large support the Presbyterians and the more extreme Protestant groups in England. Such clerics as the House was likely to approve were almost certain to vote against episcopacy. The Remonstrance seemed to good Anglicans and loyal subjects of Charles I a hostile manifesto, and must have distressed the moderates who hoped that a fair verdict on the religious question might be arrived at by free discussion of all points of view.

The supporters of the Remonstrance pressed it hotly. During the summer of 1641 the sympathy of the nation seemed to be shifting from Parliament to the King. The Commons must either temper its zeal for power or quicken popular enthusiasm for its aims. To insist on grievances was one effective way of winning adherents. Few Englishmen were quite satisfied with things as they were; to point out how much

was wrong and to blame it all on the King and his advisers
was obviously good politics. The leaders of the House knew,
even if Falkland did not, that the surest weapon was an appeal to passion and prejudice. Tempered arguments might
charm scholars, but the scholars were far outnumbered by
those with whom invective, exaggeration, or even downright
falsehood, worked magic.

Falkland and Hyde fought together against the Remonstrance. Their disagreement in the spring had not impaired
their friendship, and now, in the face of a changed situation,
they were again voting together. Hyde opposed the Remonstrance in part because of its hostile tone toward Charles. He
declared: "Wee stand upon our liberties for the kings sake,
least hee should bee king of meane subjects, or wee subjects
of a meane king." Reform he favored, but reform within the
limits of decent loyalty. Falkland sounded the same stop.
The Remonstrance, he said, accused the sovereign of con-
cealing delinquents, surely too grave a charge for subjects to
make lightly. But the religious issue interested him most, and
he tried to explain to the House that the High-Church bishops
were not Catholics but "Arminians" who "agree noe more
with papists then with protestants." This was true, but the
real issues were political, and politicians did not care what
an "Arminian" really was as long as they could use the term
to identify Laud with Rome and so arouse the people against
him. Falkland forgot the excitement of his colleagues and
went to work like an intellectual critic, trying to straighten
out confusions in their thought. The Scottish campaign had
been called "The Bishops' War," and the phrase had become
a battle cry against episcopacy. To combat it there were
needed some equally resounding words to be repeated in the
bishops' defense. What Falkland offered instead was a pre-
cise explanation that only one bishop had spoken of the
"bellum episcopale" and that to accuse all of them of the
same attitude was absurd. It was, but not as absurd as to

suppose that such comments would interest many members of the Commons. To lecture about theological distinctions and the origin of a phrase was, under the circumstances, so ridiculous as to approach the sublime.

Nor, to judge from the brief notes that survive, did Falkland's speech on the Remonstrance go explicitly into what could be urged against its immediate usefulness. Sir John Colepeper, who spoke later, was wiser, and hammered on the political aspects which were those most likely to influence votes. He argued that the people would be offended by the plan to change the government of the church, and went on to say that a declaration from the Commons alone, without the consent of the Lords, would go "but on on[e] legg." The House was bound, he felt, to address itself only to the Lords and the King. This was pointed up practically by the assertion that the Remonstrance would make for discord in the nation and be "daingerous for the publique peace." He and Falkland agreed as to the need of defeating the Remonstrance, but he talked like a politician and Falkland like an academic.

They were beaten, and about midnight the House passed the Remonstrance. The margin was only eleven votes. The Commons was clearly split into two parties of almost equal strength. How radical the division was came out even more plainly after the vote on the Remonstrance itself. It was at once proposed that it be printed. This would make it an obvious "complaint" to the nation against the King and a document of party politics instead of a state paper designed for the guidance of the government. Those who had voted against its passage, Falkland and his group, now fought the motion to print it. Geoffrey Palmer, "a man of great reputation, and much esteemed in the house," demanded that, if the Remonstrance were printed, he "and all the rest" might protest. The minority rallied round him, and in a few minutes the House was in an uproar. Palmer's friends shouted, "All! All!"

and the word maddened those who had worked for the Remonstrance in order to enhance their prestige with the people. According to Warwick, only Hampden's coolness prevented bloodshed. He shifted the debate from the right of the minority to protest, to the question of whether Palmer could speak for "all." These tactics mercifully sidetracked the main issue long enough for angry men to recover control of themselves and put up their swords.

As Falkland and Hyde walked home through the dark streets, there was much to discuss. Hyde, no doubt, was ready with diagnoses and counsel. Falkland listened—he had never cared to advise his friend. For Hyde it was obvious that hereafter the House would vote in two groups—the extremists on one side, and the supporters of constitutional monarchy on the other. The thing to do was to choose a party and to fight for it. That was a bitter pill for Falkland. He had built up his reverence for Parliament on the theory that it proceeded by calm discussion of the evidence, and rose above mere partisanship, acting not as allegiance to one of two political creeds required but always in accordance with the conclusions of free and intelligent debate. As a moderate, siding now with Charles and now with Pym, he had voted as his conscience decreed. If Hyde were right he might be forced henceforth either to condemn himself to futility or to support the tenets of one party through thick and thin, even when his sceptical turn of mind and his rational standards made such support seem like betrayal of himself.

On the religious issue he was already in agreement with the "royalists" in the Commons. He had expressed his belief that the church as it stood might be easily reformed, and that then it could serve to advance learning and to provide a foundation for the ideally tolerant communion he hoped for. He distrusted the extreme Protestant sects because of their dogmatism, and he disliked their attempt to tear down Anglicanism with no apparent agreement as to what was to replace it. He had heard Colepeper challenge the enemies of the church to define the new ecclesiastical system they favored, and he had heard D'Ewes's reply: "It hath been objected that before we alter the old government of the Church we should establish a new one. For that it may be answered that before a new house be builded where an old one stood, the old one must first be removed." That was nonsense. The "new house" might at least be planned before the old was torn down, and, unless it was, no sensible man could be sure that any change was worth while. To Falkland men like D'Ewes seemed to advocate a leap in the dark, the result of which no one could predict, and in the face of their folly he turned to the defenders of the *status quo*. Others shared his feeling, and one of the great causes for the formation of a "royalist" party in the House was the attack made on the Church of England by Pym and his followers. The religious question might not be the most serious, but it appealed most directly to men's sentiments, and involved Falkland's dearest principles.

Very soon after his speech on the Bishops' Bill, in the spring of 1641, he had had proof that the plan to do away with episcopal government, "root and branch," was by no means dead. A new bill was brought in, "the object of which was the absolute extinction of Episcopacy." Falkland opposed it. His speech was more direct and more effective than the one he had given on February 8. Then he had seemed to blow hot and cold, condemning bad bishops but defending good ones. Now the question was clear cut. Were all bishops, good or bad, to go, leaving the church to someone else? In his attack on this programme, Falkland reiterated his distrust of too radical innovation. "Whosoever desires this totall change of our present Government, desires it either out of a conceit that [it] is *unlawfull*, or *inconvenient*." The episcopal system, he was sure, could not be proved unlawful. As to its being inconvenient, he insisted that anything in it which worked badly could be amended "without destroying the whole." Parliament had already clipped the "Nails" and "Tongues" of the evil bishops, and had only to set up proper regulations in order to insure that episcopal power would not again be abused. But, even if the existing church government were "inconvenient," there were worse inconveniences to be feared in drastic change. A man voting for the "destruction" of Anglicanism must "be sure that he destroys not that, which he likes better than that which shall succeed it." To vote for "blind uncertainty" was to vote foolishly, opening the way to "all the inconveniences, which any Government hath" and also to those "which any Government may have." Once the church was destroyed, it could not be restored, he insisted, without "a miracle in State, like that of the resurrection to Nature." It was all summed up in "the inconvenience of change itself, which," said Falkland, "is so great an inconvenience, when the Change is great and suddain, that in such cases, when it is not necessary to change, it is necessary not to change." The loyalties that underlay his attitude came out in his: "We have lived long happily, and gloriously, under this Form of Government; Episcopacy hath very well agreed with the constitution of our Laws, with the disposition of our People: how any other will do, I the lesse know, because I know not of any other, of which so much as any other Monarchy hath had any experience."

Falkland did not believe that the people wanted to destroy the church, and shrewdly pointed out that those who were content were unlikely to make as much noise as those who were not. That was true, and was one of the weaknesses of the conservatives in Parliament. The malcontents, their heads buzzing with a sense of their wrongs, were tireless in their attendance at debates. The more complacent advocates of things as they were, were tempted away from town by their horses and hounds. The long sessions of the Commons were tiresome, and they deserted them, lured away by friends

who, whatever the plight of the nation, still found no difficulty in buying good food and wine for elaborate dinner tables
in great houses. Falkland remarked that those "who hated
bishops hated them worse than the devil, and that they who
loved them did not love them so well as their dinner."

If his hostility to change can be disparaged as the weakness of timidity, or the fruit of coldly unimaginative intellectualism, there is none the less much in his speech defending episcopacy which reasserts principles both liberal and
positive. To ruin the bishops would in many cases, he felt,
be to ruin the most learned. There was a duty to support
men who could further scholarship. Bishops were not tied
down to the duties of a parish; they could keep alive knowledge of "Arts and Languages," and make themselves expert
in controversy. If there were no bishops, who would have
the "great leasure and great means" these things required?
If there was no one, most books would "remain rather as of
ornament, then as of use." Protestantism would then be helpless before its foes. Could even good preaching be hoped for,
if preaching were "separated from generall Learning?"

No less positive was his interest in tolerance. Against the
bishops were ranged its chief enemies. He saw and commented
on their violence (prudently exempting his fellow members
of Parliament, who, he said, were "to be hoped to be freer
then ordinary, from vulgar passions") and he hinted that their
dogmas, pressed too far, would drive out of the church "not
our worst" but "our most learned Ministers," and would
"send a greater Colonie to New England, then it hath been
said this Bill will recall from thence." He wound up with
a frontal attack, twitting his opponents with their eagerness
to destroy and their reluctance to say how they expected to
rebuild. "To this," he declared, "I can speak but by guesse,
and groping, because I have no light given me . . . I hope I
shall be excused for shooting at random, since you will set
me up no Butt to shoot at." He drove this general comment

home with a specific denunciation of Scottish Presbyterianism for which, he must have learned by now, many of his colleagues longed. He held that the Presbyterians were as intolerant as any bishop, and as guilty of absurd pretensions to divine right. They want, Falkland said, "to meet when they please, to treat of what they please, to excommunicate whom they please, even Parliaments themselves; so far are they from receiving either rules or punishments from them." They sought "unlimited . . . Independent authority," which would be dangerous to "the Liberty of the Subject and the Priviledge of Parliament." The argument that the Presbyterians claimed authority only in spiritual matters, Falkland brushed aside, saying: "Arbitrary Government being the worst of Governments, and our Bodies being worse than our Souls, it will be strange to set up that over the second, of which we were so impatient over the first . . . If you make the Lyon judge (and the Clergy, assisted by the people, is Lyon enough) it was a wise fear of the Foxe's, lest he might call a knubb a horn. And sure . . . they will in this case be Judges, not onely of that which is Spiritual, but of what it is that is so: and the people, receiving instruction from no other, will take the most Temporal matter to be Spiritual, if they tell them it is so." This was plain speaking, almost as plain in its mild contempt for the people as in its dislike for Presbyterian intolerance.

In spite of Falkland's opposition the bill was read twice. The second time the margin in its favor was thirty-one, out of two hundred and forty-seven votes. It was then sent to a committee, of which Hyde, probably because it was hoped that he could thus be partially silenced, was chosen chairman. He managed to delay progress throughout the summer, making sure that the King knew of his work. Parliament adjourned from September 9 to October 20, and when it reassembled no attempt was made to revive the bill. Instead, on October 21, another was introduced, excluding the bishops

from Parliament. It passed the Commons in two days. Falkland in March had voted for a measure substantially the
same; now he was in opposition. Hyde, no doubt, was pleased,
the more so since those who had rejoiced at his difference
with his friend months before, now had to admit that they
had laughed too soon. Hampden directly taxed Falkland with
his change of front. Falkland's retort was that Hampden had
"persuaded" him "to believe many things which he had since
found to be untrue, and therefore he had changed his opinion in many particulars, as well to things as to persons."
Hampden's saying, in the spring, that if the bill against the
bishops' voting in the Lords were passed, there would be no
further assaults on the church, had seemed to Falkland a
good reason for voting for it, but that bill had been thrown
out by the Lords so that Hampden's conditions were not met,
and, as Falkland knew all too well, Anglicanism had since
been repeatedly attacked.

On the religious question, then, Falkland was in the autumn
of 1641 in direct opposition to the most powerful leaders
in the House, and to that extent already aligned with the
King's party. But to champion episcopacy was not to go all
the way with the more ardent royalists. There were other
problems for the Commons to discuss, and probably on those
Falkland would have liked to vote without party ties, deciding
every question on its "merits." But the Remonstrance proved
that this would be difficult if not impossible. As Professor
Laski has said: "When a system is fighting for its life, it has
no time for the habits of a debating society. The passion of
conflict makes reason its slave. Those dominate the political scene who are prepared to use the means which will
accomplish the end. In such a period there is rarely the prospect of either tolerance or rationalism." [3] Such a condition
would be horrible to Falkland.

---

[3] H. J. Laski, *The Rise of Liberalism* (N. Y., 1931), p. 282.

He must have had a growing realization that neither with the King nor with the Commons was there much hope for a worshipper of reason. The events of the past few months were enough to outline the lesson. There had been a day in May when the sudden creaking of a board in the gallery had brought on a hysterical tempest in the House. A member shouted that he smelled gunpowder, and there was a stampede for the door. The excitement spread into the city, and the militia marched hastily as far as Covent Garden before the absurd scare was explained. A month later a debate in the Commons led to violence, and even when order was restored it lasted for only a few minutes. On the profound question of whether candles might be brought in to light the hall without a positive order of the House, the members lost their tempers, and the luckless Sergeant-at-Arms had his cloak ripped from his back. William Lenthall said afterwards that he had not expected to get out alive. In October Pym received in the House a letter, enclosing a rag filthy with the discharge of a plague sore, and a threat that if disease did not do its work he would be stabbed to death. Outside the House, and sometimes at its very doors, mobs tried what a show of mass violence might do to dictate political action, and some members of Parliament, at least, seemed to approve. In the King's palace, too, nerves were raw, and one terrifying night a crowd outside raised a panic within. Catholic courtiers hurried to their confessors; worldly men hid their jewels; and the most gallant marked on the palace stairs the best positions for defense. If the presence or absence of candles in the House was to be decided by force, if a snapping board frightened men out of their wits, Parliament was not in a rational frame of mind. The confidence in intellect which Falkland had felt in the quiet days at Great Tew must have begun to wither. The Scottish campaign had been enough to raise doubts; the sight of what could now happen in the House, at the palace, or in the streets packed with rioters, reinforced the sinister moral.

His defeat on the Grand Remonstrance did not, of course, end Falkland's career in Parliament. There were still issues to be voted upon, still ways of making his opinion count, still straws to clutch at in a desperate effort to save himself from complete disillusion. He still had influence, and possibly it might even now be useful. In spite of his bad voice, his speeches had been praised, and had won votes. Read today, their prose seems mannered, and their only stylistic merit seems to lie in a few pungent phrases. But his contemporaries admired the "wit" with which he wrote and spoke sentences which too often seem to us to sacrifice clarity to form, and expressiveness to rhetorical convention.[4] The extremists in the House, though they may have despised his conservatism, had to respect his talents, and knew that he might still be a force to reckon with. If he stuck to high thinking, aloof from politics, he would, as things were going, be ignored, but if he deserted theory far enough to work wholeheartedly with a party he might influence many votes.

Hyde was a practical man, believing that a strong party could be formed for King and church, and he did what he

---

[4] Falkland's writings were said to show "great Learning, Reasons and Judgement" and "an incomparable happy mixture of so much of that Great, Beautiful, Charming thing, call'd *Wit*; that the measures of *Decorum* would admit no more . . . And therefore *Sir P.* thought that the publication of that *Lords* writings would be serviceable to future Writers, as a standard for their measures to be govern'd by"; Sir P. Pett, ed., *The Genuine Remains of That Learned Prelate Dr. Thomas Barlow* (London, 1693), p. 325, wrongly numbered 335. Andrew Marvell cites Falkland's speeches as examples of good "History and Oratory"; *The Rehearsall Transpros'd: The Second Part* (London, 1673), pp. 387-388. D. Lloyd, *State-Worthies* (2d ed.; London, 1679), p. 940, says of Falkland: "Much was the gall always in his Ink, and very sharp his Pen; but even, flowing, and full his Style." Gilbert Burnet praised his "sharpness of style" and the "full weight of reason" in his "discourses"; Swift was ready to concur; J. Swift, *Prose Works* (ed. T. Scott; London, 1898–1908), X, 303.

could to enlist Falkland. For Lucius Cary to desert a friend
was foreign to his nature. Moreover, if Hyde was right in believing that England's only hope was the defense of constitutional monarchy against all attacks, even if this meant acting
now and then otherwise than by purely rational theories, how
could his friend resist him? Hyde knew Falkland well enough
to play his cards shrewdly. He played them even with the
King, and it was surely in large part because of him that
Charles I finally put the problem of choosing a party before
Falkland in terms that admitted of no compromise.

During the summer the King had come to look tenderly
on Edward Hyde. He had all too few friends, and many of
those he had were politically inexpert. Hyde was a trained
lawyer, and a skilful tactician in Parliament. He had had a
hand in much that the Commons had done against the King's
will, but his fundamental loyalty to monarchy and church
was beyond suspicion. He had talked with Charles early in
the summer, and had promised to combat the Root and
Branch Bill, proving himself later as good as his word. His
obstruction of the bill in committee justified "the king's
taking notice of him." On August 10, Charles went to Scotland, after protests from the House, in which Falkland joined,
but even during his absence his admiration for Hyde increased. Secretary Nicholas wrote him that when the Commons proposed that royal appointments "of all Officers,
Councellors, Amb'dors, and Ministers" should hereafter require Parliamentary approval, "the Lo: ffalkland" and "Mr
Ed. Hide . . . stood as Champions in maynten'nce of" the King's
"Prerogative." Hyde was proud when Nicholas showed him
a letter from Charles, praising him for his "great zeal." And
when the Remonstrance had been printed, he endeared himself further by preparing an answer to it. All this Falkland
knew, and he should have realized that since Hyde had the
King's ear, his own virtues were sure to be expounded to
Charles. Yet he was surprised when, late in December, the

King offered to him and to Sir John Colepeper, seats on the Privy Council. The invitation confronted Falkland with a more weighty problem than he had ever had to decide. His loyalty was to the institution of monarchy, rather than to the monarch himself, and he was not a great admirer of Charles I. Certainly the King was no disciple of reason, and on occasion he was a hypocrite. He "many times obstinately adhered to many conclusions, which did not naturally result from good premises, and did love to argue many things to which he would not so positively adhere." Falkland idolized truth and hated "all dissimulation." He saw no excuse for admiring the courtiers, and "had not the court in great reverence." He believed that the sovereign must make concessions to save the nation, and, although he thought that Charles "would in the end be prevailed with to yield to what was pressed," he was tormented by foreboding that the King "would fall into great misfortune." That fear, no doubt, arose from his suspicions of Charles's character, and under its spell he felt sure that if he chose the royal service he would ruin himself. And when he said "ruin" he must have thought as much of the sacrifice of his ideals as of the risk of having his worldly fortunes crumble with the King's.

He made up his mind to refuse the appointment to the Council, and then changed it again. If reason was, for the moment, an unsafe reliance, it was natural to fall back upon feelings, temperamental likes and dislikes. His impetuous love for action made him hate to pull out from the centre of conflict. His pride made him resent the idea that he might be suspected of cowardice, if he declined the King's offer. Some of his deepest instincts were touched by Charles's assertion that "all these tumults and disorders have only risen from the meaner sort of people, and . . . the Affections of the better . . . part . . . have ever been Loyal and Affectionate." How little Falkland understood the "meaner sort" he had made plain years ago in his "Elegie" on Morison, and he betrayed the same blindness more than once thereafter. Thus he "suffered himself . . . to be overruled by the advice and persuasions of his friends," chiefly, of course, Hyde. By New Year's Day, 1642, he was serving with the Council.

His decision has brought down denunciations from one group of historians, and from another extravagant praise for choosing at last the path of righteousness. Lloyd, writing soon after the Restoration in a warm glow of royalist feeling, says that Falkland, after being among "the Demagogues that had been for twelve years silenced, and were now to play the prize in Parliament, and shew their little twit-twat," and after carrying "things beyond the moderation and decency of that Assembly, which he made too hot for himself," gloriously repented, was swayed by "cooler thoughts," and turned to "countermining the main props of Westminster . . . laying open the little pretensions" of Parliament, "whereby poor people were insnared in their Civil and Religious Liberty." This serves as the type for many later judgments, but on the other side are such verdicts as Forster's. He maintains that Falkland "was far more of an apostate than Strafford, for his heart was really with the Parliament from the first . . . and never, to the very end, did" he "sincerely embrace" the King's cause. But his heart was with Parliament only so long as it seemed to him superior to petty motives. When his faith in its high-mindedness went, it no longer claimed his heart. But Mr. Forster was right, no doubt, in suggesting that when Falkland became a conservative champion of the church and King, he left his deepest aspirations unsatisfied.

Looked at without partisan bias, he seems in no real sense to have turned his coat in 1642. As Mr. Jones has written: "The Anglican constitutionalists stood where they had always stood; they merely faced about to resist innovation from below in the same spirit in which they had resisted it from above." Their doctrines may have been outmoded, and their respect for forms of law too great, but they were consistent and judged Parliament by the same criteria they had applied to the King. Their relation to the Commons changed not because their principles shifted, but because, in order to defend those principles in a new situation, they chose to run "the risk of despotism rather than abandon the Monarchy to complete domination by a Parliament." [5]

Falkland's weakness lay in his inability to find premises sufficiently broad to give a basis for rational support of any but the conservative position. The law, the constitution, the established order, he saw as fixed goods, and he rarely thought beyond them. Had he been able to admit that, given a changing world, there might be national needs not provided for by older laws, or changes in the governmental and social structure demanded by the existence of new problems, he might have reasoned his way to serving Parliament instead of the King. Gardiner said: "To be moderate in any real sense of the word, requires the highest powers of the imagination. He who would reconcile adverse parties must possess something more than a love of peace and a contempt of extreme doctrines. He must have a clear and sympathetic perception of that which is best and noblest on either side, and it was [in] the perception of anything good or noble in Puritanism that Falkland and his associates were entirely lacking." What he convinced himself of, by the intellectual standards he revered, was dictated by his premises. They, in turn, were prescribed for him, as for everyone who thinks, to some extent by his prejudices and emotions. His breeding in a loyal household, his position as a landowner, and his natural liking for the established order of society, related to his sceptical suspicion of change, supplied him with the axioms on which he tried to erect logical conclusions.

He was whole-hearted in his attempt. To say that he was

---

[5] I. D. Jones, *The English Revolution*, 1603–1714 (London, 1931), pp. 61-62.

"too large-minded to take a mere party mould" and "too clear-sighted to make a great party leader" is to pay tribute to his effort to act rationally according to his premises. If "he could not work out the results of a special political principle, and push it to its extreme consequences regardless of other principles," it was because of his insistence on what he construed as reason. His moderation, his religious tolerance, and his struggle to think clearly, showed qualities in him which generations after him professed to respect and sometimes acted on, but in the critical time in which he lived they had little chance of success.[6] Men might pay lip-service to his lofty theories, but forgot about them in the stress of politics. His cause was that of orderly thought and learning against passion and arrogant ignorance—a cause always likely to lose except when those concerned are so indifferent to the issues that feeling can be kept in bounds. But the issues of Falkland's day touched selfishnesses, fears, and hatreds, and were tied in with men's love for their purses and their bewildered restlessness in a period of shifting values, moral, intellectual and economic. They were so linked at every point with the deepest sources of emotion that only a man with a genius for statesmanship, in the fullest sense, could hope to solve them by cold logic. Falkland was not such a genius. His mental range was too circumscribed by the assumptions his training and experience had taught him to make, and the men with whom he had to deal felt too intensely to be as rational as he. He had to yield. In entering the King's service he ad-

---

[6] S. R. Gardiner, Great Civil War, I, 7. Cf., Id., p. 218: "[Falkland's] heart was large enough to embrace all that was noble on either side," and the same writer's History, VIII, 257-258: "The comprehensiveness of his heart was not supported by comprehensiveness of brain. The desire for reconciliation . . . did not lead up to the reconciling thought which would have satisfied the reasonable desires of both parties." According to E. Wingfield-Stratford, History of English Patriotism (London, 1913), I, 329, Falkland "had breadth without depth, he was without fire, without iron, without a star, in short, he was a hero of Matthew Arnold." Cf. Arnold's essay "Falkland" in Mixed Essays (N. Y., 1879), pp. 205-236.

mitted frankly that it was only by abandoning his hope of being consistently moderate and rational, free of partisan ties, that he could hope to make his ideas prevail. It was only by compromising with his principles and joining a party that he could hope to put any of them into effect.

He has been charged with seeing what was wrong but failing to propose a remedy. His fault was not quite that. His remedy, so far as the church went, was positive and clearly stated; in other matters his programme was like Bacon's: "It were good . . . that men in their innovations would follow the example of time itself; which . . . innovateth greatly, but quietly, and by degrees scarce to be perceived." He wanted to progress toward reforms in the state, but hoped to base every measure on thoughtful discussion, protected from the contamination of conscious prejudice. He offered remedies, but remedies that were not practicable in the midst of political turmoil. His creed was not negative but positive, but it made too few concessions to human weakness. He addressed himself to men who felt more than they thought, and preferred action to talk. They formed parties to express concretely their emotions and their faiths, and in loyalty to them lost interest in such sober counsels as Falkland urged.

In joining the Privy Council he did not, of course, abandon his doctrines. Even though official allegiance might hereafter limit his freedom somewhat, he could, as a servant of the King, still work for the preservation of the constitution and the church, and against war. Whatever was or was not the way out of the situation, he could see no excuse for bloodshed. Like his old friend, Chillingworth, he made an ideal of peace.[7] Right and wrong, truth and falsehood, justice and injustice, could not be determined by war, in which force, not reason, carried the day. If Charles would live up to his

---

[7] B. Whitelocke, *Memorials of the English Affairs* (Oxford, 1853), I, 215, calls Falkland "a passionate promoter of all endeavours of peace betwixt the king and parliament."

promise to do nothing without the advice of the new counsellors, Colepeper and Falkland, there was a chance that constitutional government, Anglicanism, and peace could be saved. But Falkland had serious doubts of the King, and pessimistic misgivings as to whether his advice would be heard. He entered the Council reluctantly, and within a few days found his worst fears justified.

Things had been going more and more badly. Mobs had tried to enforce what Pym called "their just desires" by open violence. The bishops no longer dared to take their seats in the Lords, but adversity did not teach some of them Christian meekness, and their defiant attitude made matters worse. As one of them said, "they had a Good Game of 30 playd into their hand, but would play againe, and they were out." Charles frightened and embittered his enemies by his frank reliance on armed retainers. Worse, he lost his head, and without consulting Falkland, Hyde, or Colepeper, tried a desperate venture. He called for the impeachment as traitors of five members of the Commons—Pym, Hampden, Holles, Hazlerigg, and Strode. To the list was added one from the upper house, Edward Montagu, Viscount Mandeville, brother of Walter Montagu and a connection of Falkland's; the others were men with whom he had often voted during the past year.

The Lords did not act at once on the impeachments, but Charles pressed on recklessly. He sent to the Commons on January 3 an order for the arrest of the five members. The House appointed a committee of four, including both Falkland and Colepeper, to tell the King that the affair was "of great Consequence," concerned "the Priviledge of Parliament," and would be taken into serious "Consideration." On the next day Falkland reported to the House that Charles had asked whether the Commons expected a reply and had been told that the only duty of the committee was to deliver the message. The King then asked Falkland and the rest what they thought "as private Persons." To this they said, "they conceived the House did expect an Answer."

The answer it got was worse than none. On the afternoon of the 4th, Charles drove from Whitehall toward Parliament, followed by several hundred armed men. A bystander guessed what he intended, and ran ahead to warn the Commons. The five members were hustled out and smuggled down the river by boat, to take refuge in the city. When Charles, a few minutes later, boldly entered the House, while his followers crowded the lobby, he saw at once that his coup had failed. "All the birds" were "flown," and he had to withdraw with the best grace he could, after protesting that he had meant to act "in a legal and fair way." Cries of "Privilege, privilege!" echoed from the House, and there were surly mutterings from the King's men, who would have liked to let bullets prove to Parliament that the sovereign was supreme. Sir Simonds D'Ewes hurried home to make his will, and he was but one of many who saw dire peril ahead.

Parliament held the whip hand. Within a week the accused members were again in their seats, and Charles had deserted Whitehall. He spent the night of the 10th with his wife and children uncomfortably at Hampton Court. On the next day he began openly to prepare his defenses. He made the Earl of Newcastle governor of Hull, where there was an important stock of munitions, and sent off a messenger to prepare the town for the Earl's arrival. But Pym had good spies, and even before the royal emissary left town, another from Parliament was well on the road to Hull, with orders to Sir John Hotham to hold the city and to turn over his authority to no one until he had instructions from the Lords and Commons. At Kingston royalists gathered, obviously threatening the county's ammunition stored in the town. Parliament retaliated by calling on the nation to protect itself against armed aggression, summoning the militia to its service, and asking that it be commanded hereafter by Lord

Lieutenants selected not by Charles but by the Houses.

The King wavered between making concessions and attempts to reassert his authority. By the middle of February he had agreed to the exclusion of the bishops from the Lords, had promised to drop the prosecution of the members of the Houses, and had yielded on other points. But on the 23rd it was known that he had sent the Queen and her daughter abroad and that they were safely at sea, taking with them the crown jewels. Five days later he agreed to put the militia under officers nominated by Parliament, but insisted that their commands might be terminated at his pleasure. To the request that he stay near Westminster, he retorted that it was no longer "safe and honourable" for him to do so, and on March 3 he started for York.

Falkland's initiation into the King's service was a drastic corrective for any illusions he may have had as to Charles's wisdom or his willingness to take his advice. The attempt to arrest the members proved how foolish he could be. He had promised to consult Falkland and Colepeper at every point, but they were told nothing of the plans for the impeachment. Neither was Hyde. But Lord George Digby, now a favorite of the Queen, had been consulted, and it was with his counsel that Charles acted. Digby, no pattern of wisdom, was far less astute than Falkland or Hyde, far less honest, and far more self-seeking. So long as he had the King's ear, moderate counsellors had to work against odds. Falkland distrusted him, and dared not speak as candidly to him as to Colepeper or Hyde. Digby was largely governed by "ambition and vanity." Though he was talented and brilliant, "a graceful and beautiful person" and an eloquent speaker in spite of his affected manner, Hyde thought him the "unfittest man alive to conduct" great affairs. Falkland's fierce love of honesty was enough to alienate him from Digby, who had proved his indifference to truth. He had agreed to move in the Lords the commitment of Mandeville, but in-

stead "never spake the least word" and pretended surprise
when the plan for impeachment was revealed. He even whispered in Mandeville's ear "that the King was very mischiev-
ously advised, and that it should go very hard but he would
know whence that counsel proceeded." Dissimulation could
no farther go, since the advice had come from Digby himself.

On the surface, however, he was friendly enough to Falkland, Colepeper, and Hyde, whom he had urged Charles
to advance. Often he was guided by them, but he was fatally
prone to think "difficult things very easy," and did "not consider possible consequences" when a scheme tickled his
"fancy" or catered to his lust for personal glory. This, coupled
with his evasive insincerity, enabled him to consult with the
others and seem to agree with them, only to rush off independently and without warning in pursuit of some alternative
plan of his own, more satisfying to his ambition. The King
was unfit "to be served by such a counsellor, being too easily
inclined to sudden enterprises, and as easily amazed when
they were entered upon." Charles's plot against his enemies
in Parliament proved how dangerous Digby's influence could
be, and was the worst of auguries for Falkland's success in
his new relation to his sovereign.

The affair of the "Five Members" was a "discouragement"
which "made a deep impression on" Cary. It proved how
unreliable Charles was; it weakened the King's position with
the people; and it was the sort of thing which, if repeated,
must destroy any influence Falkland still had in the Commons. He knew that in December rioters at the House of
Lords had climbed up on tables to denounce him and his
friends as "persons disaffected to the kingdom." He knew that
many of those who still thought well of him were distressed
by his joining the Council, and blamed Hyde for it. He knew
that any rashness of the King might be laid at his door, even
if his advice had never been asked.

Perhaps the best thing he could have done would have been

to give up his office, now that the King had not kept his word. No doubt he did think of this. Hyde says that all that kept Falkland loyal was "abstracted consideration of . . . duty and conscience, and of the present ill condition the King was in." Charles seemed remorseful, and Falkland may have imagined that he had had a change of heart. But probably what did most to keep him with the King was his feeling that even if the sovereign broke promises and acted foolishly, there was nothing better to be hoped for among his foes. Even a misguided monarch might be preferred to a frenzied mob, and an errant sovereign to an errant Parliament, now clearly representative of only a small minority of the nation. Whatever the reason, Falkland in spite of the slight put upon him in the first days of his service not only went on with Charles but tied himself up to the King more closely still by accepting office as Secretary of State.

It took all Hyde's persuasions to bring him to this, and the nature of those persuasions indicated his state of mind. He still preserved some respect for Parliament, and still had no "veneration for the Court, but only such a loyalty to the person of the King as the law required from him." He protested that he was "totally unacquainted with business, and the forms of it" so that he was unfit for a secretaryship. His pride winced at the idea that he would be accused of having defended the bishops in order to win high office. He was afraid lest Charles "expect such a submission and resignation of himself and his own reason and judgment to his commands, as he should never give or pretend to give." His conscience rebelled, since "he was so severe an adorer of truth that he could as easily have given himself leave to steal as to dissemble, or to suffer any man to think that he would do anything which he resolved not to do; which he thought a more mischievous kind of lying than a positive averring what could be most easily contradicted." Hyde had trouble in disarming such scruples. He promised that he would help in the technical side of the secretaryship, and then fell back on two appeals to his friend. One was that a refusal of duty under Charles would be construed as dislike of the royal cause and so an advantage to its enemies. The other was positive, to the effect that Falkland could be of great use in keeping the King well posted as to the state of the kingdom and in supplying him with good advice to offset the bad he was sure to get. Hyde also insisted that by being close to the throne, Falkland could do better work for Charles in Parliament where even yet "he was too well known to have it believed that he attained to" the secretaryship "by any unworthy means or application."

There was a further argument, probably more potent still. Falkland was no coward and throughout his life the daring that led to the challenge to Willoughby asserted itself whenever there was any chance to display it. Nor could he endure being thought less than brave. His pride was touched by the suggestion that if he did not become Secretary, his critics would say he was afraid of the House of Commons. That would be unbearable, "for as he had a full appetite of fame by just and generous actions, so he had an equal contempt of it by any servile expedients." Once again, since reason offered no clear verdict, he fell back naturally on feeling, and was swayed by his hatred of ever giving even the appearance of timidity.

Thus "he submitted to the King's command, and became" on January 8 "his Secretary, with as humble and devout an acknowledgment of the greatness of the obligation as could be expressed, and as true a sense of it in his heart." Probably, however, his sense of duty did not quite stifle his doubts, and certainly he was rigid in his resolve not to compromise with his conscience. He knew that if he were to do all that an efficient Secretary of State might, he would have to stoop to tactics he loathed. "He must either do that which would be a great disquiet to his own nature, or leave that undone which was most necessary to be done." He knew "that the most just and honest men did every day that which he could not give himself leave to do." As an "exact and strict . . . observer of justice and truth" he could never condescend to "applications to the weakness of other men, and those arts and insinuations which are necessary for discoveries and prevention of ill." He might sacrifice enough of his standards to take sides when only by taking sides could anything be done, but he would not retreat an inch from his strict code of honesty. Practical men reproached him for his scruples, but he refused to use spies, except those who later worked in actual warfare, and he would never open letters addressed to others even when they were believed to contain matter dangerous to the state. He insisted that spies must be so dishonest as to be unworthy of any trust, and that prying into others' letters was "such a violation of the law of nature that no qualification by office could justify a single person in the trespass." Sometimes "the necessity and iniquity of the time" made it necessary to do the things he hated, but he declined to have any hand in them, leaving base methods to others, "so unwilling he was to resign any thing in his nature to an obligation in his office."

Admirable as his principles were, his clinging to them in a time of strife was pathetically academic, and must have handicapped his usefulness as Secretary of State. If Charles was attracted by Falkland's honesty, he had to pay a stiff price for it, since it was risky to have his officers more scrupulous than his enemies, who cheerfully used spies and peeked into letters. But in other respects Falkland was fully qualified for his new post. He was "sufficiently versed in languages to understand any that is used in business and to make himself again understood," and he was without question incorruptible.

How lofty his standards were, and how deeply rooted his doubts, appears in his behavior toward the King. Others flattered him and veiled their criticisms with fair words, but the new secretary was plain-spoken to the point of rudeness. Earlier, when the members of the Commons had been asked to express their thanks to one of their number whose work Falkland disapproved, he had not only refused to take off his hat as the others did, but had clamped it down on his head, with his hands pressed tightly over the crown. Similarly, since he did not trust Charles, he treated him brusquely. He hated servility, and even before he joined the Council, his answers to the King's questions had been "more negligent . . . than might be expected; as if he cared only that his actions should be just, not that they should be acceptable, and that his majesty should think that they proceeded only from the impulsion of conscience, without any sympathy in his affections." "From a person of so perfect a habit of generous and obsequious compliance with all good men" this might well have been taken by Charles "as more than an ordinary averseness to his service." And when Falkland did accept office, he did so with such apparent bad grace that the King could hardly form "any notable expectation of his departing from the severity of his own nature." He was not deferential before his royal master, and "contradicted him with . . . bluntness, and by sharp sentences," so that "his majesty often complained; and cared less to confer with" Falkland "in private, and was less persuaded by him, than his . . . great parts and wisdom, would have required." He could not wholly respect Charles nor could he completely justify the royal cause. Lacking entire confidence, he could not throw himself into his task whole-heartedly enough to come as close to the King as a truly valuable adviser should, nor make full use of the only means by which he could be thoroughly effective. He had chosen a party and a career within it, but he still set other values higher than its success.

He was most helpful in his influence on Hyde and Colepeper. Before the King left London he asked these two and

Falkland "to meet constantly together, and consult upon his affairs, and conduct them the best way they could in the parliament, and to give him constant advice what he was to do, without which, he declared again very solemnly, he would make no step in the parliament." Night after night they met at Hyde's house in Westminster, and without Falkland they would have fared badly. Hyde was his close friend, as honest in his way as he, but with a readier sense for political necessities. Colepeper was harder to deal with. Trained as a soldier, he had "a rough nature, a hot head, and . . . great courage" proved "in many quarrels and duels." He was "proud and ambitious, and very much disposed to improve his fortune . . . by industry and thrift, without stooping to any corrupt ways." He was no scholar, nor was he a polished courtier. He had "never sacrificed to the muses, or conversed in any polite company." As a simple country gentleman he had no use for the fanaticism that quickened the leaders of Parliament, and "did not love the persons of those who were the violent managers." His god was common sense, which inclined him to conservative respect for the *status quo*, and, when the decision seemed to be between rebellion and loyalty, he chose loyalty. He joined the Council when Falkland did, and when the latter was made Secretary, he became Chancellor of the Exchequer. In office he revealed dangerous weaknesses. He was quick to see what was wrong, but he was rarely able to plan wisely. He was unfortunately given to a "very tragical way in expressing himself," and colored what he said to suit his hearers. He increased the Queen's alarm by his lurid pictures of dangers ahead, and with the King, "who was naturally very sanguine," he was apt to play the optimist. His fellow counsellors had always to reckon with his dogmatic confidence in his own schemes, the more so since he, rather than they, had Charles's ear. Falkland's ungraciousness did not endear him to the King; Hyde had no office at court, and was distrusted by Parliament, so that he talked to Charles "only in

the dark ... upon emergent occasions." Colepeper was thus
usually the spokesman of the triumvirate, and it was essential
that his colleagues keep on friendly terms with him. He "was
warm and positive in debates," and had a hot temper. So had
Hyde. Falkland had to moderate their discussions. Fortunately
both had "always much deference" to him, so that he could
allay the "passions, to which they were ... inclined." Without
his evenness of disposition and cool concentration on the
rational, there might have been disastrous disagreements
among the three.

Had Charles observed better his vow always to listen to
them, and had Parliament been in a mood to heed their
advice, they might have done much. But the Queen had views
of her own, and so had Digby, and both now and then proved
less wise than Hyde and Falkland but more powerful with
the King. His enemies in the Commons knew of the meetings at Hyde's house and, scenting plots against Parliament,
did their best to discredit the three advisers. The House
listened to letters, purporting to be from a Catholic, which
said, "Falkland and Culpeper are friends to our side, at least-
wise they will do us no hurt." The documents were forged,
but served to stir up against Hyde's friends the bitter anti-
Catholic feeling of the King's opponents. After Digby fled
to the continent he was, on February 22, accused of treason;
and Falkland, going every morning to visit Hyde, and seen
every evening by Pym's agents, must have known that he
might soon have to face the same charge.

He was not to be intimidated in his search for some peaceful solution of the nation's problems. When the bill excluding the bishops from the House of Lords was passed, he
seems to have urged the King to sign it, joining with Colepeper against Hyde. In the spring of 1641 he had voted for a
similar measure, and in the autumn against. He wavered because it seemed to him comparatively unimportant whether
the bishops voted in Parliament or not. He hoped in 1642

that if Charles conceded this point he might conciliate some of his foes, and stave off more radical attacks on the church. Hyde was against giving in.[8] His reverence for the established legal order, as he understood it, was one argument; another was his shrewd perception that by approving the bill against the bishops the King would seem to endorse the act of a minority which had terrorized its enemies and flouted the proper usages of government. Whether or not Falkland's attitude was as wise as Hyde's—probably it was not—his readiness to compromise was characteristic of his policy throughout the first stormy months of 1642. Peace was the great end —peace and relief from an atmosphere of threats and violence which blocked thoughtful statesmanship.

Usually, however, Falkland and Hyde saw eye to eye, as they did in opposing the King's departure for the north, and worked together to keep Charles in the light of a consistent defender of constitutional principle, yielding all he could in the interests of harmony, and resisting only when the law was clearly on his side. They were beaten by the King's indecision, by the rash importunities of his wife and Digby, and by the intolerance of a Parliament zealous for complete reconstruction of the state. For months the battle was waged with words. Charles issued pleas, often written by Falkland or Hyde. The Parliament countered with other statements, and went on doing what it pleased. Royal supporters found it daily more dangerous to enter the Houses, and when the King went to York many of them deserted Westminster to follow him or to seek safety in the country. Both parties were busily arming, all the time loudly asserting their desire for peace. Charles, under Hyde's guidance, excused his preparations as necessary to protect his rights against arbitrary government by a minority calling itself a Parliament.

---

[8] Clarendon, *History*, I, 565-570, strongly suggests that Hyde was the only one of the three trusted counsellors to argue against the Bishops' Exclusion Bill.

There is no doubt that the traditional position of the sovereign was threatened. The Nineteen Propositions, "ordered to be delivered to the king on" June 1, 1642, were later called "the principal foundation" of the Civil War, and sum up what the active remainder of the Lords and Commons wanted. Privy counsellors, all important state officers, and commanders of fortresses, were to be appointed subject to parliamentary approval; the education and marriages of the royal children were to be regulated by the Houses; the laws against Catholics were to be enforced, and Catholic nobles were to be excluded from the upper House; the national church was to be made over as Parliament decreed; control of the militia was to be left to the Houses; they must judge all delinquents; and if new peers were created they could not vote in the Lords unless the whole Parliament agreed.

Of course Charles rejected the Propositions, and his appeal for the traditional order, and, especially, the church, won him friends. With him sided those who feared that "the lower classes" were learning their strength and hoped to

> "Teach the nobles how to crouch,
> And keepe the gentry downe."

Others, less alarmed by possible social changes, were governed by love of the church. "A majority of the peers and greater landlords" stood out for Charles, if for no other reason than because what they regarded as their proper privileges seemed more likely to be saved under him than under Parliament. Against them, and him, were ranged middle-class "upstart merchants and shopkeepers," many of them puritanically inclined, and "men with any kind of grievance—political, social, or economic." [9] Among these were some capitalists and men of property and rank. Religion, business, and class consciousness, were stronger incentives than reason or legal

---

[9] G. Davies, *op. cit.*, pp. 123, 124-126.

doctrine. Even Falkland, for all his intellectual scrupulousness, must have had instinctive prejudices which allied him with the King. Those prejudices, no doubt, he expertly rationalized. Were not politely educated men a better hope for England than an ignorant rabble? If so, should not the "upper" classes be maintained against the "lower"? Would not an upset of the social order open the gates to the uninstructed enemies of truth?

However he felt, there was little that Falkland could do. That the King's plight was desperate should have been clear when in April he appeared before Hull and was refused admission to the town. This cut him off from munitions he knew he might soon need, and it gave him the measure of his authority with some of his more defiant subjects. Whatever forms of speech Parliament used, it was plain that he faced open rebellion. His friends in London learned the same lesson in other ways. They were able to accomplish little and faced constant threats. In March Falkland wrote to Hyde, who was resting in the country, in terms that showed how deeply they were both suspected and how definite were the plans to ruin them. Soon afterward they got wind of a proposal to accuse them, with Colepeper, of treason. They knew that if they were ever all three in the Commons at the same time, they would run the risk of arrest. They could not all stay away without abandoning their duty, and so they arranged that for weeks one of them was always in his seat but all three never were. Obviously they lived in a state of exhausting strain, and any illusions Falkland may still have had about the power of reason in politics must have been sadly dimmed. Tired out by endless talks with his friends late at night, disgusted by the mobs, revolted by the plain signs that hot heads ruled Parliament, disturbed by constant fear of being jailed, and too busy to think far beyond the exigencies of the moment, he may now and then have crept wearily back to his wife and children for a few days of quiet at Aldenham or

Great Tew. But even there was no real peace—at the most there could be simply brief forgetfulness.

In April the King decided that he needed Hyde, and sent for him to join him at York. Hyde waited till the Lord Keeper, Littleton, had sent the Great Seal of the kingdom to Charles and had agreed to follow himself. Then he undertook to make his way to the north. In order to escape Parliament's vigilance, he pled ill health, and went to Ditchley, in Oxfordshire, where he stayed at the house of Lady Lee, a connection by marriage of Sir Henry Lee, who had been the favorite great-uncle of Falkland's mother. George Morley, Falkland's friend in the days at Great Tew, on the morning when it was known that Littleton had gone to the King, picked up the news that Hyde was to be promptly accused of treason. He went straight to Falkland, who sent off a letter to Ditchley, urging Hyde to hurry to York. That was difficult, since the main roads were sure to be watched, and the others were hard to trace. But another old friend, William Chillingworth, volunteered as a guide. For all his rationalism and his moderation, he, like Falkland, had been moved by the danger of intolerant Puritanism, and had come out frankly as a royalist. His brother had a farm near Coventry, and to it he and Hyde sent horses. On the next day Lady Lee had them driven there in her coach. Thence by back roads and "unusual ways" they rode the long journey to Yorkshire.

Parliament wanted to arrest the loyal gentlemen who joined Charles, but he forbade them to heed its summons. As soon as it was known that he was eager to protect the faithful, "persons of all conditions and from all places flocked to York, and many members of both houses of Parliament . . . repaired to his majesty." Thus Hyde, when he appeared at last with the King, found himself among friends. To be sure he received a summons to come back to the Commons, but he answered it with an empty evasion, saying that he would return whenever Charles gave leave.

Falkland and Colepeper, left alone in London, hung on there as long as they could. They drew up a reply to the Nineteen Propositions, and sent it to Hyde at York to be published. Then they yielded at last to the hopelessness of the situation in Parliament, and made their way to the King. The past months had been bitter for Falkland, and his nerves were on edge, so that, almost as soon as he got to York, he lost his temper with Hyde. That prudent soul had not printed the answer to the Propositions, because "there were some expressions in it . . . prejudicial to the king," and because Colepeper, in what he wrote, seemed to deny the bishops the place which Hyde thought the constitution gave them. Falkland flared up angrily, and declared that Hyde objected to the answer because he had not written it himself—a thoroughly ungenerous accusation. His friend, of course, heaped coals of fire on his head, and at once sent the document to the press. Falkland recovered his self-control, the quarrel blew over, and its only significance is as a sign of Falkland's nervous instability after his disillusioning months in London. Hard work, often going for naught; the spectacle of political selfishness and violence; and the ever growing realization that no intellectual standards were likely to be of much use, had worn him down. For his sensitive nature almost worse were the breaking of friendships and the pitting of one Englishman against another, which were the inevitable prelude to revolution.

They were dramatized for him in a single episode. When Charles left London he ordered the Earls of Essex and Holland to accompany him. Parliament forbade them to go. They chose to stay rather than to risk losing the confidence of the Houses, and, no doubt, because they understood that there was nothing to be gained by giving an excuse for further parliamentary complaints against the King. But Charles was in one of his more reckless moods, and the Queen, whose favorite Holland once had been, now hated him and was

infuriated by his insubordination. Her persuasions and
Charles's ruffled dignity led him to demand that Littleton,
as Lord Keeper, get Essex and Holland to give up their offices
at court. Littleton refused, fearing Parliament's vengeance
if he obeyed. Thereupon the King wrote Falkland, ordering
him to notify the Earls of their dismissal. Falkland thought
Charles's insistence was unwise, and both Essex and Holland
were his friends. With them he had served in the Scottish
war, and even though Holland's part in that futile campaign
had been inglorious, Essex, at least, had done all he could
with perfect loyalty. It was hard to be asked to serve the King
by injuring two friends, particularly since it was a task that
any underling might have done. It was the harder since to
carry out the order would surely alienate Falkland further
from Parliament. But, when he took the secretaryship, he
must have decided grimly that he must obey whenever he
honestly could, and probably his knowledge that to do so
in this case would be dangerous for him personally was an
argument for not hanging back. So he went to Essex and
Holland, waited while they debated what to do, and then
received their insignia of office. They said little, but Falkland
was too shrewd not to see that, officially at least, the Earls
were now his enemies, and that the King had lost the allegiance of two men who, in their different ways, might have
served him well. He was right. Within a few months Essex
was commander-in-chief of the parliamentary forces, and the
King had declared him a traitor. Friendship and old loyalties
were breaking before the first warning gusts of civil war.
What civil war meant had been brought tragically home to
Falkland by the news that his brother, Lorenzo, with whom
he had liked to debate theology at his mother's house, had
died fighting against insurgents in Ireland.

In the face of forebodings, and in spite of the King's occasional bursts of headstrong wilfulness, Falkland, Hyde and
Colepeper held their ground, and did all that they could to

counteract Charles's own folly and the Queen's pleas for drastic action against the "rebels." Now and then they were successful, as they were when they managed to keep Charles from treating Littleton as he had treated Essex and Holland, but too often their advice counted for little. However disappointed they were they gave every sign of complete loyalty. They joined in signing protestations of devotion to Charles, larded with assurances as to his longing for peace, and both Falkland and Colepeper promised to supply horses for his army. This was consistent enough with their principles, since they believed that the King must arm against Parliament in order to guard himself and his authority against attack, and had convinced themselves that he did so with no intention to provoke war. Yet war was in the air. For Falkland the prospect was a nightmare.

The best refuge was work. In writing letters, messages, and statements for the King he could momentarily forget how trivial words are in troubled times. While they were being written, at least, protestations of Charles's yearning for peace, his nobility of principle, and his reliance on his legal rights, carried conviction enough to keep doubts at bay. To be sure, all Falkland's labor—and he must have come painfully to recognize it—could only postpone hostilities, but it was some comfort to try every means of settlement before admitting that England's fate depended on pikes and solid shot. It might be useless for him to write graceful answers to loyal subjects who addressed the King, but in "this carnival of half-truths" [10] it was satisfying to express his mind, as he did when he dilated on the earnest wish of the royal party "that all hostility may cease, cease for ever, and a blessed and happy accommodation and peace be made; that God's honour and the Protestant religion may be maintained; that the just privileges of Parliament, and the laws of the land, may be

---

[10] J. Buchan, op. cit., p. 118.

upheld and put in execution." Less lofty in tone, but equally valid as a statement of Falkland's feeling was his assertion that "the very Protestant religion itself" suffered "scorn and contempt . . . by Brownists, Anabaptists, and sectaries, who in truth have destroyed the civil peace too." This might be admitted if Falkland's definition of "Protestant religion" was, but it was no answer to the "sectaries" who saw even in moderate Anglicanism a betrayal of all that the words should mean. Similarly Falkland declared that "the known laws of the land" were "the only excellent rule," and the only defense against "extravagant arbitrary power," though this might be brushed aside by those who disagreed as to the nature of the "known laws," or wanted to go beyond them, and had no fear of "arbitrary power" if it was used in their interest. Whether talk about Charles I's "great affection to justice and peace, and his care of the freedom (which is the principal privilege) of Parliament," and about his determination to govern only by "the known and established laws of the land" and "to stand and fall together with the law," meant anything, depended on how much his professions could be trusted. No doubt Falkland persuaded himself that his master was sincere in them, and Charles must have approved what his secretary wrote. But the King was all the time listening to other points of view, and had pretty well lost his ability to convince anybody, except the determinedly loyal, that he always meant what he said. He joked once about Falkland's style, saying that he had two secretaries, one dull and one witty, and preferred the work of the dull one. "My Lord Carleton," he said, "brought me my own sense in my own words; but my Lord Faulkland most commonly brought me my instructions in so fine a dress, that I did not alwaies own them." Was it just that he resented having his own prose polished by a secretary, or was it that Falkland now and then made honestly explicit statements when the King would have preferred to hedge?

Anyhow there was little leisure now for words. Charles's second attempt, in July, to regain Hull, this time by using Digby to persuade the governor, Sir John Hotham, to give up the town, was the sort of scheme which Parliament looked on as a hostile plot. The King characteristically delayed action too long. Hotham changed his mind, and the royalists got nothing but increased hatred and suspicion from Parliament. On July 15 there was actual bloodshed at Manchester, when Lord Strange drove his troop of horses through a group of townsmen, raising forces for Parliament, and killed one man. There was a skirmish before Hull; Lord George Goring came over to the King and seized Portsmouth for him. All over the country men took up arms. Guns were hauled along narrow roads, and town walls and private houses were fortified. On August 9, Essex and his officers were proclaimed traitors, but a pardon was offered to any who submitted within a week. Three days later the Commons swore its members to live and die with Essex, and on the 18th declared that all who helped Charles were guilty of treason. Goring was besieged at Portsmouth, and the Marquis of Hertford in Sherburne. Even before that the King had given notice that on the 22nd he would raise his standard in Nottingham as a rallying point for a loyal army.

On that day the King, the Prince of Wales, the Duke of York, and Prince Rupert, Charles's nephew, rode to Nottingham for the ceremony. Sir Edmund Verney, a connection of Falkland's through the Lees, had charge of the standard. In the early twilight its staff was planted in the ground, and the royal herald stepped forward to read a declaration from the King. Charles, perhaps overcome at the last moment by a sense of how irrevocable was the step he was about to take, interrupted, and made a last flurried correction of some phrases. The herald had trouble reading the scribbled changes, and stumbled and halted as he pronounced the words of the Lord's anointed. A cold rain swept over the town, and the wet banner blew out sluggishly. The King's retainers threw their hats in the air, and shouted, "God save King Charles and hang up the Roundheads" but "melancholic men observed many ill presages." There were pitifully few troops and "no conflux of men" eager to show their loyalty. Charles himself was sad and could not conceal it. Falkland, who had stayed behind to look out for the King's affairs at York, may well have regarded the raising of the standard as proof that his foreboding of ruin had been prophetic. There could now be no alternative to war, and for a man who thought as he did, war was ruin. The banner of the King, rising above a muddy field at Nottingham, was the symbol of a new despair.

He fought against it, trying still to hope. He must have rejoiced to hear that on the 25th Charles, with difficulty persuaded by his Council, agreed to try once more for peace. The Earls of Southampton and Dorset, Colepeper, and Sir William Uvedale, Falkland's brother-in-law, were sent to Parliament to ask that commissioners be appointed to discuss terms. They were sharply refused. The Lords and Commons demanded that the standard be taken down and the King's declaration of the treason of his enemies be revoked, before there could be any talk of settlement.

Falkland arrived at Nottingham to find Hyde busily trying to cheer the King, lest his low spirits depress his followers. He also discovered that Charles, rebuffed by Parliament, was determined to make no more overtures. Hyde and Falkland urged him to swallow his pride and go to London, in order to appear in Parliament himself as a sign of his complete readiness to deal openly. This was too much for the royal pride, but the King did agree to one last effort for harmony, and sent Falkland himself to Westminster, with assurances that if Parliament would withdraw its accusation of the King's adherents as traitors, he would recall his proclamations against its members and take down his standard. He would then treat for peace, "ready to grant any thing that" might "be really for the good of" his subjects. His "chief desire, in this world," he protested, would be "to beget a good understanding and mutual confidence" with the "two Houses of Parliament." Probably Falkland had also secret instructions to say that Charles would "consent to a thorough reformation of religion" and to anything else that his people "could reasonably desire." But vague promises were futile, and Falkland could get no concessions. Parliament reasserted its intention to punish the King's supporters, and thus aided him, perhaps, by driving more royalists to his banner, since only by his victory could they be saved from condign punishment for their opposition to Pym.

At Northampton Falkland was distressed by the "great pride" of his erstwhile commander, Essex, "who would scarce take notice of him." More disturbing still was his meeting with Hampden, one of the leaders he had admired most in the Commons. Now he was at the head of a cavalry regiment. When they met both men dismounted and walked away from the troopers into a field beside the road. That was the way to proceed in dark times, Falkland felt—a few minutes' sober talk would be better than days of fighting. But Hampden swiftly undeceived him. He was full of "violence and acrimony of spirit" and in no mood for temperate debate. His evident hatred for "the government and the person of the King" was final proof that "very much blood must be spilt" and one side or the other have "an entire conquest . . . before peace could ever be made." Under the stress of emotion men might be false to their real characters, Falkland thought, and he believed "it was hardly possible that" Hampden "should have all the pride in his hearte which he acted and made show of." But that pride, genuine or not, demonstrated the vanity of attempts for peace.

At Nottingham, when Falkland returned, stories were being told of how the royal standard had blown down, dragging the King's banner in the mud, and of how the wind had raged so that for two days it could not be set up again. In the face of crisis, everything seemed an omen. But for Falkland no omens were needed to drive deeper into his heart his feeling of imminent catastrophe. Essex's arrogant disregard of old friendship, and Hampden's tense invective were enough to reveal that the future was committed to violence and hate.

VIII

"OUT OF IT ERE NIGHT"

Falkland with the King's Army, September,
1642–September, 1643

"FROM the entrance into this unnatural war," wrote Clarendon, Falkland's "natural cheerfulness and vivacity grew clouded, and a kind of sadness and dejection of spirit stole upon him which he had never been used to." Ten years before he had been eager for military command; now he was with the King, in arms and holding high office, but bitterly discontent. In 1630 he had longed to prove his daring, but the intervening years had taught him other ambitions that haunted him even when they no longer seemed possible to realize. The wonder is not that he was melancholy, but that he could endure his lot at all.

He had dreamed that he and Hyde and those who thought with them might avert war, but now war was upon them, and the King was surrounded by men whose first goal was to win battles. Prince Rupert, the son of Charles's sister, Elizabeth of Bohemia, was foremost among them. Twenty-three years old, tall, handsome, valiant, already experienced in the field, he was admirably equipped to become a figure of romance, but not to understand the "politicians" like Hyde and Falkland. How could his uncle, an anointed monarch, be anything but right? Were not Englishmen who dared to resist his will, traitors? They deserved no better than to be ridden down by royal troopers, and for that Rupert had great talents. So long as he had cavalry to train, and a chance to use it; so long as there were towns to capture, and he might display his skill in arms, he need not trouble his head about the rights and wrongs of this strange quarrel. Falkland would have been happier had he been able to adopt Rupert's creed, but since he could not, he must have feared the Prince's influence with the King.

To be sure, Clarendon has it that Falkland's chief hope was that one victory would end the war. If so, Rupert was the man to win it, provided always that his pride could be somehow curbed. His sense of his own importance, and Charles's weakness in deferring to him, started the campaign with a handicap. Wisely the King had appointed Robert Bertie, Earl of Lindsay, as his commander-in-chief. The Earl was a seasoned soldier, and "had very many friends and very few enemies." But Rupert rebelled against taking orders from anyone but Charles—was he not a prince of the blood royal? Moreover, he had radical ideas about the use of cavalry, and wanted to put them into effect unhampered by any superior officer schooled in older methods. He persuaded his uncle, therefore, to give him orders directly, independent of Lindsay, thus virtually removing the cavalry from the control of the commander-in-chief. Bertie resented this, and said so, and within a few weeks Falkland had his own taste of the Prince's determination to let nothing—not even military expediency—stand in the way of vanity.

The Viscount was sent to him with instructions from Charles. Rupert "took it very ill, and expostulated with Falkland for giving him orders." The Secretary, of course, was imperturbable, and merely remarked that "it was his office to signify what the king bad him; which he should always do," and that the Prince "in neglecting it neglected the King." Clarendon adds that Rupert "could not have directed his passion against any man who would feel it or regard it less" than Lucius Cary. Yet, even though he was too intelligent to be angry, the episode must have disturbed Falkland. It showed how gravely the King's enterprise was threatened by "unhappy jealousy and division between the principal officers."

Nor were all Charles's officers really ardent. Some of them had qualms as to the complete justice of the royal cause, and yielded only to what they felt was the duty of allegiance. Henry Spencer, Earl of Sunderland, like Falkland a student and strict in morals, wrote home to his wife, Dorothy Sidney, at Penshurst, that the King was "averse to Peace," under the influence of Digby and Rupert, and so opposed the desires of better men. As for himself, Spencer wrote: "I am unsatisfied with the Proceedings here . . . Neither is there wanting Daily, handsom Occasion to retire, were it not for grin[n]ing Honour. For let Occasion be never so handsome, unless a Man were resolved to fight on the Parliament Side, which, for my Part, I had rather be hanged, it will be said without Doubt, that a Man is afraid to fight. If there could be an Expedient found, to salve the Punctilio of Honour, I would not continue here an Hour. The Discontent that I, and many other honest Men, receive Daily, is beyond Expression." A "Punctilio of Honour" was too slim a basis for whole-hearted devotion. Sir Edmund Verney's similar comment has become classic. "You," he told Hyde, "have satisfaction in your conscience that you are in the right; that the king ought not to grant what is required of him; and so you do your duty and your business together; but for my part, I do not like the quarrel, and do heartily wish that the king would yield and consent to what they desire; so that my conscience is only concerned in honour and in gratitude to follow my master. I have eaten his bread, and served him near thirty years, and will not do so base a thing as to forsake him; and choose rather to lose my life (which I am sure I shall do) to preserve and defend those things which are against my conscience to preserve and defend: for I will deal freely with you, I have no reverence for the bishops, for whom this quarrel subsists."

Others recoiled from the idea of a war against Englishmen on English soil. Sir Benjamin Rudyard said: "We cannot fight here as they do in Germany, in that great, large, vast Continent; where although there be War in some parts of it, yet there are many other remote quiet places . . . We must fight as in a Cock-pit, we are surrounded with the Sea. We have no stronger Holds, than our own Sculls, and our own Ribs, to keep out Enemies; so that the whole Kingdom will suddenly be but one flame." These words emphasize one of the major terrors of civil strife.

Even on the Parliamentary side, men had their doubts. Sir William Waller looked on the conflict with "perfect hatred" because it was a "war without an enemy," which he entered with reluctance. He felt that he was "upon the stage," forced to act the part assigned him in the "tragedy." All he hoped for was to serve "in a way of honour, and without personal animosities." But probably Parliament could count on sources of strength denied to the King's army. One was the religious fervor with which some of its adherents fought, sure that their cause was that of Christ and Protestantism against Popery and godlessness. Another was the fact that as rebels they were easily whipped up to a fanatic enthusiasm that was hard to instil in many of their opponents, who were contending not for an imagined Utopia but for the tame realities of the existing order, and were mainly inspired by conventional loyalty, reverence for tradition, and fear of change. There were on both sides educated and thoughtful men who hated war, but in one party their voices were drowned out by the shouts of downright revolutionaries, ready to pay whatever price in blood was exacted for success; and in the other the prudent and temperate, since the King's whole case was supposed to rest on reason and law, found it hard to reconcile themselves to seeking a decision by violence. The royalists were undoubtedly handicapped also because they misunderstood the spirit of their enemies. A loyal gentleman found it fatally easy to suppose that all the disloyal were mere rogues; a courtier, taught to believe that success in war was the prerogative of men of breeding, trained in courts, naturally assumed that rebels must be bad soldiers. With such theories, too many of the King's party, Falkland among them, underestimated the ferocity of the struggle.

After Rupert had won a skirmish at Powick Bridge, near Worcester, a "rencounter" which was "of unspeakable advantage . . . to the King" and made the Prince's name "very terrible" to his enemies, Falkland wrote an account of it to the Earl of Cumberland. He told how the Parliamentary troops fled, but some of their officers, "Gentlemen, (more sensible of honour than the rest) fought valiantly." Wounded to death was Edwin Sandys, a nephew of George Sandys, Falkland's old friend. Falkland declared, and no doubt believed, that Sandys repented fighting in "so bad a cause, which he was drawne into as well by his own ambition as by the perswasion of other men." Another "Gentleman," the story goes on, confessed he was a rebel "for gain and sinister ends." This, to Falkland, proved of the Parliamentarians what was surely true of some royalists—"that the hearts of these men goe not along with their actions." Apart from a few of good family—and the implication is that all of them saw the error of their ways—the defeated were "of meane quality" and "raw Souldiers," "Taylors," "Embroyderers and the like." The blindness that underlies Falkland's assumption that men of "meane quality" were easy to beat, and that such gentlemen as there were with Parliament were turning away from it, was the same he had shown in writing of beggars in his "Elegie," and the same that was hinted at in Randol's sermon before him in Burford Church, when the preacher complacently assumed that the lower orders had no real part in the state except in so far as they conformed to the dictates of their betters. It was dangerous for a royal officer in 1642 to see so little. Even Falkland suspected it might be, and he did warn Cumberland that the King's men might suffer from their "great Sinnes" and their "slight esteeme . . . of Parliament forces." But that was a small part of the danger. To scorn not only the power, but the motives and aims of "Taylors" and "Embroyderers"; to understand nothing of the possible justice of their wish for a radically changed position in English life; was to be almost incapable of any statesmanlike attempt to settle peacefully a conflict in which social and economic as well as political and religious issues were woven into the texture of chaos.

The affair at Powick Bridge must have weakened Falkland's hope that one victory could end the war. There had been a victory, but the war went on. His account of the fight was burned by order of Parliament, and the story of Sandys's repentance was denied. Optimism could feed only on dreams that the next triumph might accomplish more. In the meanwhile there was nothing to do but to go on marching with the King, from Nottingham to Stafford and Shrewsbury, and then toward London, distressed by the lack of unity in the command of the army, and painfully aware of scruples as to the complete rightness of Charles's cause. Falkland may well have been shocked by the intemperate behavior of the gayer officers and the rank and file. As his friend Henry Hammond put it later, preaching before the King, "As long as God-damme's leads the vann and the-Devil-confound-me's brings up the rear" Charles "must needs be routed in all his enterprizes." Clarendon said "one side seemed to fight for monarchy with the weapons of confusion, and the other to destroy the King and government with all the principles and regularity of monarchy." No truth could have been more unpalatable to Falkland, who loved "principles and regularity" as much as he hated confusion.

However little he liked the careless cavaliers, who squabbled about rank and privileges and thought England's problems could be solved in battle, however imperfectly he trusted Charles, and however out of place he felt among men who had none of his gravity of temper and no realization that the war was tragedy, he had gone too far to turn back. He sold one of his estates to raise money for the King; he was an exile from London; in September what was left of the Parliament he had once admired branded him as a traitor. Essex was instructed to promise "Clemency and Favour" to any royalist who recanted and joined the Parliamentarians, but specially exempted from mercy were "all Persons who stand impeach'd in Parliament of Treason" and a group of others, including both Hyde and Falkland. The Commons voted that he might no longer continue "a Member of this House."

A contemporary pamphlet asked some awkward questions about this. "We would be glad to know," wrote its author, "what was the cause of turning the Lord Faulkland, Sir John Culpepper . . . and divers others out of the Houses (for they were voted out by scores hand over head), unlesse it were because they spake more reason than the more violent party could answer; and therefore it was come to that passe, that (cleane contrary to the use, yea, and the honor of Parliaments too) things were not debated by reason and strength of argument, but by putting it to the question and carrying it by most voices, where the greatest number were so far from understanding many times the force of arguments, that they did not, after the vote was past, conceive the state or sense of the question, but thought it was enough for them to vote with Master Pymm or Master Hampden by . . . faith; and if they differed (as seldom they did), then, crosse or pyle, vote at venture." The contrast between reason and thoughtless voting at the behest of party leaders was for Falkland the contrast between truth and error, hope and hopelessness. Parliament had chosen the false gods, and hated him because he refused to worship its idols.

After September, 1642, no reconciliation was possible. Before then it might have been, had Falkland been able to include in his conception of what was reasonable the ideas of men who were ready to abandon the law as he defined it in order to meet needs for which they felt the old rules did not provide. His failure to comprehend their premises may have been narrow conservatism, but even had he managed to justify Parliament's aims, it is hard to see how he could have ever approved its methods. Whatever the premises and whatever the issues, surely he thought that "strength of argument" and "understanding" should decide, not political emotionalism or voting "at venture." Nor could he easily have kept his faith in a Parliament that now included only those of the legally elected members who agreed with the leaders or as yet had not been driven out by the harsh tactics of the partisan. But was his new affiliation any better? Did "strength of argument" govern the King? How much weight did it have with Rupert? Even if Charles's armies prevailed would the jealousies and vanities and ambitions of the court be forgotten in a renaissance of reason? Falkland was too much the sceptic to be able to answer "Yes."

On October 21, the King was at Southam, in the full tide of an advance on London. The next night he was at Edgecott, where he had word from Rupert that Essex was at Kineton, only a few miles away. Charles could hardly hope to escape a battle, and drew up his army along the high land of Edgehill. But Essex was too wise to attack, and waited calmly in the plain below. So long as he stayed there, the royalists could not safely move, nor easily get supplies. The King must come down and fight. Through the morning of the 23rd he assembled his troops, and just after midday marched them down the slope of Edgehill under cover of guns posted above. Many of them were in high spirits. Sure that Essex commanded a rabble, not an army, and that gentlemen and nobles fighting for the sovereign could rout a rebellious flock of baseborn "Taylors" and "Embroyderers," they looked forward to an easy victory. Like Falkland they believed that it might end the war; unlike him many of them thought that ending the war would heal the nation's wounds.

Charles's troops, for all their confidence, went crippled to the fight. The Earl of Lindsay, smarting at having the cavalry given to Rupert, left the chief command nominally to Patrick Ruthven, Earl of Forth, and actually to the Prince. He said that "he did not look upon himself as general, and . . . would be in the head of his regiment as a private colonel, where he would die." For all Rupert's brilliance, the last minute shifts of authority made for disorder and for bad feeling among the many who loved Lindsay.

In the plain the line was formed with Lindsay and the infantry in the centre, Rupert and most of the cavalry on the right, and a smaller body of horse, led by Henry Wilmot, on the left. Ruthven rode with him. So did Falkland, who quite naturally did not wish to follow the Prince. Opposite Wilmot on the Parliamentary side were three regiments of horse, one as a reserve. It was a bright October afternoon, and as he took his place in the line Falkland mercifully "forgot that he was Secretary of State," forgot his intellectual dilemma, and wanted simply "to be where there would probably be most to do." With his horse's flanks warm between his knees, and his ears filled with the clicking of bits and stirrups and the creaking of leather as his comrades settled themselves in their saddles, there was every temptation to stop thinking. It was even possible to delight sensuously in the scene before him—the level field, broken only on the left, just in front of him, by hedges and ditches, and splashed with color where Essex's troops, wearing orange scarves, spread across it. The air was crisp and the scent of the grass trampled by hooves called back memories of tilled fields in Oxfordshire. Even Rupert was a splendid figure, riding up and down before the lines, erect on his great horse. In size and dignity of bearing he seemed a prince indeed, and inspired confidence as he gave orders to charge in the new way he favored—at top speed, never stopping to fire volleys. Surely this was better than a secretary's desk, better than endless disputes at the Council, better than dreary compounding of phrases to prove that though England was at war all would be well if only the King and his gravest advisers were given their way. Here was the best anaesthetic for scepticism as to whether anything—even fighting for Charles I— was better than inane futility. At last Falkland was to have his chance to show himself worthy of Henry Morison in valor as well as wit, his chance to live up to the soldierly ideal his father had taught him to love.

Then, after a last moment of tense excitement, while he reined in his horse, waiting the order to charge, he was riding hard, racing with the troopers pressed close to him on either side, deafened by the thunder of hooves on the turf, and tasting the dust that swept up about his straining horse. Muskets crackled from the hedges and ditches, and bullets sang past his ears. He had no time to look back to the hill where Hyde, with the King and the princes, watched the first real test of the royal army. All he knew was that Wilmot's advance, checked only momentarily till Essex's snipers could be driven out of their cover, swept all before it. As he told Hyde afterward, "he saw no enemy that day of the horse that made any resistance."

On the right Rupert's men swept hilariously on. Either they were out of control, or Rupert was foolish, for instead of turning to charge again or to support the rest of the royal line, they plunged happily on to the village of Kineton, a full mile from the field, and fell to plundering the Parliament's baggage train. Worse, the King's cavalry reserves could not resist the sight of Rupert's triumphant gallop, and rode hotly after him. Even Charles's own body-guard, entirely made up of gentlemen, followed, eager to wipe out the taunts of their companions, who said they were readier to be admired than to fight and had called them "The Troop of Shew."

Wilmot handled his men better than the Prince, and got them back to the field still in comparatively good order, but too late. Apparently two of the Parliament's cavalry regiments had pulled aside to let the charge pass, and its effect had been only on the reserves. Thus, after the first royalist advance, Lindsay and the infantry were left to face not only Essex's foot but part of his cavalry. Sir William Balfour drove his troop through the King's defenders far enough to cut the traces on the royal cannons. Charles's foot-guards, surrounding his standard, carried by Sir Edmund Verney, were led by Lindsay himself. He fought well and kept his promise to die as a colonel, falling with a mortal wound. Verney was killed, and the standard was taken. By the time his cavalry rode back from its first charges, Charles's plight was desperate. Two regiments alone held his front, and Essex was preparing a new attack. Falkland saw the situation and begged Wilmot to charge again. But the horses were jaded and their riders drenched with sweat, nor was Wilmot of heroic stuff. "My lord, we have got the day, and let us live to enjoy the fruit thereof," he said. They had not got the day, though they had made a triumphant charge through or past the Parliamentarians opposite them on the field. But to Wilmot it seemed better to keep a whole skin, even if the King were beaten, than to risk life itself, as Falkland wanted to, on the chance of victory.

Fortunately the gathering darkness prevented much further action. One gallant follower of the King did recover the captured standard by whipping an orange scarf about his shoulders and masquerading as one of Essex's officers, but this was the only royal success in the last minutes of the battle. It grew darker and colder, and both armies held their positions. Lindsay was dying in the hands of the enemy; his son was a prisoner, too. Verney had been seen to fall, defending the standard. George Stuart, Lord D'Aubigny, was dead, and some fifteen hundred or two thousand more of those who had so proudly arrayed themselves for Charles earlier in the day. Sir Jacob

Astley was wounded, and Sir Nicholas Byron, Colonel Charles Gerard, and Sir George Strowde. These had been with the infantry; "of the horse there was not an officer of name who received a wound," except poor D'Aubigny. Sir Thomas Lunsford, Sir Edward Stradling, and Sir William Vavasour, of the King's guards, were prisoners. The air was thick with rumors. Everywhere men were seeking missing friends, doing their best to dress wounds, looking for food, or for some shelter from the numbing frost. Above all the noise of the camp came insistently the cries of the wounded left on the field, writhing in pools of bloody mud.

A few bushes and fragments of wood were heaped together and lighted, and Charles and his counsellors sat getting what comfort they could from the blaze. Some urged leaving the field. Others thought that Essex had gone and that in the morning Charles would have a clear road to London. But only the most sanguine could persist in thinking that the fight had been won, and Falkland can have had little with which to console himself. He had done his part, and had ridden bravely. He had urged a second charge that might have turned the scale, and had been ready to throw himself recklessly into it. Moreover, for all the excitement of battle he had not forgotten his humanity. Some Parliamentarians had "thrown away their arms" in their flight, and his companions had fallen upon them. This was perhaps sound military practice—a soldier who lived to run away might fight again—but it seemed to Falkland useless brutality and but one more way of increasing hatred. His defense of his helpless enemies, by which "he was like to have incurred great peril," made him seem like a man who "came into the field only out of curiosity to see the face of danger, and charity to prevent the shedding of blood." Such charity seemed to him, and to those who were as thoughtful and chivalrous as he, a very proper virtue for a soldier of the King, fighting against Englishmen in the name of peace; to the hard-headed soldiers and to those who hated the very name of Parliament, it seemed quixotic nonsense. For their opinion Falkland cared little, no doubt, but he did care about the result of the day, because victory might have meant peace. Since victory was at best doubtful, his work had gone for nothing, and through the bitterly cold night he saw opening before him further vistas of a loathsome war.

In the morning things looked worse. There had been no "refreshment of victual or provision for the soldiers." A third of the royal infantry was missing, and many of the cavalry. Those that were left "were so tired with duty, and weakened with want of meat, and shrunk up with the cruel cold of the night" that there could be no hope of action. About noon there was definite news that Lindsay was dead—dead in a cottage, lying "in his blood" "upon a little straw." As Falkland went back that night with Hyde and Colepeper to Culworth, where they had spent the night before the battle with Lindsay, he must have sincerely mourned the Earl, who had been both his commander and his friend. He must have wondered whether Rupert, for all the magnificence of his bearing and the gallantry of his charge, could ever be as wise a leader as Lindsay might have been, and whether the Prince's pride had not been one source of the King's ill success.

D'Aubigny's death moved Falkland, too, and he declared that he was "very much affected by the consideration of my poore Lady Aubignie's condition," even before he read it, "sensibly expressed," in a letter from Lady Dungarvan. Katherine Howard, Lady D'Aubigny, was his distant cousin. Lady Dungarvan, her friend and his, had married young Richard Boyle. She was the daughter of the Earl of Cumberland, whom the King had left as his commander-in-chief in Yorkshire. To her in London Falkland wrote several times during 1642. She asked him to do services for her—or, perhaps, her father—at court, and he eagerly responded, constantly inquiring from her about her sister-in-law, Katherine Boyle, whom he had known in Ireland. She was now Viscountess Ranelagh, celebrated for her "vast reach . . . of knowledge" and her liberality of mind. She was in Ireland, in danger from the rebels there, and Falkland had only such scattered reports of her as he could get through Lady Dungarvan. With the latter he could keep in touch only by letters, which were often opened and confiscated before they reached her hands. When they were the pamphleteers made the most of it. In September, 1642, they told London gossips of "a Letter read in the House of Commons written from the Lord Faulkland to a Lady his special friend." No "mouldy sawes of flatt philosophie" could deceive him as to the insane barbarity of a war which turned some friends into enemies, cut him off from others like Lady Ranelagh or Lady Dungarvan, "a very fine-speaking lady, and a good woman," and destroyed such men as Lindsay and Verney. He felt that in war, "a time of so much sadnesse and solitarinesse, a companion of good humour is no little diuersion, and in a time of so much rancour and malignity one that can loue very well is no little Jewell," but war, with exquisite cruelty, separated friends when they most needed one another.

Of all those from whom he was now isolated, the one who probably best deserved to be called "his special friend" was Lady Sophia Murray, the daughter of John, Earl of Annandale, who had been a trusted adviser of James I. Her brother James was now Earl in his turn, and a Scottish supporter of Charles. For Lady Sophia, Falkland "had an extraordinary esteem," and he "exceedingly loved her conversation, as most of the persons of eminent parts of that time did; for she was in her understanding, and discretion, and wit, and modesty, above most women." His intimacy with her was talked about maliciously, and mischievous tongues called her his mistress, but it is only generous to accept Hyde's statement that "they who knew either the lord or the lady, knew well that neither of them was capable of an ill imagination," and his assurance that Falkland was ever "kind" to his wife and "loved his children with more affection and fondness than most fathers."

Lady Sophia was, Hyde continues, "of the most unspotted, unblemished virtue; never married, of an extraordinary talent of mind, but of no alluring beauty; nor of a constitution of tolerable health, being in a deep consumption." She seems to have stayed in London when the King took the field, so that now Falkland's friendship could express itself only in letters, while he chafed at being cut off from the charms of "her conversation." [1]

He must, then, have been heavy hearted after Edgehill. No one agreed as to who had won the fight, and neither side wanted to go on with it. Essex withdrew to Warwick, and on Wednesday, the 26th, the King marshalled his army again. His enemies had carried off the honors for discipline and organization, but had left his army, now led by Ruthven, free to move on to Oxford. Banbury capitulated, and there was excited confusion in London. In Parliament, especially in the Lords, advocates of peace began to speak out, and on the 29th, the day of Charles's arrival at Oxford, the upper house listened to a proposal to negotiate with him, while Waller urged the concurrence of the Commons. But no one knew how peace was to be had, and Rupert was trying to persuade the King to march quickly against London and, by striking one decisive blow, crush the rebels. He may well have been right, and have seen more clearly than the more cautious advisers who ob-

---

[1] Aubrey, I, 152, tells a story of "Mris . . . Moray," whom he calls Falkland's "mistresse." Clarendon, *Life*, I, 202-203, refers to this story, but does not name the "noble lady." Dr. Shepard H. Werlein, Jr., has proved that "Mris . . . Moray," named by Aubrey and alluded to by Clarendon, was Lady Sophia Murray, who was implicated in "Waller's Plot" (pp. 248-250 post). See his unpublished thesis in the Harvard College Library, *Edmund Waller: A Study of His Life and Works*, especially p. 249, note 3. Unfortunately Dr. Werlein identifies Lady Murray wrongly as the daughter of the Earl of Arundel, following J. Sanford, *Studies and Illustrations of the Great Rebellion* (London, 1858), p. 562. According to one story she was the "Amoret" addressed by Waller in his verses. Cf. E. Waller, *Poems* (ed. G. Thorn Drury; London, 1893), p. 307, and Sir J. B. Paul, ed., *The Scots Peerage* (Edinburgh, 1904–1914), I, 227-229.

jected to his plan. If it was to succeed, it must be carried out at once. Rupert, after Edgehill, was sure that he could take Westminster, capture the unruly Parliament, and occupy Whitehall, with only his cavalry and part of the infantry. But Hyde and Falkland wanted no more bloodshed since there seemed to be a chance for peace by treaty. Nor was Rupert trusted. The Earl of Bristol was sure that the Prince would burn London if he got there, and was not London English still?

Falkland stated his position in a letter to Lady Dungarvan, written on November 2. "Wee are remouing to Redding," he wrote, "That is within 30 miles of your La^p, neerer by 100 then I durst hope not long since euer to have come." His next sentence, "I would willingly flatter my selfe with an opinion of possibility that a Treaty may yett end all" shows what he longed for, and how slender was his hope of getting it. He added bitterly: "This filthy warre . . . takes away the Joy of England" and "must utterly lose us Ireland." Nor could he agree with Rupert as to the best means of stopping it, for he wrote: "Neuer to see London or to enter it by force are equally dreadfull to mee." The only shred of hope was that an amicable discussion might bring peace before the army was allowed to fight its way into the city.

Charles characteristically made no clean-cut decision about Rupert's scheme. He delayed his march until Essex managed to pass him and get in to London. That lost the advantage which Rupert had hoped to use. Then, on November 3, the Parliament's envoy, sent to talk of peace, was confronted by the royal army moving at last against the capital, too late for military effectiveness, but quite soon enough to destroy confidence in the sincerity of the King's desire for peace. On the 4th he was in Reading, and had the Parliament's message, but he delayed answering it until the 6th. He then agreed to meet emissaries from the Houses, but refused to deal with one of those whom they suggested. He gained more ill will by this, and supplied his enemies with new grounds for suspecting that his talk of reconciliation was only a pretext to cover an attack on London. Essex was ordered to defend the city. On the 11th Charles replied to the Parliament's suggestions for an agreement, but said nothing about an armistice. Essex, however, was instructed to take no hostile action, and the King was asked to consent to a cessation of hostilities. To that Hyde and Falkland would no doubt have agreed at once, but Charles was now excited by what seemed the success of his advance, and before his message, promising to negotiate, was delivered in the city, he had allowed Rupert to attack Brentford. The Prince's men captured and sacked the town. London felt the threat at its very gates, and thousands of men rallied to Essex, marching out with him to bar the royalists' course at Turnham Green. There was nothing for the King to do but to leave Brentford to the Parliament's troops, raw recruits many of them, but far too numerous for his small force.

His greatest loss in the affair was not military but political. By continuing his march while writing about terms of peace, he violated no specific agreement, and by military standards acted properly enough. Tactically, however, he was foolish, if he wanted concord, since to achieve it he must convince his restless subjects that he was eager to heal the breach and resolved not to use force except in self-defense. He might have assured them of his good intentions by avoiding any appearance of aggression until the parleyings had finished; as it was, his care for peace seemed mere pretense. Acting too late, as he had ever since Edgehill, he moved his army to Reading, and calmly proposed to resume discussion of a settlement. Nothing came of it, naturally; he had too effectively destroyed Parliament's trust in him. To Falkland was given the ticklish task of explaining in "a declaration" why the King had acted as he had. The result was a painfully unimpressive document

—even Hyde seemed later eager to have it understood that not he but Falkland had written it. Its chief plea was that Charles had advanced to Brentford to save himself from being surrounded by his enemies, "so gross a perversion of geographical fact, that it is difficult to understand how he expected to gain for it even momentary credence." The only way to excuse Falkland is to suppose that he wrote dutifully from the King's dictation and that he was too ill informed of the actual position of the armies to see how specious the argument was.

Thus ingloriously ended the first campaign of the Civil War, and Charles and his court, attended by Falkland, took up their quarters in Oxford, where the loyalty of the University promised a secure refuge. Under other circumstances living there among scholars and libraries would have delighted Falkland. Great Tew was only a few miles away; he had many friends within easy riding distance; Thomas Barlow was at Oxford; Gilbert Sheldon was with the King, and so were John Earle, as tutor to the prince, and Henry Killigrew as an army chaplain. Jasper Mayne, too, was probably at Christ Church where Charles made his headquarters; Endymion Porter was with him; and there were many other old acquaintances in the town. Some had frequented Great Tew, or London in the days of Jonson; others were men of affairs or courtiers whom Falkland had known in Parliament or since he joined the Council; still others were connections of his family or his wife's. There was time for a dinner with Barlow and George Morley, at which they talked about such subjects as the character of Dr. Joshua Hoyle, Falkland's erstwhile teacher at Dublin, whom he called "a person of some few weak parts, but of very many strong infirmities." There was even leisure to bet with the King, who insisted that he could recognize Hyde's style anywhere, and to win an angel from him by proving he could not. But these were mere interludes, and if Falkland now and then dined with old friends, pulled down vol-

umes from the Bodleian shelves, or found an hour or two for
talk with some scholarly theologian about the place of reason
in divinity, there were few such chances to forget the present
in the past. Even the sight of some of his friends called painfully to mind how many others were removed from him by
the war. Suckling had fled to France and there was no recent
news of him. Selden had stayed on in the Commons, and
earlier in the year had voted against the legality of the Com-
missions of Array by which the King tried to keep some control of the militia. To be sure, when Falkland wrote him about
it, he defended himself on the ground that he was maintaining
a principle that in other matters could be applied in Charles's
behalf, but it was plain that he was sceptical of the motives
which had led Falkland and others to join the King. Hobbes,
timidly sure that mathematicians had no place in war, had
gone to Paris. Edmund Waller was in London, perhaps kept
there by fear of Parliament, perhaps by his belief that he could
serve Charles best among his enemies. Henry Hammond was
in Kent, at Penshurst, with Lady Spencer and her mother;
Hales was still at Eton, clinging to scholarly retirement and
trying not to notice Rupert's guns planted not far from his
windows. Sir Benjamin Rudyard had stayed in Parliament,
ineffectively discoursing about moderation and peace. Of the
Boyle children, remembered from his boyhood in Ireland, the
eldest had been killed fighting the Irish rebels. Richard, his
brother, fought in the same cause, but kept his seat in the
Commons. Davenant had left England in 1641 but had
stolen back and joined the Earl of Newcastle in the north, becoming his Lieutenant-General of Ordnance, which provoked
Sir Philip Warwick to write that Newcastle "had the misfortune to have somewhat of the Poet in him" and that "this
inclination of his own, and such . . . witty society" as Davenant's, "diverted many counsels, and lost many opportunities."
Still others of Falkland's friends, and they were those most

lost to him, were frank supporters of Parliament—like Thomas May, who still sat in the Commons, and, of course, Essex and Hampden, who were actually in arms against the King.

Oxford itself was changed, and for the worse. Libraries, students, and scholars, were still there, but the students drilled and dug trenches with more enthusiasm than they read, and scholars were ousted from their studies by courtiers. It was hard to work quietly in a town in which the hooves of cavalry clattered constantly past college gates, and the streets and quadrangles were thronged with men and women in the latest court fashions, doing their best to make Oxford another Whitehall. There must be fortifications, at Magdalen, and trenches near Wadham and St. John's. New College must serve as a powder magazine; in other colleges, too, munitions were being stored. Whenever Rupert made a successful raid into the countryside, the towers rocked with pealing bells, but at other times timid lovers of peace who walked in the fields about the town looked nervously down every road, imagining dangers, seeing Essex's soldiers in every whirl of dust and conspirators and rebels in every unfamiliar face.

Beneath the surface there were more sinister forces. The "politicians," the moderates who wanted peace by peaceful means, were still pitted against the military men who saw war simply as war, and had no use for wordy debates when there was a chance to prove the King's justice and wisdom by riding down in battle all Englishmen who dared to question them. Worse still were the fortune hunters—men not at all eager to risk their lives, but fluent in protestations of honor and loyalty. They hoped that their talk might bring rewards of titles and court offices even though they never soiled their clothes in the vulgar contacts of actual strife. There were ladies in scores, wives and mistresses, some of them self-forgetful in honest allegiance to the King, and others using ready wit and complaisant bodies as weapons in political intrigue. Poor Charles said, early in his stay at Oxford, that there was no one but Hyde whom he could trust. If he meant that, it was a confession of the intolerable weakness of his followers. He lived in the midst of their vanity and ambition, and the efforts of his best advisers were too often thwarted by the bickerings and jealousies of the worst. Hyde may not have been the only man he could trust, but he was one of the pitifully few.

All this was hard for Falkland to endure and he grew more melancholy day by day. Brentford had been the straw that destroyed his last pretense of cheerfulness. It may have been because he realized that Rupert's boldness had ruined the chance for a treaty; it may have been because he saw that the declaration he had had to write explained nothing except Charles's readiness to save his face without reference to truth. In any case, "those indispositions which had before touched him grew into a perfect habit of uncheerfulness; and he, who had been so exactly unreserved and affable to all men . . . and held any cloudiness and less pleasantness of the visage a kind of rudeness or incivility, became on a sudden less communicable, and thence very sad, pale, and exceedingly affected with the spleen. In his clothes and habit, which he had intended before always with more neatness and industry and expense than is usual to so great a mind, he was not now only incurious but too negligent; and in his reception of suitors, and the necessary or casual addresses to his place, so quick and sharp and severe, that there wanted not some men (who were strangers to his nature and disposition) who believed him proud and imperious, from which no mortal man was ever more free." Nervously exhausted, on the edge of melancholia, he could no longer masquerade. He liked "good and worthy and entire" characters, and hated "ill men." Many of those with whom he had to deal were neither good nor worthy, and in his desperate frame of mind he saw no reason to hide his dislike for them.

A lively rumor ran around in October that he had been sent on a secret mission to Ireland. The story may have started because he hoped to find some service outside of the immediate environment of the King.[2] Certainly he must have longed at times to be far away from the machinations of the court. His closest associates, Hyde and Colepeper, were not above petty quarreling. Charles wanted to make Hyde a Secretary of State, since he had "prepared and drawn" all but two of the royal declarations thus far issued, since he was faithful, and since he was more likely than Falkland to be affable. Hyde prudently refused. At about the same time Sir Charles Caesar, the Master of the Rolls, died. Colepeper had long had an eye on his office, and now asked for it. He was "violently opposed by many, partly out of ill-will to him, (for he had not the faculty of getting himself much loved,) and as much out of good husbandry, and to supply the king's necessities with a good sum of money, which Dr. Duck was ready to lay down for the office." But Charles had promised the Mastership to Colepeper, and kept his word. Falkland thereupon urged that Hyde succeed Colepeper as Chancellor of the Exchequer. The King agreed, but Colepeper was angry. His simple plan had been to hold both the Chancellorship and the Mastership. Moreover, he was jealous of Hyde's influence and "had no mind he should be upon the same level with him; and believed he would have too much credit in the council." He stubbornly delayed resigning until Falkland and Digby "expostulated very warmly with him." He gave in then, and Hyde became Chancellor, was sworn of the Privy Council, and knighted. Charles fatuously supposed "nobody was angry at his preferment." Actually Parliament hated the very name of Hyde, Colepeper felt cheated, and other courtiers were envious. Older lawyers thought Hyde was an upstart who "had run too fast," and

---

[2] Edward Reed wrote Sir John Coke, Oct. 10, 1642: "My Lord of Falkland is sent by the King into Ireland"; on Oct. 17, Don Jayme Nochera wrote from London to Luke Wadding in Rome that Charles had sent Falkland to Ireland with the title of justice and an "extraordinary commission"; and on Nov. 1, Hugh Bourke wrote from Brussels to Wadding, repeating the story. *Hist. Mss. Comm.*, Report XII, Appendix, Part 2, p. 323, Report on Franciscan Manuscripts, pp. 205, 212-213.

the Queen herself, who had not been consulted, was annoyed at having an important place given to one who was no favorite of hers and indeed was the more ready to take the Chancellorship because she had had nothing to do with the appointment. Where there was jealousy of Sir Edward Hyde there was jealousy of Viscount Falkland. The rift between him and some of the King's other advisers was widened by the promotion of his friend.

Through the winter of 1642–43 the King's troops were active, and had their share of victories. Victories were well enough, but they decided nothing, and took a horrible toll. Sidney Godolphin—poet, scholar, and gentleman, and Falkland's close friend—had stayed in the Commons as long as he safely could, and on leaving warned his colleagues "that by a war the parliament would expose itself to unknown dangers; for," he said, "when the cards are once shuffled, no man knows what the game will be." So physically sensitive that he shrank from bad weather and had amused his companions at Great Tew by his flights from rain and wind, it was major heroism for him to enter a brutal "game" which he disapproved. But he was too gallant to hide at home while others fought, and too chivalrous in his loyalty to Charles not to come out in his defense. He braved cold, sleet, and all the hardships of a long campaign with Sir Ralph Hopton in the west of England, venturing his small body with all the daring of the most callous trooper. At Chagford, early in 1643, he was killed. The cards were indeed madly shuffled.

The only relief for Falkland, and that at best a transitory one, was to turn from the news of battle and the lists of brave Englishmen who had fallen, to the letters that came from London telling that the supporters of a plan for ending the conflict seemed to be gaining ground even within Parliament. There were many negotiations, all quite as futile as the one which had been ended by the affair at Brentford, but each seeming, while it lasted, the one bright prospect for the future. They alone broke Falkland's gloom. It was only "when there was any overture . . . of peace" that he became once more "erect and vigorous." Inevitably he fell back into deeper depression when the bargaining led to nothing.

Sir Thomas Roe wrote to him in March: "This only I will lay, that if you must or shall make war successfully, you must set peace in the first rank, you must show that she is ravished from you, and your arms are only employed to rescue the beloved of all men." Roe yearned to have the King concede enough to make agreement possible, and wrote again, on April 6, that a group in London blamed Falkland for blocking the way to a settlement. Falkland's reply, delayed because of his bad health, said, "My desire of peace, and my opinion of the way to it agree wholly with yours, and I wish the second followed—but both sides must then contribute—that the first might be obtained." In other words, like Roe, he disliked strife, and hoped, like him, that concessions on both sides might end it. But by April 14, four days before Falkland's answer to Roe, the Parliament's commissioners had been recalled from Oxford, breaking off conferences which had gone on vainly for weeks. Parliament had agreed to ask for an armistice of twenty days, and Charles had had word of this on March 1. At the same time he had heard of his wife's safe return to England with munitions and funds. He promptly wrote her that the Parliament's proposals were too unreasonable to grant, and added, "The distractions of the rebels are such that so many fine designs are laid open to us we know not which first to undertake." On the 6th he told Parliament that the terms of the armistice did not provide for "freedom of trade," and asked that the ships defending the kingdom be put under officers of his choosing. He also insisted that while the truce lasted no one should be jailed except according to known laws. This provision sounded innocent, but actually struck at the

Parliament's attempts to collect taxes by imprisoning those who would not pay. Charles's message was taken in London as a virtual refusal of offers for peace. To give up both the fleet and the revenue from taxes would make his enemies helpless. Moreover, the King's letter to the Queen was captured and made public. His reference to "fine designs" was taken to mean that he was working underhandedly by plots the while he talked solemnly of conciliation. None the less the Houses persevered, and on March 18 sent fresh orders to their commissioners at Oxford. Charles liked the new proposals as little as the old, and still demanded, in effect, that the navy and the forts be turned over to him as a preliminary to negotiation. Thereupon Roe declared, "The last message of his Majesty hath utterly discomposed even all those who seriously pursued and grasped after the hopes of accommodation. They pretend to have no ground nor subject left them to continue their endeavours . . . Yielding . . . is often the true way to perfect victory."

The commissioners expected support, as did Roe, from Falkland. All the while that he was, as Secretary, working on the formal discussions, they privately used "all the means they could . . . in conferences with" him and Hyde to have Charles persuaded to meet them half way. Plainly Cary was known to want a settlement and the "peace party" had high hopes of him. Left to himself he would surely have put peace in the "first rank" and have been content to compromise generously in the interests of harmony.

But the King, elated by the thought of the fresh supplies brought by the Queen, and dictated to by her and her favorites as well as by soldiers of Rupert's stripe, was only half-hearted in his desire to make terms. What he really wanted was to starve his foes, and then to treat with them while they were too helpless to exact more than he cared to grant. Rashly he had promised his wife never to come to terms with the rebels without "her interposition and mediation." That vow guaranteed that he could never yield much. Inevitably he listened less and less to counsellors like Hyde and the others who honestly sought peace above all else. As for Falkland, his brusqueness to Charles, which came close to rudeness, was almost enough by itself to make his advice go unheard.

In February commissioners had come from Scotland to discuss the possibility of a treaty with the King. They were much concerned with religious issues, and presented "a long paper" attacking episcopacy and advocating Presbyterianism. Charles wanted to answer them in detail. Falkland, at the Council table, lost patience, and challenged some of the King's arguments "as not valid to support the subject." He spoke his mind with "quickness of wit, (as his notions were always sharp, and expressed with notable vivacity)." Charles grew hot, reproaching "all who were of" Falkland's "mind with want of affection for the church." Hyde smoothed things over, but Charles was not the man to approve completely a Secretary who disputed his ecclesiastical views and was so liberal in religion as to seem unorthodox. The Scottish commissioners got nowhere, and the angry scene with Falkland probably weakened Charles's faith in him.

The long winter at Oxford brought only further disappointment to Falkland. Peace was as far off as ever, and war as cruel. He was still a counsellor but his advice was least likely to be taken on the matters he cared for most. The Queen was coming, and he knew how little sympathy his opinions would have from her. He was sick, and weary. All that he had taught himself to care for most, was out of reach—reason, by which he had fondly dreamed that he might live, seemed illusory now. He had nothing else in which he could vigorously believe, and was thrown back upon what he could cobble together out of rudimentary feelings and acquired loyalties, out of fears and instinctive impulses. He was afraid of fanaticism and of social upheaval, whether he knew it or not; he kept, even in depression, his uneasy desire to prove his physical prowess; and, even though he could not justify it intellectually, he had not forgotten the conventional courtier's creed by which his father had lived. By it he could subsist, but it gave him no final respite from uncertainty.[3]

His stress of mind was no aid to clear thinking, and he, like other men in troubled times, blundered now and then. So he did in connection with an attempt to conquer London by a "fine design." Early in 1643 his friend, Sir Edmund Waller, had come to Oxford as one of the Parliament's commissioners. His head was buzzing with a great scheme by which the royal supporters in London and the lovers of peace might unite to put an end to the war. The result was "Waller's Plot." It may have been designed originally as a mere measure of passsive resistance on the part of those in London who hoped to stop bloodshed by withdrawing all support from the Houses, and this may have been all that Waller and Falkland talked about in Oxford. But at the same time there was formed a plan to bring about an armed rising in London, which, aided by a small force sent by Charles, might deliver the city and the Parliament into his hands. Hyde insists that the two projects were separate, and that Falkland was concerned only with the one for peaceful conquest. Pym, however, declared later that there was but one conspiracy, to be carried out by force, and maintained that Falkland managed the correspondence between Oxford and the schemers in the capital.

There can be no question that Falkland knew of the plan to organize in London opposition to Parliament, and that he

---

[3] "When the King threw his cap over the windmill and . . . Pym replied with open war, men had to choose their sides. They decided less by pure reason than by that instinctive form of reasoning based on subconscious and inherited opinions of the past which is known as temperament . . . Traditional loyalty to an acknowledged sovereign . . . the determination of the Church to stand . . . against the schismatics . . . pure passive conservatism which desired to see no violent change—all found their expression in the support of the Loyalist cause"; M. Woods, *History of the Tory Party in the Seventeenth and Eighteenth Centuries* (London, 1924), pp. 9–10.

did his best to aid. It is barely possible that he did not recognize that the design was linked with a plot for an armed revolt against the Houses, but if he did not he must have been singularly blind. In March the King had issued a Commission of Array, empowering Sir Nicholas Crisp and others to raise troops in London. In May this Commission, enclosed in a small box was sent to the city from Oxford, tied "about the thighs" of Falkland's friend, Lady D'Aubigny. According to Hyde she did not know what the box contained. Perhaps Falkland did not, but if he managed, all the time that "Waller's Plot" was hatching, to send and receive messages from those engaged in it in London, without seeing that more than peaceful resistance to Parliament was involved, the secret must have been extraordinarily well kept, or he so preoccupied with his own troubles that he was alert to nothing else. It seems far more probable, Hyde to the contrary, that he knew what was on foot, and thought the plot was a permissible act of war. So it was, perhaps, but it was utterly inconsistent with Falkland's assertion in November that he did not want to enter London by force. Perhaps since then he had come to believe that peace could be had only by bloodshed, and that the end justified the means. Even so, he was clutching at straws. The plot obviously ran grave risk of failure, and failure would, as the event proved, make matters worse.

The secret leaked out. Waller saved his skin by abjectly humbling himself before Parliament and by testifying volubly against his fellow plotters, two of whom were put to death. The whole shabby business increased hostility toward the King and deepened the general distrust of his honesty. Pym and his party came out of the affair with new solidarity. The friends of the King and lovers of peace were frightened and disorganized.

Such a result was the last thing Falkland wanted, and must have deepened his depression. He could blame himself for his part, however slight, in a scheme that instead of hastening

peace had delayed it. Moreover there was for him an agoniz-
ing twist of the knife in the wound when the full consequences
of the plot were known. Waller was in danger of his life, but
that could be endured since he had chosen to take the risk
and by his behavior afterward had left little room for sympathy. The men who died would presumably have met the
same fate even if Falkland had known nothing of their acts.
But his dear friend Lady Sophia Murray was also in the toils
and for that he could blame himself.

To her he had probably written often during the war, trying affectionately to bridge the gap between them while she
was in London and he in Oxford. Certainly during the maturing of "Waller's Plot" he sent her a letter in cipher, in which
he wrote that the Earl of Northumberland was on the side of
the conspirators. Waller had helped her to decode the letter
and had confessed. Along with Lady D'Aubigny, she was arrested and haled before the Parliament's Committee of Safety.
Lady D'Aubigny protested that she had known nothing of the
conspiracy; Lady Sophia simply refused to testify. She defied
the Committee, saying, "I do not mean to give an account to
such fellows as you are!" She would not implicate herself or
Falkland, and in spite of her "consumption" courageously
voiced her disdain for Parliament. She was threatened with a
court-martial, and committed to custody. She appeared before
the Committee on June 29; Falkland must have heard the
news soon afterward, and have begun to torture himself with
the thought that his indiscretion had brought into danger a
woman for whom he had, at the very least, "an extraordinary
esteem." No crime could have seemed baser to him. He had
been brought up to be chivalrous toward women, and he had
worshipped the ideal of friendship. His sense that he had betrayed Lady Sophia into the hands of her enemies was a
crowning grief added to a heavy load. Nor was there any relief
from it throughout the summer of 1643. She was a prisoner,

her health was bad, and captivity might well make it worse or even threaten her life.[4]

Even attempts at diversion worked out badly. There is a story that during his months at Oxford Falkland went one day with the king to the Bodleian Library, and suggested that they amuse themselves by trying to read the future in the pages of Virgil. It was an old superstitious device. A volume was to be opened at random, and the passage revealed was to be taken, with whatever interpretation was needed, as an oracle of events to come. Charles tried his hand and hit on lines which he had Abraham Cowley translate for him. They read:

> "By a bold peoples stubborn arms opprest,
> Forc'd to forsake the land which he possest
> . . . . let him in vain
> Seek help, and see his friends unjustly slain:
> Let him to bold unequall terms submitt,
> In hopes to save his crown, yet loose both it
> And Life at once."

The passage was already painfully pat, and its prophecy startling. According to the tale, Falkland also tried his own luck. He lighted on verses which Dryden later rendered:

> "Thou hast fail'd thy plighted Word,
> To fight with caution, not to tempt the Sword:
> I warn'd thee, but in vain, for well I knew,
> What Perils youthful Ardour would pursue:
> That boiling blood would carry thee too far;
> Young as thou wert in Dangers, raw to War!
> O curst essay of Arms, disastrous Doom,
> Prelude of bloody Fields, and Fights to come."

---

[4] Gardiner, *Great Civil War*, I, 158, says that after Lady Murray defied the committee "no further attempt was made to inflict any penalty" upon her. But S. H. Werlein, *op. cit.*, relying on *Journals of the House of Commons*, III, 228, shows she was still in custody on Sept. 5.

This might chill the most rational. It was all very well to shrug and say "Superstitious nonsense!" Such nonsense is potent in times of nervous strain. If the story of the visit to the Bodleian is true—and there seems to be no reason to reject it completely—neither Charles nor Falkland can have got much comfort from it.

Virgil's lines, whether or not Falkland actually hit on them at Oxford, were curiously true of him. "Youthful ardour," "boiling blood," "tempting the sword"—the phrases perfectly described one side of his character. Perhaps he was happiest now when it was uppermost, when he could drop all pretenses of "fighting with caution" and give himself up to the enjoyment of dangerous action. Thereby he could silence his too busy intellect, and abandon futile reasoning in the midst of a "curst essay," on the edge of "disastrous doom." If there were to be "bloody fields and fights," and there were sure to be, why not let "boiling blood" be his talisman?

The prophecy of continued war was made more certain by the Queen's arrival at Oxford. With her at court, intrigues were livelier than ever, and disagreements in the Council warmer and more frequent. Falkland went grimly on, doing his best to bring order out of chaos, still hoping against hope that folly might bow before reason, but it was a thankless task, and may have stimulated a suspicion that the only emotional solace he could hope for was in striking hard blows for the King on a bloody field.

That hope was hardly better than none. There were too many reminders of better things; too many proofs of the essential horror of war. On June 18, at Chalgrove Field, John Hampden's men met Rupert's, and Hampden was fatally wounded. A week later he died. There were plenty of Royalists who saw his death as "a great deliverance to the nation," but the Parliamentarians felt that "every honest man" had "a share in the losse, and . . . in the sorrowe," for Hampden had been "a gallant man, an honest man, an able man, and take all

. . . nott to any man liueinge second." Hardly more than a year earlier Falkland had admired him. Later he had swung round to doubt his wisdom in Parliament, and later still had been resentful of the arrogance with which Hampden treated him. But none the less, Hampden had been brave, and far worthier than many who outlived him. His fate was one more of the scalding ironies of war. There was even irony in the lines engraved on the setting of a carnelian, found on his body:

> "Against my King I never fight
> But for my King and Country's right."

Had Hampden believed that? Could Falkland believe it? Surely war had created an ugly paradox.

In his melancholy—a melancholy now patent to everyone —Falkland when with his friends did not hide his emotion, and after brooding silences would suddenly break in with "a shrill and sad accent" crying out "Peace, peace!" He could not sleep. "Passionately" he used to say that "the view of the calamities and desolation the kingdom did and must endure" —shades of Virgil!—"would shortly break his heart."

It was no remedy for a breaking heart to think of Lady Sophia Murray, coughing away her strength as a prisoner in London. It was no help to see Henry Jermyn, now Lord St. Albans—was he actually the Queen's lover?—and others of her favorites, using every art to please her and to influence the King. They behaved as if the Civil War were a game devised to display how gracefully courtiers could serve a royal mistress, and ranged themselves against advisers like Hyde, who thought less of intrigue than of law. To contend with the Queen's friends was like slaving in a treadmill. Falkland learned, like Thomas Fuller, the "affliction attending moderate men" who "have not an active party to side with them and favour them. Men of great stature will quickly be made porters to a king, and those diminutively little, dwarfs to a queen, whilst such who are of a middle height may get themselves masters where they can. The moderate man, eminent for no excess or extravagancy in his judgment, will have few patrons to protect, or persons to adhere unto him." Even if "the very work of moderation" was "the wages of moderation," it was hard to be content with that, when everyone squabbled or schemed in his own interests. The whole atmosphere seemed tainted.

In midsummer Falkland had to go with Charles to Bristol to patch up a dispute between the Marquis of Hertford and Prince Rupert. The Prince had captured the town, but Hertford, who disliked him, resented his acting alone in signing the articles for the surrender, and appointed Sir Ralph Hopton as governor without confiding in Rupert. The latter promptly asked the King to "bestow the government of that city, reduced by him, upon himself." Charles, ignorant of the quarrel, agreed. Then Hertford protested, and there was nothing to do but to travel to Bristol. With the King went the Duke of Richmond, and the three counsellors, Hyde, Colepeper, and Falkland. Those three stayed at Hyde's estate for a night in the course of their journey, and no doubt recalled the weeks in London when every evening they had met to talk and plan with far more optimism than was left them now.

At Bristol the difficulty with Rupert and Hertford was cleared up after a fashion. The Prince was given the governorship, but Hopton was made his second in command. Hertford was persuaded to go back to Oxford with Charles. But "whisperings or murmurings" continued, and there was still another disagreement to arbitrate, once more between Colepeper and Hyde. It was bad enough when generals bickered; it was worse when pacific counsellors fell out. Hyde, as Chancellor of the Exchequer, undertook to regulate the customs service of Bristol, "the only port of trade within the king's quarters." But he found that one Ashburnham, "a groom of the bedchamber . . . with the assistance and advice of sir John Colepeper" had taken charge "as a means to raise a present sum of money for . . . the army." Hyde was outraged. Falkland had to intercede again "and expostulated . . . with the king with some warmth," and even more fervently with Colepeper and Ashburnham. He accused them of "violation of the friendship they professed to" Hyde, "and an invasion of his office; which no man bears easily." Charles was shrewd enough to see that "mischief . . . would ensue" if there should be an apparent breach "amongst those he so entirely trusted," and he persuaded them to keep the semblance of harmony at least, even if there was actually "jealousy or coldness between" Hyde and Colepeper, as many believed there was.

Now if ever the King needed a united council. He had to make a critical decision as to his campaign. Things had been going well with his armies. Should he try to unite all his forces and take advantage of what seemed to be Parliament's confusion and discouragement by moving against London? Would it be safe? It might open the way for his enemies in the west, and it was by no means sure that the King's troops in that area would leave it. The Cornishmen who had served Charles well "were too much inclined to mutiny, and had expressed a peremptory aversion to . . . joining and marching with the King's army." And, as always, there were coupled with serious military considerations, petty pleas weighing down one scale or the other. If, for example, the armies were united against London, Prince Maurice, Rupert's brother, "could have been but a private colonel," though he now held high command in the west. Therefore Charles let him stay with the Earl of Carnarvon in Dorsetshire. Hertford was kept out of mischief in attendance on the King. He and Maurice could not get on, and "there were persons about them who would foment their" rancor. Moreover, Clarendon thought, Charles preferred to "reduce his people by the power of his army" rather "than by the persuasions of his Council," and saw that the Prince was more likely than Hertford to work for this. Hertford disapproved, but did not complain. Hyde, and presumably Falkland, regretted Charles's decision, and must have been disturbed once more by the extent to which personal animosities determined policy.

The next question was what to do with the troops that remained to march with the King. Should Charles stake everything on preparing an advance against London, eventually calling Newcastle and his army down from the north, and recalling Maurice and Carnarvon from the west to join in the essay? There was much to be said for the plan, and the Queen and her disciples favored it. But there were arguments on the other side. Carnarvon and Maurice were at odds. In the north, as well as in the west, the troops were reluctant to march out of their home counties. Worst of all, the town of Gloucester was in the hands of Parliament. If it remained so, while the King approached London, his armies might be threatened in the rear. It was decided, therefore, to march against it, partly on the ground that Massey, the governor of the town, seemed to be ready to turn his coat and surrender his garrison to Charles. Gossip has it that Falkland was largely responsible for the attempt on Gloucester, but there is no evidence that he was. Another story makes Colepeper the chief agent in persuading the King. Even Rupert, always on the side of swift action, seems to have been reconciled to delaying long enough to conquer Massey's stronghold, but many disagreed. Spencer wrote home from Oxford: "The King's sudden Resolution of going before *Glocester*, hath extreamely disappointed me, for when I went from *Bristow*, on *Munday* [August 7] . . . he was resolved to come hether this Day. . . . The King's Going to *Gloucester*, is in the Opinion of most very unadvised. I find the Queen is unsattisfied with it; so is all the People of Quality. I am not able to give you any Account, upon what Grounds the King took this Resolution." The only thing certain is that Charles, once again, had to act without united support.

Unfortunately, before he appeared at Gloucester, the Parliamentarians within the walls had the whip hand. Massey's

morale was strengthened, and he began active preparations
for defense. Gloucester was no longer likely to be an easy
prize. On August 10 the King drew up his army on a hill outside the walls, and sent a summons to the town, promising
pardon to its inhabitants if they would submit. If they would
not, they would compel him to use force. Two hours were allowed for an answer. Before the time was up a pair of citizens
returned with the royal messenger. They had "lean, pale,
sharp, and bald visages," "faces . . . strange and unusual." The
gayer of the courtiers tittered at their ridiculous "garb and
posture." Hyde's heart sank, for, he thought, "it was impossible such ambassadors should bring less than a defiance." In
other words they were clearly not well bred and looked like
Puritans—quite enough to identify them as hostile to the
King. "Without any circumstances of duty or good manners"
they piped up bravely "in a pert, shrill, undismayed accent"
and gave Charles "insolent and seditious answers" to all that
he asked. With them they brought a document from Massey,
the Mayor, and many of the townsfolk. It completely rejected
the King's summons. After delivering it the two messengers
put on their hats, adorned with orange ribbons, and marched
off without waiting to see how the sovereign received this
proof of Gloucester's mettle. The sight of the two angular
figures, proving themselves utterly ignorant of etiquette, and
turning their backs on the King as proudly as if they were
monarchs themselves, was too much for the courtiers. They
laughed openly, but in a few minutes the messengers were inside the town, and here and there "in the suburbs" smoke
began to rise, then flames, and soon the watching royalists
saw Gloucester ringed by blazing buildings. It was plain that
Massey expected a siege and was taking the precaution of
destroying all that he could not defend. This was serious. The
courtiers put on sober faces. If the town resisted, it would
take time to capture it. To lose time was to give Essex more
opportunity to block the march on London. Yet the King,

after his manifesto, could not leave Gloucester unsubdued without making himself a laughing-stock.

"The soldiers of the best experience" trotted off for a reconnaissance and told the King "that they should be able in less than ten days . . . to win" the town. The council of war was unanimous in its advice to try. The decision was a boon to Pym. The taking of Bristol had dismayed Parliament, and the House of Lords had seized the occasion to suggest new projects for ending hostilities. But the violent party had prevailed once more, and now that the King's halt at Gloucester gave time, worked to strengthen their armies. Many of the Lords who most favored a treaty decided they could do nothing more, and set out to join Charles. The Earl of Portland and Lord Lovelace came directly to him as, soon after, did Lord Conway. The Earl of Clare hesitated in Worcestershire until he was sure that the King would receive him. The Queen's erstwhile favorite, the Earl of Holland, with the Earl of Bedford, got as far as Wallingford where they were stopped by the royal garrison.

The Queen, thoroughly annoyed by the delay at Gloucester, set the tone for the counsellors at Oxford. They were far enough from the army to be sanguine about its success if it only would push on, and, snug at the University, they believed that the royalists' triumph at Bristol had at last given them the upper hand. Charles had to ride over from Gloucester to decide how the Earls of Holland and Bedford should be treated, and found the court uncompromising. The Queen hated the idea of tolerating traitors to whom she had once been kind, and when the Council met, only Hyde and one other had a word to say for the repentant Earls. The rest were for turning them scornfully away. No doubt Hyde was right in urging that if they were kindly received, more might follow their example and return to the King, but in the Council prejudice and feeling carried the day. Torn between his respect for Hyde and his desire to please his wife and her friends,

Charles pleased nobody. The Earls were admitted to Oxford, but were snubbed by the courtiers, and on the 18th, the day after the King went back to the siege, they set out after him, hoping more from his favor than from a circle in which the Queen was supreme. At Gloucester even Rupert was agreeable, and Charles was at least polite to Clare, Bedford and Holland. The first two adapted themselves meekly to the royal entourage, but Holland would be content with nothing less than a court office, and was ridiculed for his pains. Even during a siege, when every wasted hour counted against the King, ambition and vanity bred discord among those whose only hope was harmony.

Hyde remained in Oxford, while Falkland, at Gloucester, had his first taste of trench warfare. Ugly as it was, it distracted him from the inanities of futile negotiations and the constant reminders that Charles was threatened, if not doomed, by the pettiness of his officers and counsellors. Falkland threw himself into fighting as if it were a sport in which the risks were part of the fun. His daring smacked of desperation. Hyde was worried by the reports he got. He wrote his friend, protesting against "the daringness of his spirit," a "daringness" that suggested readiness to throw life away. Hyde was not alone. Others "reprehended" Falkland "for exposing his person unnecessarily to danger, (as he delighted to visit the trenches and nearest approaches, and to discover what the enemy did)," and told him that it was his duty as Secretary to be less foolhardy. But he replied "merrily," masking his real feeling, that "his office could not take away the privileges of his age"— he was thirty-three—"and that a Secretary in war might be present at the greatest secret of danger." More seriously he added that his known love of peace made it necessary for him to "be more active in enterprizes of hazard than other men, that all might see that his impatiency for peace proceeded not from . . . fear." This was part of the truth certainly; more of it was implicit in his writing to Hyde "some melancholic things of the time." The hopelessness of his mood made him set a low price on life.

That mood was broken now and then, no doubt. It must have been pleasant to see William Davenant again, when the poet at last found his way to Gloucester. Better still was Chillingworth's companionship. He had changed rôles, and from being a divine and an expounder of rational religion, had become an amateur engineer. He could forget the intellectual misgivings raised by the chaotic times in the "Diligence and Satisfaction" with which he devoted himself to the construction of "sundry imperfect, chargeable and troublesom Engines to assault the lower part of" the besieged town. Chillingworth got his idea for them from reading of Roman war machines. In one way at least, perhaps in only one, could scholarship be of use in war. How could Falkland turn to account his delvings in church history, or his confident conclusions against claims to religious infallibility, in a struggle in which both sides virtually professed to be infallible, and no one wanted to stop fighting long enough to debate theology?

No one, that is, except a few chosen spirits. Chillingworth was one, of course, and Henry Spencer another. At the latter's quarters, a "little private Cottage," he entertained Falkland and Chillingworth at supper one night during the siege. For one evening they reverted to the ways of Great Tew, and disputed busily about "Socinianism." Apparently Chillingworth took the extreme rational position, and although he probably did not argue for Socinian heresy, in the strict sense, he pressed the claims of reason over faith farther than Falkland would allow. In the midst of the confusion of war and the wreckage of his confidence in the supremacy of intellectual principles, it was important to cherish any loyalty that survived. One such, for Falkland, was to the Church of England. He still thought that it might express the nobility of Protestantism and that even as it stood it was the best shield against the Puritans' narrow dogmas. If Chillingworth's talk challenged the essentials of Anglicanism—and his cool logic easily ran into that—Falkland must combat him. Spencer, who listened, felt that the Viscount, not the engineer, had the best of the argument.

Such retreats into theorizing helped to make the siege bearable. But if there was at times "much good Company," there were also "the Noise and Tintamarre of Guns and Drums," and "horrid Spectacles." Men were injured by missiles thrown from the walls. Englishmen bled to death on English soil. The English countryside reeked with carnage. The ears of anyone who ventured into the trenches were assaulted by the "hideous Crys of . . . hurt Men." There was loneliness, too—Spencer said he was more solitary than ever before in his life. The officers lived in cottages scattered about the country near Gloucester, and to go back to one of them at night was to be wrapped in silence almost as oppressive as the din before the town. The farmhouses, the smoke rising white from kitchen chimneys, the scent of the fields at sunset, were unchanged by war. As Spencer put it, there were almost within sight of Gloucester, all "the Marks of Peace."

The marks of peace! For men tired of battle they were the landmarks of memory. They made Spencer think back, longing for Penshurst; Falkland must have dreamed of Great Tew. Memories could be bitter, and the present corrupted the past. Falkland could not forget all that had happened since he flew his hawk in the fields outside Dublin, marvelled at Ben Jonson's wit, proudly displayed his bride at the court of Elizabeth of Bohemia, or talked gaily at his crowded dinner table at Great Tew. Then he had been happy, sure of his "own private sense," fancying he saw "the Sun at noon." But it had brought neither heat nor light, and he had been left still "wintred and frozen" in "the wayes of" barren "understanding." Faith was shaken, and happiness had fled.

Both his father and mother had lived by faith. Sir Henry had not thought much about his, but had managed to keep his assurance that to observe the forms of devotion to his sovereign and to profit from them when he could, gave a sufficient excuse for life. Lady Elizabeth had found in her church the answer to all her riddles, and had served it unterrified by the world. Had Falkland been able to accept his father's values, he might have become, as he once hoped to, a courtier and soldier, able to take part even in a civil war without uneasy speculations as to final verities. Or had he been able, like his mother, to accept once and for all a revelation too lofty to be threatened by the mind, he might have won content, even in 1643, as a fanatic fighting for his creed or as a retired saint dazzled by a vision of eternal reality that eclipsed the ephemeral day dreams of his more sordid fellow men. But, defeated in his hopes of following in his father's steps, and prevented from feeling as his mother did, partly because she outraged his father and partly because his generation grew up among challenges to unthinking credence, he had tried to make his own way as a scholar, schooling himself to believe that in learning, free discussion, and the sanctity of intellect, was the one sesame to truth. His creed had called for moderation, tolerance, and charity for other men's ideas. It had refined and enriched his temper; it had developed his talent for friendship. It had given him for a few years the joy of faith— faith in what the English church might become, faith in essential Protestantism, faith that reason, God's gift to man, could make man worthy of God. Living by that he had dedicated himself to friendship, honor, justice, and cardinal Christianity, unafraid. Minor doubts had then been easy to brush aside. What if now and then he did have to distrust the King? What if he was himself occasionally unjustly dealt with? What if the Scottish campaign proved how silly men could be? There were reasonable heads enough to turn the scale, and for a few months in Parliament he had been sure that in politics they could make their dreams come true. He had rejoiced in the vision of an England governed by reason embodied in law;

of an Anglican establishment rooted in learning, tolerance, and the precepts of Christ.

Then the whole structure had collapsed. Not reason but passion had prevailed in Parliament. Blind fanaticism, unthinking loyalties, selfishness, fear, and vanity, had swept the board. The successful man seemed but the

> "Savage Beast, whose mind
> From Reason to self-Love declin'd,
> Delights to prey upon his Kind."

Honesty was sacrificed for political effect; tolerance was forgotten in strife; battles left no time for books. He had been suspected as an enemy of the church he adored, first by the Archbishop and then by the King. He had been mocked for his scrupulous morality. He had been called a coward because he loved peace, and had been ignored because he thought clear thinking should precede action. Clinging still to his faith, he had been beaten at every turn. His principles had forced him to be sceptical, to weigh the evidence, to seek painfully for the right decision before he made any, and thence had swarmed doubts—of the King, of the courtiers, of the wisdom of war, of the power of reason to rescue an anguished England, doubts even of himself. Had he been wrong in his faith? Could men be rational only in laboratories, dealing with senseless clay, or in studies, proving out of books that reason was as potent as faith? The mind could work only from premises, and in the affairs of men what premises were valid? How carry the light of the intellect deep enough into a welter of instincts, habits, and emotions, to reveal anything from which deductions could honestly be made? The royalists might prate of reason, but so did their foes. So did all men who were eager to mask self-interest under a kinder name. Did even Falkland's own thinking start from axioms that were quite secure? Did not his loyalty to his class, his misunderstanding of the less fortunate, and his ignorance of impulses he had never felt and faiths he had never worshipped, account for most of the conclusions that he believed he reached by reason? If so, what of his opponents, who, starting from different data, thought their way to other ends? What of those who made no pretense of being rational but lived frankly by emotion and faith? They might be blind, but they did at least live confidently, blessedly sure of themselves. Even if wedded to folly they were spared his troubled days and sleepless nights.

No doubt he never fully faced all these questions, but some of them must have cropped up when the "marks of peace" drove his thoughts back to better times. He was not superhuman and was as helpless as most men to diagnose his own disease. But some of its causes were too obvious to ignore. One hope after another had been thwarted; hope for Parliament, hope for a triumph of truth in church and state, hope that Charles might yield to sober counsel—hope for peace. His intellectual creed had gone far to make him helpless before those whose beliefs crowded out thought. Perhaps he could still learn from them. He might surrender to instinct and emotion. He might teach himself to fight for the joy of fighting. That would satisfy part of his nature, and by bravery he could honor the memory of Henry Morison and of his father. The more defiantly he risked his life the less time there would be to reflect on what he had made of it. If in risking it, he lost it, that might be best of all. Death might offer the one victory still within his reach; it might be the only cure for the torture of incertitude.

Some cure he sorely needed. The siege dragged on, and every day it lasted weakened the King. Essex was at the head of an army commissioned to relieve Gloucester, and whether or not he succeeded he could still hold the road to London. Nor was this the worst news that came for Falkland from the city. There were tidings of Lady Sophia Murray. She was still "in custody" and her health was failing fast. On September

5, perhaps out of compassion for her sickness, Parliament voted to set her free, provided that she left London and promised not to return. By the time Falkland heard this, he must have heard that she was in the last stages of her disease. She was apparently too weak to be moved even as far as Oxford where her friends were, and where Falkland might have seen her once more. The thought of her plight was torture to him. Largely because of his act she had been kept to face death as a prisoner. He could not now defend himself by logic; his emotions were too deeply stirred. For once feeling was all—a remorseful agony not long to be borne.

The night of September 4 had been stormy. Above the roar of the wind the sound of cannon rolled over the countryside near Prestbury Hill, not far from Gloucester. The townsfolk did not hear it, but it was the signal for their relief. Essex was at hand. The next morning the King's army gave up the siege. The royalists had no means of knowing how near surrender the town was. There were only three barrels of powder left within the walls. But, in ignorance of this, Charles's officers acted wisely in deciding to move. Away from the town his cavalry could operate, and Essex was a long way from his base in London. By taking a strong position the King might cut off his retreat and wipe out his force. Thus, on the day when Parliament agreed to release Lady Sophia, Falkland left Gloucester and began a march that he knew must soon lead to a critical—perhaps even a final—struggle.

Essex entered Gloucester on the 8th. On the day before, Charles had installed himself at Sudley Castle, commanding the road by which Essex had come. On the 11th the Parliamentarians were in Tewkesbury. For several days both armies jockeyed for position, but on the 15th Essex struck boldly southward, captured a store of royal provisions in Cirencester, and marched on to the southwest, toward the London road leading through Newbury. On the 18th Rupert was in time to head him off at Aldbourn Chase, and that night the King spent at Newbury. Essex must fight his way past him if he was to get to London. Everyone realized on the 19th that the morrow would bring battle.

According to tradition Falkland slept that night in the house of Mr. Head in Cheap Street, Newbury. Recent news from London must have told him that Lady Sophia was now on the point of death. She succumbed finally on the 20th, but well before that her case must have been called hopeless.[5] Grief for her overwhelmed Falkland. He prepared for the fight at Newbury like a man despairing of life. During the long months of war he had become increasingly careless of his dress, but this morning he called for clean linen. He declared that he was weary of the times but would "be out of it ere night." Hyde loyally supposed this meant he was sure that the war would end with a victory at Newbury; others, twenty-four hours later, looked back on the words as Falkland's vow to end his misery by death.

He took communion from Doctor Twisse, the rector of Newbury, and then rode out to take his place with Sir John Byron's cavalry on the right of the royal line. They faced a slope, broken by hedges, held by the Parliamentary left. Sir Nicholas Byron led his brigade of foot to drive the enemy out. Of twelve ensigns in one infantry regiment "eleven were brought off the field hurt." The task was too great and the soldiers began to shout, "Horse! Horse!" Sir John rode up with his two cavalry regiments, and halted them while he looked over the ground.

His advance was blocked by "a high quick hedge" with "no passage into it, but by a narrow gap." There was hot fighting all about, but the Parliament's troops were holding their own and commanded the opening in the hedge. Cavalry attempt-

---

[5] *Journals of the House of Commons*, III, 249. Clarendon says that Lady Murray "died the same day, and, as some computed it, in the same hour that" Falkland "was killed"; Clarendon, *Life*, I, 202.

ing to ride through must straggle out in single file, a perfect target for gunfire. Byron saw that unless the breach could be widened or Essex's musketeers dislodged, a charge would be suicide. He kept his men back, but as they reined in their horses, one officer broke suddenly forward, like a hawk slipped by its keeper, and spurred directly into the gap. The horse plunged, stumbled, and fell with thrashing hooves. As it came down, its rider threw up his hands convulsively, and then slumped in the saddle as if crushed beneath an intolerable weight. A few minutes later when the opening in the hedge had been enlarged, the rest of Byron's men swept through, but Falkland lay beside the fallen horse, shot through the stomach. He had died "as much of the time as of the bullet."

That night the mist which had often typified for him the forces that hid the light of truth, lay cold and white over the battlefield. Through it, as in their element, moved dark shapes, and when Falkland's body was found the next day, it had been stripped bare by the vandals who had been the first attendants upon fallen reason. The corpse, "trod-upon, and mangled" could only be identified by a servant who recognized a mole on his master's neck.

The news of his friend's fate brought desolation to Sir Edward Hyde. For him, as for Swift later, it "moved grief to the highest excess." Nor was Hyde the only man at Oxford to mourn. Wherever there were lovers of peace and advocates of moderation, Falkland's fall seemed the loss of a leader, who had gallantly though vainly done his best to turn the cruel tide of passion.

Lucius Cary's small body was reverently brought off the bloody field of Newbury on the back of one of the King's own chargers, and was carried home to Lady Lettice, to be buried in the little church at Great Tew. His grave was very near the house in which he had for a few precious years joined other men, as serious and as honest as he, in worship of the authority of reason. There he had tasted the only freedom from conflict he had ever known, briefly secured from doubt by faith in the omnipotence of truth.

But in 1643 there was no peace. The echoes of war carried even to Great Tew. Newbury had cost many lives besides Falkland's—Spencer's for one—and Charles had been beaten again. Falkland had found the way to be "out of it ere night," but England still bled. Armies marched and countermarched; courtiers intrigued; politicians schemed; fanatics ranted; and maddened Englishmen butchered their countrymen. Widows sorrowed and villagers stared bitterly at burned houses and ruined crops. Victory was as tragic as defeat; peace came only with exhaustion. Passion and greed sat at every campfire, but the glorious vision which Falkland had evoked and had named Reason, was shunned like an unclean ghost, a will-o'-the-wisp flickering down the pathway to despair.

IX

"A VERY PROFANE WIT"

John Wilmot, Earl of Rochester, 1647-1680

LATE in July, thirty-seven years after the first battle of Newbury, John Wilmot, Earl of Rochester, lay dying in the Ranger's Lodge at Woodstock Park. He was only thirty-four, but was aged before his time. In his last painful hours, if he had kept anything of his old taste for the ironies of life, he might have smiled to see about his bed not the profligate wits he had known best, not Etherege, Sedley, Buckhurst, or Buckingham, not Mrs. Barry or any other of his mistresses, but the neglected wife of his bosom and the servants of his household, down to "the piggard-boy." At times there were even two divines—Bishop Burnet, grave, earnest and worldly, but with a worldliness far from the Earl's; and Robert Parsons, his mother's chaplain, an honest man without one tenth of the mental strength of his dying patron.

But probably Wilmot could not smile. If he remembered at all his old companions, loves, and victims, it must have been as spectres, ominous reminders of his long roll of sins. It was better not to think of them. Perhaps he could comfort himself by reflecting that to his son, at least, he had given pious advice; that to his wife he had shown a veneer of devotion even when he was most unfaithful; and that his friend, Henry Savile, and possibly a handful of others, would mourn him with unfeigned tears. If he could fix his mind on these things, he might shut out torturing thoughts of the two men whose deaths he had helped to cause, might ignore the picture of John Dryden lying on the stones of Rose Alley, bleeding from the blows of Rochester's hired ruffians. The portents of wrath to come were agonizingly real to him now, and he was helpless to exorcise them. The time had passed for mockery. It was too late to make all go with a shrug and a sneer, or a new satire. Rochester was no longer the merry sinner, but the pious convert; no longer the scorner of the church, but the candidate for salvation, pitifully laden with sins. Burnet and Parsons were no longer canting clerics, but keepers of the keys of Paradise. Pain, disease and mental conflict had done their work. His world had turned topsy-turvy. In the wreck his old arts could not save him. Wit was vain. His wooer's tongue, once so glib, was now thick with fear. Scepticism was the worst of attitudes. Nothing was left except his need to believe, to pray, to repent. It was only after leaving to the bishop and the parson a full recantation of his evil tenets, and after pleading that his writings and his collection of obscene pictures be burned, that the once reigning wit, the favorite of the court, the terror of the godly, dared to die.

He was in most ways as unlike Falkland as a man could be. Falkland had died heroically in battle, worsted in a life-long effort to turn lofty principles into action. He had constructed standards of honesty, moderation, and nobility out of his faith in a divine law of reason, which, once seen and followed, would enable man to live worthily beyond the claims of mere sense and emotion, proof against the deceitful goads of passion. Falkland failed, but not because he had been lax in striving. The pursuit of truth led him to throw life away, not because he lacked devotion in the quest, but because the goal was too far beyond actual desires and material needs of men, and because his reverence for the rational brought intellectual doubts that crippled action. Rochester began with different premises. He took life in its most obvious terms, sure about sensation and about little else. If Falkland was noble in deed, Rochester was base; what Falkland revered, Wilmot mocked.

Yet underneath there were likenesses. There were those who called Rochester a "fair soul" and "a hero." He was named "absolutely Lord of Wit," and Sir Francis Fane said that whenever he talked to him "he found himself not only a better poet, a better philosopher, but much more than these, a better Christian," because in the Earl's "*miraculous* wit and intellectual powers" was an incontrovertible proof of the immortality of the soul! The same things had been said of Falkland. The words had changed their meaning somewhat since 1643, and "wit" in Rochester's day was not quite the "wit" that rejoiced Falkland's guests at Great Tew, but both men were intellectuals, both thought more than was consistent with their happiness, and both, however little Rochester realized it, were consumed by longing for some sufficing faith. Falkland thought he found one, and tried to live by it, only to have its futility disastrously proved. Rochester worshipped at a different altar, found himself deceived, and began a fresh search in the last troubled months of his life. The aspiration was the same in both men—the same that a half-century earlier had driven Elizabeth Cary to evade rational riddles in submission to Rome.

Even John Evelyn, little as he liked rakes, saw that Wilmot had a mind. Dining one day with "My Lord Treasurer," his fellow guest was, he says, "My lord Rochester, a very profane wit." Very profane, surely, but as surely a wit—and a wit not merely as wits went in London of the 1670's but in the sense which passes current whenever men praise intellect. To be sure, he veiled his quality from all but those who knew him best. Those Englishmen who heard of him at all, during his short life, were most apt to hear of him simply as a creature of vice. Even in London, outside the limits of the court, there can have been few who thought of him except as the perfect pattern of well-bred debauchery.

It was in London, where Evelyn met him, that Rochester flourished. True, he loved his lodge at Woodstock, a few miles from Great Tew, and he had its walls adorned with pictures that must have shocked staid Gilbert Burnet. He was granted the house in the face of counter claims by Lord Lovelace, and whiled away much time in the exercise of his nominal duties as Ranger of Woodstock Park. His more famous exploits, however, took place elsewhere. There was Newmarket, which he frequented apparently only because the court was as dissipated there as in town. He visited and wrote of Tunbridge Wells, but called it:

"The Rendezvouze of Fools, Buffons and Praters,
Cuckolds, Whores, Citizens, their Wives and Daughters."

But it was London, and in London the court, the playhouse, the tavern, or the brothel, that spurred him to the deeds which have brought obloquy to his memory, albeit special lustre to his repentance. There he made himself famous—or infamous; it was about his London adventures that contemporary gossip was most explicit.

There, too, he proved his wit. The foibles of his fellow poets and playwrights, the inanities and viciousness of the court, Charles II's mistresses, and even royal Charles himself, were targets for his satires. Most of them reek of spite, and any nobler motive is usually far to seek. He seems to have found in London little to elevate his thoughts, little that inspired his Muse to anything but savagely coarse abuse, or lyrics in which lewdness is adorned with melody and grace of phrase. But there was no hiding his intelligence, and even those who smarted under his lashing couplets had grudgingly to admire his skilful brain.

It was his body, though, not his brain, that was most talked about. Samuel Pepys, in 1668, went to Whitehall and "saw all the ladies, and heard the silly discourse of the King, with his people about him, telling a story of my Lord Rochester's having of his clothes stole, while he was with a wench; and his gold all gone, but his clothes found afterwards stuffed into a feather bed by the wench that stole them." The Rochester of this note appears elsewhere in Pepys's diary, and was the Rochester most commonly spoken of in the "silly discourse" of the King and court. Because he did not write sober tracts on theology, or labor over grave speeches in Parliament, as Falkland had; because he had replaced Falkland's chivalry and sobriety of conduct by a picturesquely passionate interest in wenches or any other means of grasping sensual delight, it was easy to forget that, like Falkland, he was a wit, and that he had a better side than Pepys could comprehend.

Perhaps the better side was saved for the country—Aubrey maintained that there "he was generally civill enough." Surely the poor Earl spoke truly when he used to say that whenever he got as far as Brentford on his way to town "the devill entred into him and never left him till he came into the country again." Possibly in his house at Adderbury or the lodge at Woodstock he might meditate and study as gravely as Falkland at Great Tew, but he derived no principle strong enough to resist the teasings of sense. Once in the city, women, and the physical joys he could command of them; the bottle and the gaiety it provoked—perhaps even the temporary oblivion it brought—offered quick rewards. Bodily pleasure was good, and he knew how to get it. There was a sure premise for action. What if other premises were less secure, what if his mind restlessly wandered off to ponder values not measurable in terms of sense? He could always muffle its questionings in drunkenness, in his ecstasies with his newest mistress, or in the exhaustion that followed on a long debauch. As much as Falkland, perhaps, he wanted to be rational, but to be rational involved proceeding logically from valid axioms. Rochester came quickly to doubt the validity of anything his body could not feel.

At first his body served him well. He came to court in 1665, "a Graceful and well shaped" boy of seventeen, "tall . . . a little too slender," of "a very faire, cleare rosie complexion." He was both handsome and "exactly well bred, modest in behavior, of an easy natural civility," and Graces rather than devils seemed most likely to be his attendant spirits. "His Conversation was easie and obliging," but even as a boy "he had a strange Vivacity of thought, and vigour of expression." His wit had a "subtility and sublimity both, that were scarce imitable." Such traits recommended him at once to the gay lords and light ladies at Whitehall, and they took him to their hearts the more readily because his blood was good, and his training what the standards of his class required.

He had been born at Ditchley in Oxfordshire, on April 1, 1647. His mother, Anne St. John, had married first Sir Henry Lee, who was a connection of Lucius Cary's mother and had inherited estates from her great-uncle, an elder Sir Henry.[1] Lady Lee, after the death of her husband, went on living at Ditchley, and sheltered Edward Hyde there, after he left Falkland in London on his way to York with Chillingworth in 1642. Later, Sir Henry Wilmot, under whom Falkland fought his first battle, married her, and John Wilmot was their first child. The elder Wilmot, though reluctant to risk his life at Edgehill, atoned by helping Charles II to escape after his defeat at Worcester. He was rewarded with an earldom in 1652. He died in 1658 when John, the heir to his title, was almost

---

[1] J. Hayward, ed., *Collected Works of John Wilmot, Earl of Rochester* (London, 1926) p. li. says Rochester came to court in 1664, but V. De Sola Pinto, *Rochester, Portrait of a Restoration Poet* (London, 1935) p. 43, fixes the date as the spring of 1665. J. Prinz, *John Wilmot, Earl of Rochester, His Life and Writings* (Leipzig, 1927) p. 22, gives the date of the Earl's birth as April 10, but I follow De Sola Pinto (pp. 3; 271, note 7) who has April 1, relying on J. Gadbury, *Ephemeris* (London, 1698).

eleven. The boy grew up in the same countryside that Falkland knew in his childhood, and went to school at Burford, where Lucius Cary was born and lived before 1622 with the Tanfields. So far as it was possible in a politically changed England, John Wilmot was brought up as courtiers' sons had been for generations. He had his private tutors, as well as the Burford school, and must have been taught to reverence the crown and distrust the Puritans, to reckon worth in terms of rank and property, and to think and act accordingly. He went to Oxford in 1660, and while there wrote two poems, one celebrating the arrival of Charles II and the return of monarchy to England, and the other mourning the death of the Princess of Orange. In the former he said:

> "Forgive this distant Homage, which does meet
> Your blest approach on sedentary feet:
> And though my Youth, not patient yet to bear
> The weight of Arms, denies me to appear
> In steel before you, yet, Great SIR, approve
> My Manly Wishes, and more vigorous Love;
> In whom a cold Respect were Treason to
> A Fathers Ashes, greater than to You;
> Whose one Ambition 'tis for to be known
> By daring Loyalty your *Wilmot's* Son."

Looking back on the Civil War he saw in it "traiterous Mischief" and a "Black Design" by Charles I's enemies. This was the same language that Henry Cary, first Viscount Falkland, had used; the same that his son, Lucius, Sir Henry Wilmot, Sir Edward Hyde, and all loyal royalists had repeated for years. Charles II was a king hedged about by restraints unknown in his father's heyday, and the courtiers were no longer as powerful as they once had been, but the old phrases and the old willingness to let words determine behavior, still marked the sons whom the faithful supporters of the Stuarts had tutored in their creed.

That creed, of course, John Wilmot knew by heart, but the old elements in it were now mixed with new. For one thing it had come to be a sign of breeding to despise the moral strictness, which the Puritans had professed. For another, the more intellectual cavaliers were now priding themselves on being reasonable, with different definitions than Falkland had recognized. There had been much uproar about "patriotism," "liberty," and "true religion," during the Civil War and the troubled years that followed. Talk of ideals, of faith, of immutable and transcendent laws, had been rife, and all the while the friends of Charles I had been in exile or under a cloud at home. The whole period had been exhausting, and now that loyal families were again in the sunshine of a king's favor they tended to be contemptuous of idealisms, to be cynical about theories, to be wary of abstract doctrine, and to give up speculating about higher values, content with the tangible blessings accessible to those who had titles and wealth. For all Falkland's devout instincts, his rationalism had worked to lessen the place of revelation and faith, and, consequently, of emotion, in religion. The fiery exaltation of Donne's sermons and the mystic yearnings of the "metaphysical poets," were being supplanted by the lucubrations of even-tempered and cool-headed preachers and versifiers, who thought of morality in terms of concrete conduct and of faith not as a reaching toward mystery but as a tranquil acceptance of such Christian tenets as appealed to men of the world. In a day when science seemed to be offering more and more certainties, scepticism weighted the scales in favor of observable data rather than divine revelation. Thomas Hobbes had written trenchantly to prove that only material measures were valid, that man was a selfish animal, that "spirit" and "faith" and "religious feeling," in the old senses of the words, were unworthy of a sensible being. To be sure, habits were hard to stamp out, and many thoughtful men still tried to conceive of the world in a way that gave scientifically acceptable data their proper place but reserved room for notions of a divinely ordained, unifying principle, above the surface manifestations of life. Probably even the young Earl of Rochester started with such ideas.

If so, he did not puzzle himself unduly about them while he was at Oxford, and showed there signs of readiness to enjoy life as it came without worrying as to what ineffable meaning might lie behind it. It was pleasant to be a nobleman's son at the University; it was pleasant to know that by virtue of his family he was looked upon kindly by the great. Charles II must have taken his youthful verses as grateful incense, auguring well for a monarch who suspected he might need just such "daring loyalty" as the elder Earl of Rochester had offered to his father and himself. It was natural that when, in September, 1661, Oxford conferred a degree upon young Wilmot, hopeful scion of a faithful family, Sir Edward Hyde, now Earl of Clarendon, went beyond his formal duties as Chancellor of the University, and kissed the fourteen-year-old student on the left cheek "very affectionately" as he awarded him his academic honors.

Fresh from this tribute to his deserts, Wilmot set out to finish his education by travel, especially in Italy. On the journey he succumbed to what he called the "tricks" of Dr. Balfour, his travelling companion and tutor. The crafty Scottish physician knew how to appeal to his protégé's mind, and "drew him to read such Books, as were most likely to bring him back to love Learning and Study." He taught Wilmot to delight in reading, a lesson he never quite forgot. At court the youthful Earl was supposed to have "a thorough acquaintance with all Classick Authors," "a thing very rare (if not peculiar to him) among those of his quality."

Now John Evelyn was old enough and wise enough to see that Charles II's circle at Whitehall was no place for a scholar or a moralist. After a busy day in town, marked by an abundance of "spirituous drinks, as punch, etc." and some "incomparably good" canary, and after seeing given before his Majesty "a lewd play," he gladly "came home to be private a little, not at all affecting the life and hurry of the court." Falkland had early in his career come to very much the same opinion of the tamer gaieties of Charles I's palace, and had retreated to the country. Not so John Wilmot. If he was temperate in 1665, he was temperate by the exercise of will. Dined and fêted in London, he found restraint irksome and was bored by what he remembered of Dr. Balfour's precepts. Very soon he became one for whom the presence of incomparable canary was no argument for leaving town. In a crush of "jolly blades racing, dancing, feasting, and revelling, more resembling a luxurious and abandoned rout, than a Christian Court," he lingered happily, basking in the warmth of his welcome. Wine loosed his tongue, and his love of excitement flew away with his prudence.

It was well enough that he should fall in love with Elizabeth Malet, a Somersetshire heiress, but when the King's intercession failed to win her family's consent to her marriage with Wilmot, already a royal favorite, his rashness startled the most seasoned habitués of Whitehall. On May 28, 1665, Pepys told Lady Sandwich "a story of my Lord Rochester's running away on Friday night last with Mrs. Mallett, the great beauty and fortune of the North." She had supped at court with Mrs. Stewart, and set out for home in her coach, escorted by her grandfather, Lord Hawley, Gentleman of the Bedchamber to the Duke of York. At Charing Cross there was a sudden din in the street, and the horses were sharply pulled up. The carriage was surrounded by armed riders. The heiress was unceremoniously pulled out. Hawley watched helplessly while she was thrust into another coach drawn up beside them. Her grandfather had a glimpse of her seated between two women, before, with a clatter of hooves, horses, coach, heiress and all, disappeared into the darkness.

Poor Hawley hurried furiously back to Whitehall to tell his story. The King was "mighty angry," guessing at once, as

they got pleasure, and no amount of conjecturing about higher goods proved to his senses that such goods existed.

In this frame of mind he devoted himself to recapturing Elizabeth Malet. He married her in January, 1667, and afterward, as Gentleman of the Royal Bedchamber, holder of a captaincy of horse, Gamekeeper for Oxfordshire, and a peer of the realm, went his way not at all hampered by matrimony. Married or not, he could be witty and reckless, and love and drink like the gayest bachelor, measuring good and evil by physical pleasure or pain. The pleasures need not always be obvious. It was often pleasant to do anything that made him feel powerful, or more clever or daring than others; it was fun to be notorious; fun to shock the respectable, horrify the pious, and make the vicious envious of his greater proficiency in vice.

In January, 1669, Lady Sunderland wrote to Martha Giffard: "This has been a very quarrelsome week, before the King my Ld. of Rochester forgot his dutye so much as to strike Tome Keeligrew, he was in a case not to know what he did but he is forbid the court." There had been a dinner at the Dutch Ambassador's, where the King and his company "drank, and were pretty merry." "There," said Pepys, "was that worthy fellow my lord of Rochester." Killigrew, a seasoned dramatist, and for years a pet of the King, was there too, full of "mirth and raillery." His talk offended Wilmot, who, regardless of Charles's presence, boxed his ears. This did "much give offense to the people . . . at Court, to see how cheap the King" made himself. Pepys, noticing that Charles, only a few weeks later, "did publickly walk up and down" with Rochester, "as free as ever," remarked that it was "to the King's everlasting shame" to be intimate with "so idle a rogue." In fact, the sovereign, still in his thirties, and the young lord, who was only twenty-one, seemed to be boon companions, and when it came to repartee Rochester was apt to carry off the honors. There was no real "love lost between them." The Earl's attitude toward

Charles was often one of downright scorn. None the less, the King, although he may have sometimes disliked his precocious subject and must often have feared his tongue, sorely missed his cleverness when he was not at court. So, though Rochester's excesses of speech or act often brought royal wrath upon his handsome head, and sometimes banishments, he was always received again in order that he might enliven the palace by highly spiced jesting, gay songs, wild pranks, and the circulation of satires, often filthy but almost always adroit. Thus, even his attack on Killigrew was forgiven, although because of it or some other offense Charles decided that a brief exile would be salutary for the Earl. In March, Wilmot went to France, after "most solemnly," but how ironically no one knows, asking pardon of young Henry Killigrew for the insult to his father.

In November he was at court again in the midst of a quarrel with Lord Mulgrave. An eager gossip wrote on the 24th, "Mulgrave and Rochester went away on Monday in order to fight, and no news of either of them since." News of the duel, when it did come, was not flattering to Wilmot. Apparently he did his best to turn the meeting into a burlesque of the conventional affair of honor, and rejoiced in making sport of the duellists' ritual and even in exhibiting his own superiority to the current rules for seeming brave. Mulgrave was bewildered. According to him his adversary virtually refused to fight, alleging that he was so weak from disease "that he found himself unfit." In the presence of witnesses and in the face of warnings that tongues would wag, he let the duel be called off. Mulgrave's second wrote an account of the incident, which "was never in the least contradicted or resented by the Lord Rochester" and "intirely ruined his reputation as to Courage."

His perverse pleasure in flouting polite codes in this case started the legend that he was a coward. That hardly agreed with his naval record, or with his readiness to fight on other occasions, and there was courage of a sort in his contempt for what gossip said of him. He was loyal to whim, if whim promised a new sensation, even if thereby he got a reputation as a poltroon. But he reserved the right to feel insulted when he chose. Some years later, stung by a satire which alluded to his début as a duellist, he undertook to vindicate his honor by hiring a gang to chastise John Dryden. Rochester can hardly have been sure that the "poet squab" wrote the offending verses, for they were pretty generally suspected to be Mulgrave's, but Dryden was in favor with Mulgrave and Wilmot elected to wound the patron through the poet. Moreover, he had long been no friend of Dryden, though in 1673 he had seen fit to patronize him and to accept his fulsome praise.

Wilmot was kind to Dryden as long as it amused him to be so, and then threw him over. He took up and cast off in turn, Settle, Crowne, Lee, and Otway, giving to each the success that his favor conferred only to let each taste the bitterness of a sneering rejection at last. Perhaps the assault on Dryden was simply a veiled attack on Mulgrave, but it probably came partly from cruel vanity. To give pain sometimes brought pleasure; it was certainly enjoyable to be admired and feared as the arbiter of poetic reputations and a tyrant over hireling wits.[2]

In 1675, a deputy-lieutenant for Somerset, the recipient of a pension of £1000, and appointed to the Rangership of Woodstock Park, he had grown audacious in his taste for amusement. Returning one night to Whitehall, with Lord Buckhurst and others, "comeing in from their revells," his wavering gaze was caught by the glass spheres housing some costly chronometers set up in the palace gardens. They were treasured as the work of a skilful Jesuit astronomer, and a

---

[2] For Rochester as a patron, see J. Prinz, *John Wilmot*, Chap. II, especially his defense of the Earl, pp. 90–91; and De Sola Pinto, *Rochester*, pp. 114–121. But see also R. G. Ham, *Otway and Lee, Biography from a Baroque Age* (New Haven, 1931), pp. 56–57, 67.

watchman was supposed always to guard them. What happened to him is not related, but the Earl cried to the "dials," "Dost thou stand there to——time?" and then, pushing them down, no doubt was greatly solaced by the crash of their destruction.

By March, 1676, his "Satyr against Mankind" was being read, and its fierce contempt for humanity, as well as its skilful adaptation of Boileau's verses, was winning him the renewed reprobation of the godly and the applause of the sated court. The poem began:

"Were I, who to my cost already am,
One of those strange, prodigious Creatures Man,
A Spirit free, to chuse for my own share,
What sort of Flesh and Blood I pleas'd to wear,
I'd be a Dog, a Monkey, or a Bear,
Or any thing, but that vain Animal,
Who is so proud of being rational.
The Senses are too gross; and he'll contrive
A sixth, to contradict the other five:
And before certain Instinct, will preferr
Reason, which fifty times for one does err—
Reason, an *Ignis fatuus* of the Mind,
Which leaves the Light of Nature, Sense, behind . . .
Whilst the misguided Follower climbs with pain,
Mountains of Whimseys, heapt in his own Brain,
Stumbling from thought to thought, falls headlong down
Into Doubt's boundless sea."

Here was a deadly thrust for anyone who still believed, as Falkland had, in the power and sanctity of reason. The senses were all; in them was the only "light of nature"—in them and in "Instinct" the only certainty. To read and think was vain. "Bladders of Philosophy" helped no one to keep afloat in "Doubt's boundless sea." Rochester might almost have used Falkland, whose writing he knew by reputation at least, to illustrate his point that by trying to follow reason man must come to uncertainty and "eternal night." [3] "Wisdom did . . . Happiness destroy," Wilmot thought, and by his definition of happiness he may have been right. He thought it absurd to prate about reason as a "supernat'ral gift." Such notions he despised, because they misled man and made

> "a Mite
> Think he's the Image of the Infinite."

For him what Falkland had worshipped as reason was but

> "this busie puzling stirrer up of doubt,
> That frames deep Mysteries, then finds 'em out,
> Filling with frantick Crouds of thinking Fools,
> The reverend Bedlams, Colleges and Schools."

But if "reason" were properly defined he would accept it. "I own right Reason," he wrote,

> "That Reason which distinguishes by Sense,
> And gives us rules of good and ill from thence;
> That bounds Desires with a reforming Will,
> To keep them more in vigour, not to kill."

To trust the senses was reasonable, and to satisfy them. To sharpen desires, by brief restraint if need be, in order to make the pleasure of gratifying them more intense, was better than to be deluded by any airy moral principle.

He drove home his doctrine viciously. In the "Satyr against Mankind" he said:

> "many modern Coxcombs . . .
> Retire to think, 'cause they have nought to do"—

---

[3] Rochester makes one of his characters, deploring the state of love and poetry, praise "Falkland" and "Sucklings easie Pen" for their "former" achievements; J. Hayward, ed., Collected Works, p. 79. In John (Wilmot), Earl of Rochester, Poems, &c. On several Occasions (London, 1691), the "Preface to the Reader" gives a brief comparison of Boileau's original with Rochester's "Satyr against Mankind."

like Falkland at Great Tew? Elsewhere he declared that all
that is to be had "by studious search, and labour of the Brain:
By Observation, Counsel, and deep Thought," attains

> "the very Top,
> And Dignity, of Folly."

He exclaims:

> "What Thing is Man, that thus . . .
> Our selves with noise of Reason we do please—
> . . . .
> Thrice happy Beasts are, . . . because they be
> Of Reason void."

In other words, seek pleasure and avoid pain; key all values
to the sensual, and banish all perplexities about what cannot
be justified by material benefits.

For all the force with which Rochester endorsed this creed,
his lines are full of hints that the creed was ultimately mean-
ingless. He maintains that:

> "Thoughts were giv'n for Actions Government;
> Where Action ceases, Thought's impertinent,"

and that:

> "Our Sphere of Action is Lifes happiness,
> And he that thinks beyond, thinks like an Ass,"

but there are constant reminders of how far he missed happiness. He scourged humanity, insisting that amid universal
knavery all that mattered was "only who's a Knave of the first
Rate." He might be better than the rest, but he was still a
man "to his cost," and would rather be a beast. He was a man
and therefore "ridiculous"; he suffered from the "Disease" of

being human. All the pleasures of the "gaudy World" were but "shadow," they were not "sollid Joys," they brought no "true Content." Either he had not lived up to his own theories, or had found they did not after all offer peace of mind. They left quite out of account his instinctive yearning for something beyond mere sense. Persistently, though it may be unconsciously, he mixed his scorn for what was with a vague feeling of what ought to be. Persistently he judged men—and himself —by half-seen criteria outside the range of flesh. Thus, when he praised love, he fell naturally into talk of God. Love was:

> "The most generous Passion of the Mind . . .
> That Cordial-drop Heav'n in our Cup has thrown,
> To make the nauseous Draught of Life go down:
> On which one only Blessing God might raise,
> In Lands of Atheists, Subsidies of Praise:
> For none did e'er so dull, and stupid, prove,
> But felt a God, and blest his Pow'r in Love."

To grant that made it impossible to be satisfied with a mechanical vision of the relations of men and women. It lent point to his condemnation of his compatriots because

> "To an exact Perfection they have brought
> The action Love; the Passion is forgot,"

but it prevented his enjoying his own resolve to have no dealings with women except "as Men with Close-stools, to ease Nature." He accused the fair sex not simply because they had material defects, but because they were not restrained by "Heaven's sacred Laws." Really to live by easily measured standards of pleasure and pain, predicated on the responses of his animal nature, might have made him happy, could he have done so confidently. He tried, but still reflected bitterly that "none's made Great for being Good or Wise" and that "Virtue's commended, but ne'er meets Reward"—reflections that betray an awkward consciousness that somehow, somewhere, the "Good," the "Wise," and "Virtue," were significant realities, which eluded the grasp of his professed philosophy. His most acid verses sometimes sound as if he were whistling to keep his courage up, and his work almost never strikes the note of happiness or even passive content.

For one thing, perhaps, staking everything on physical sensation was risky, because the body tired, and refused to answer to any ordinary stimulus. Pleasures palled, and it might take the abnormal, the perverse, or at least the violent, to whip up exhausted nerves. The constant search for sensation might itself be tiresome—if so, pain of a sort seemed the price of pleasure. Then, too, even the most obvious bliss was not always easy to get. In the very act of love, for example, there were strange defeats. In more than one poem Rochester harped on this, and his frequent references to impotence suggest that he was troubled by the tricks of Fate that cheated lovers of delight. Possibly wine was better than love, because in the end it deadened feeling. There were times, surely, when to be unable to feel was the truest joy.

As long as his strength allowed, however, he kept plucking fiercely at every sensual string, plucking harder and harder and more and more nervously. If animals were luckier than men, he could try at least to be an animal. At Epsom, in June, 1676, with Sir George Etherege, dramatist and rake, Captain Bridges, and a certain Mr. Downs, he experimented with the pleasure of tossing a fiddler in a blanket as a reward for his contumacy in refusing to play. A barber, terrified by the uproar, tried to interfere. He too was seized. He promised that if he were set free he would lead the revellers to the handsomest woman in Epsom. They took him at his word, and he directed them to the constable's house. Thither they hurried as fast as unsteady legs would carry them. When the constable, poking his night-capped head out of the window, asked what they wanted, they told him plainly, though neither decently nor politely. More prudent than eager to preserve the peace, he sought safety in silence, but they broke in his door and thrashed him soundly. Well drubbed, he wormed out of their clutches, called the watch, and arrested his assailants. Then Etherege, with the skill of a practised writer of comedy, made an oration so persuasive that the constable gave up his prisoners and dismissed his men. By now Rochester's temper was blazing, and as soon as the constable was defenceless, he drew his sword to run him through. Downs caught his arm in time to prevent murder. The watch returned, and as the brawl became general, Rochester, Etherege, and Bridges, prudently took to their heels, leaving Downs to save himself as best he could. Some days later he died from his injuries, forcing Rochester to abscond lest he be brought too inconveniently to account. But once more he speedily made his peace with the King, if, indeed, the King troubled himself at all about so harmless an adventure of a sprightly Earl.

Wilmot's hunt for pleasure took him constantly to women. He is said to have been Nell Gwyn's lover before King Charles was. It is more certain that he conquered Mrs. Roberts, another of the royal mistresses. He wooed and won Mrs. Barry, when she was unknown to fame, and helped to prepare her for her brilliant career on the Restoration stage. He possessed her, while poor Thomas Otway sighed out his heart in devotion to the actress who made her first triumph in a play of his, charming Rochester and others of the rich and great to new generosity, but leaving the poor playwright, scorned in love, to stand sadly by with the applause ringing hollowly in his ears. No doubt Wilmot got a savage satisfaction out of creating the strange triangle in which he, the noble lover of the arts, saw his mistress shine in parts written for her by his defeated rival. No doubt, too, he really cared for Mrs. Barry. She was not beautiful, but she must have had physical charm for him, and her talents were in their way a match for his. He was a poet who knew and loved the "stormy, pathless World" of

poetry. He taught her how to make characters from that world
live for a few hours in a London playhouse; she learned how
to speak the poets' words so that they opened to others glimpses
of their visions. The Earl's relation with her lasted longer than
most of his amours. She bore him a daughter, but she was
probably not constant to him and certainly did not insist that
he be true to her. He repaid her with a love that exceeded
what he felt for any other woman—exceeded what a believer
in sense as the sole reality could easily explain.

Many others claimed him briefly. Women of the streets,
country girls, citizens' wives, ladies of the court—anyone to
whom a moment's fancy attracted him—and occasionally his
wife, though she usually stayed in Oxfordshire while he
frolicked in town. Perhaps he did love her—certainly his letters
to her preserve an even tone of courteous regard. It is debatable how much balm they brought her. She may have read
their graceful phrases as sincere expressions from a loyal,
though erring, husband; or she may have discerned, beneath
their courtly elegance, satire as bitter as in the verses he passed
from hand to hand in London. He sometimes made her unhappy, as one of her letters witnesses. "If I could have been
troubled att any thing when I had the happyness of resceiving
a letter from you," she wrote, "I should be soe because you
did not name a time when I might hope to see you: The uncertainty of which very much aflicts me. Whether this ode
kind of proceeding be to try my patience or obedyence I cannot guesse, but I will never faile of ether where my duty to
you requier them. I doe not think you design staying att Bath
now that it is like to be soe full and God knows when you
will find in your hart to leave the place you are in: pray consider with your selfe wheather this be a reasonable way of
proceeding and be pleased to lett me know what I am to expect for thear being soe short a time betwixt this and the
sitting of the Parlement I am confident you will find soe much
bussiness as will not allow you to come into the country.

Therefore pray lay your commands upon me what I am to doe and though it be to forgett my children and the long hopes I have lived in of seeing you, yet I will endeavour to obey you or in the memory only torment my selfe without giving you the trouble of puting you in mind that thear lives such a creature as your faithful humble" wife. He was wont to excuse his absences from home by pleading the necessity of his being at court, but she must have asked what that necessity was. In politics he had no share; no settled business demanded his presence in town; and the rumors about his doings there dealt chiefly with his pursuit of entertainment. Lady Rochester can hardly have needed the invective of his lines on marriage—

> "A Damn'd Wife, by inevitable Fate
> Destroys Soul, Body, Credit and Estate"—

or his remark that men marry "because 'tis th' very worst thing they can do," to appreciate a wife's place in his philosophy.

To one of his loves he wrote:

> "Such perfect Bliss, fair Chloris, we
> In our Enjoyment prove:
> 'Tis pity restless Jealousie
> Should mingle with our Love.
> Let us, since Wit has taught us how,
> Raise Pleasure to the Top:
> You Rival Bottle must allow,
> I'll suffer Rival Fop."

He added certain highly tolerant comments on his mistress's lightness in love, declaring:

> "There's not a brisk insipid Spark,
> That flutters in the Town:
> But with your wanton Eyes you mark
> Him out to be your own."

Then, by way of graceful amends for all, he adds serenely:

> "All this you freely may confess,
> Yet we ne'er disagree:
> For did you love your Pleasure less,
> You were no Match for me."

He spurned illusions as to woman's constancy or man's duty to be true. Love, like everything else worth having, was a way to pleasure, and the means to that end mattered little.

Thus when he could combine his worship of Venus with homage to Bacchus, he was in his element. So he was when with the Duke of Buckingham he hired an inn on the road to Newmarket, and played the bounteous host, getting drunk with his guests, and jovially trying to seduce every pretty maid that he could lure within his doors. To him, as indeed to Charles II, who managed no more than a half-hearted disapproval, this was heroic foolery. The betrayal of a village wench or two weighed little against the excellence of the jest. In the same village, too, was that grimmer episode, whence resulted one death and the recruiting of one more light of love for London streets. Stripped of romantic embellishment, the tale narrows down to a few sordid facts. Rochester and Buckingham heard of a jealous old miser, married to a young and lovely girl. It took only a few hours for a handsome Earl, contemptuous of all country folk, sure of the frailty of all women, and expert in excess, to disguise himself as a woman, to plead sudden illness in the street, to accept the sympathetic hospitality of the miser's wife, to seduce her, and then, adding meanness to outrage, to let her steal her husband's money as she fled with her lover. When both Rochester and Buckingham tired of her, they left her to live as best she could in town. Her husband hanged himself.

Good sport, this, as was most of the Earl's, but sport with an acrid taste, even for him. He was merry when drunk, always deft with words, always eager for a new jest, a novel debauch, anything that spiced stale pleasures.[4] Anything that touched the riddles of sex amused him, and he interested himself in the importation and use in England of certain instruments designed to console ladies unfortunate in love. To him has been attributed the authorship of a long set of verses which celebrate this victory of science in a manner ingeniously contrived to shock the strait-laced. If he wrote the notorious play, *Sodom*, as has been charged, he plunged to the extreme depths of pornography, and revealed a terrifying interest in the grossest and most repulsive aspects of sex. Moreover, if the play was his, he heightened whatever sensation he got from writing it by ironically penning a caustic—though filthy—attack upon its author. All that he wrote of love reeks of his passionate concern with the purely sexual, and the tone is usually sneering—indeed, throughout his work, gaiety is rarely unmixed with irony or scorn. [5]

Probably only in his drinking did he display single-minded gusto. He told Savile, "Of the three Businesses of this Age, *Women, Politicks and Drinking*, the *last* is the only Exercise at which you and I have not prov'd our selves *errant* Fumblers." Quite calmly he said that he had been continuously drunk for five years, a statement neither literally true nor made up out of whole cloth. Just as he swore fervently, and presumably with art, on the slightest provocation, so that it was said that oaths came almost naturally from him, he drank

---

[4] J. Wilmot, *Poetical Works* (ed. Q. Johns; The Haworth Press, 1935), p. xxviii, in its reference to Rochester's delight in "renewing his Pleasure in Sight of his Cuckold" is pertinent here.

[5] Savile's letter to Rochester, Jan. 26, 1670 in J. Prinz, *John Wilmot*, pp. 287–288, and "Signior Dildoe, 1678" in J. Hayward, ed., *Collected Works*, pp. 128–130. Prinz questions the attribution of these verses to Rochester (p. 151) and Q. Johns in his edition of J. Wilmot, *Poetical Works*, does not include them. For the "D^s" referred to in Savile's letter, see Prinz's note (pp. 287–288); Hayward's note in *Collected Works*, p. 379; and Havelock Ellis, *Studies in the Psychology of Sex* (N. Y., 1936), I, Part I, 169–170. For the question of the authorship of *Sodom*, see Prinz, pp. 166–177; Hayward, pp. xvi–xviii, argues the other side.

with entire abandon, like a man enjoying the one delight that never palled. With apparent sincerity he wrote:

> "Love a Woman! you're an Ass,
> 'Tis a most insipid Passion
> To chuse out for your Happiness,
> The silliest part of God's Creation.
>
> . . . .
>
> Farewel, Woman, I intend,
> Henceforth, ev'ry night to sit
> With my lewd well-natur'd Friend,
> Drinking to engender Wit."

His drinking did engender wit. Drunkenness roused recklessness, and when he was in his cups decency and restraint fled.

His daring in satire may have been provoked by wine, though the usual story is that he used to retire to the country to write in tranquillity his stinging assaults on the court and all his race. He said that satire could be written only when one was heated by desire for revenge. If so, he must have been often possessed by vengeful wrath against the world; he wrote "Who can abstain from *Satire* in this Age?" With a diabolically practical inspiration he clothed one of his servants in the red coat of a sentry, armed him with a musket, and had him stand night after night in the corridors of Whitehall. Lovers hastened to assignations regardless of the immobile redcoated soldier, who watched and told all he saw to the Earl of Rochester. Thus was heaped up fuel for his rage against his compatriots, and of the rage satires were born. Once he learned from a waiting-maid, for the moment his mistress, all that she had heard said by two Maids of Honor, while, she, surprised in stealing a surreptitious bath, sat shivering behind a curtain, an unwilling confidante of their indiscretions. The information she gave Wilmot made him a terror to two belles of the

court. He spared no one. The King was in his verses a monarch
who

> "Never said a foolish thing
> And never did a wise one."

He was also much that was far worse. The royal mistresses
were described in lines often quite unquotable. Charles for-
gave much in order that he too might laugh at the obscene
abuse the Earl heaped on others, but there were times when
his patience was sorely tried. It must have been, when Rochester, putting contempt into action instead of words, tried to
embrace the Duchess of Cleveland as she was stepping out of
her coach. She knocked him down—no difficult feat if, as is
probable, he was tipsy—only to have him jump up and de-
claim:

> "By Heavens! 'twas bravely done!
> First, to Attempt the Chariot of the Sun,
> And then to Fall like *Phaeton*."

Very likely his quickness saved him from exile. Another time,
though, he wrote of the King in phrases that would have been
palatable enough applied to someone else, but could not be
condoned when uttered of the Lord's anointed. When he
thus outran tolerance, he was banished, and on one such occasion came back to London in disguise.

He was a good actor. Masquerading as a beggar or a porter
he had used his histrionic ability in "mean Amours." Once, in
the guise of a poor wayfarer he had led on a vagrant to speak
ill of Lord Rochester, and then punished him by having him
plunged into a barrel of beer. Another time he had paraded
through Burford as a tinker, and instead of mending the villagers' kettles, had knocked their bottoms out. Now he chose
the garb of a mountebank physician. From a platform in the

city he harangued gaping crowds with an address just extravagant enough and just suggestively indecent enough to enthrall them. He promised cures for most of the ills which flesh is heir to, appealing especially to women. For days patients flocked to his lodgings in Tower Street, to be cheated, mocked, or wooed, as suited his fancy. The court heard of the new quack, and Miss Jennings and Miss Price, two venturesome Maids of Honor, dressed as orange girls in order that they might consult the mysterious Alexander Bendo. By accident they were frightened away before they met him, and were doubtless saved thereby from becoming forever after targets for his merciless ridicule. No monarch of Charles II's temperament could resist the charms of such a comedy, and the Earl, quite unchastened and armed with new proofs of human weakness, came back again to Whitehall. A shrewd woman who hated him declared that he never said what he thought, but made everyone believe what he said. This suggests that too much must not be deduced from his feverish merriment when he was in his cups, and perhaps his satires must be read with the same caution, but it is hard to see how they could have been so vitriolic had he not meant what he said. There were few rewards to be had from libelling the King. Sincerity alone explains the fierceness of his lampoons on the ladies and courtiers among whom he lived. If this be true his writing must give insight into his nature.

Marriage he called "but a Licens'd Way to Sin"; women were "the heavy Yoak, and Burthen of Mankind." Children were "Sottish Lumps ingender'd of all Ills" or "Supplies for Age and Graves." Of kings he said: "The most are Wolves, Goats, Sheep, or Swine." English statesmen were "ridiculous schoolboys." Edward Hyde, who had honored him as a boy, was "The Kingdom's Broker, Ruin of the State," a "Shrub of Gentry," "Chief of Sacrilege, Ambition, Lust, and Pride." Nell Gwyn he celebrated in a mock panegyric more cruel than she deserved in its slurs on her "Native dirt" and its allusions to her mother. The poets of his time were a "most unworthy generation." Chastity he satirized with a freedom only surpassed by his remarks on his own fickleness in love. What he thought of reason he had made clear in the "Satyr" on mankind. Honesty was "against all common sense," and like manners, generosity, and bravery, was but a name "by dull Fools to plague Mankind found out." He confessed:

> "In my Dear Self I centre every Thing,
> My servants, Friend, my Mistress, and My King,
> Nay Heaven and Earth to that one Point I bring."

And he announced:

> "If exposing what I take for Wit,
> To my dear self a Pleasure I beget,
> No matter though the cens'ring Criticks fret."

"Born to my self, I like my self alone," he insisted.

Religion, honor, philosophy, unselfishness, liberality, love, faithfulness—all were delusions. Wilmot inveighed against the principles that had spelled truth for Lady Elizabeth Cary, against the virtues that Jonson had praised in her son and in Sir Henry Morison, and against any attempt to discover in life reason, order, and beauty. Only one's self remained. Yet older ideas had diabolic vitality. Rochester laughed at them, or tried to laugh; argued them away; abused those who held them— and yet, in certain of his moods, they rose again to plague him. When he was tired or sick—and his health began to fail as early as 1671—he could not help pondering matters that a strict materialist should have dismissed as nonsense. He even speculated about the soul.

Somehow his "Self" was proving a weak reliance. To Henry Savile he wrote: "I . . . think the World as giddy as myself" and "care not which way it turns." Other letters are outwardly cheerful, but melancholy keeps cropping up, as in the acid of:

"We are in such a *setled Happiness*, and such merry Security
in this place, that if it were not for *Sickness*, I could pass my
time very well, between *my own ill-nature*, which inclines me
very little to pity the Misfortunes of *malicious mistaken Fools*,
and *the Policies of the Times*, which expose *new Rarities* of
that kind every day." Suffering, he could say, "It is a *miraculous thing* . . . when a Man, *half in the Grave*, cannot leave
off *playing the Fool, and the Buffoon;* but so it falls out to my
Comfort." He remarked that disease would put an end to his
"*ridiculous being.*" He kept a pet monkey, and declared: "Human Affairs are carried on at the same nonsensical rate, which
makes me . . . think it a Fault to laugh at the Monkey," which
he called a "curious Miniature of Man." More than that, he
had his portrait painted, sneering at himself and his race by
posing in the act of crowning the monkey with a laurel wreath.
He called himself "un Bougre lasse," and the "idlest Creature
living," languishing "all the Day in the tediousness of doing
nothing," almost "*mortified and dead* to the taste of *all Happiness.*" One of his letters explains: "The World, ever since I
can remember, has been still so insupportably the same, that
'twere vain to hope there were any alterations; and therefore
I can have no curiosity for News; only I wou'd be glad to know
if the Parliament be like to sit any time . . . *Livy* and Sickness
has a little inclin'd me to Policy; when I come to Town I
make no question but to change that Folly for some less;
whether Wine or Women I know not; according as my Constitution serves me." If, as he said, he centred everything in
himself, and if happiness was the goal of existence, he was in a
parlous state.

His dissatisfaction with himself and his unhappiness show
that, base as he was, he groped romantically for something
beyond baseness. He had read widely. He had written a few
lovely songs. His satire was compact and tense; its fury gave it
weight, and even when it was most extravagant, its energy
bordered on magnificence. His skill in conversation was cele-

JOHN WILMOT, EARL OF ROCHESTER,
CROWNING HIS MONKEY WITH LAUREL

Reproduced by permission of the Trustees of the National Portrait Gallery, London, from the painting by
J. Huysmans

brated, and he had humor as well as wit, revealed, for example, in the inspired refrain of his song of a young lady to her elderly lover: "Ancient person of my heart." He was a court celebrity, flattered and feared, but he called himself fool, boasted of his idleness, seldom troubled to print his verses, and included himself in his derision of mankind. Behind this there must have been thought, some sense of values that transcended those which his professed materialism allowed. If his satire came from desire for revenge, as he said it did, on what was he eager to revenge himself? If he was an unthinking sinner, with no abstract conception of virtue, why was he enraged at the very follies he permitted himself? To rail as he did at the men who revelled with him, or at Charles II or Edward Hyde, he must have put them and himself into comparison with some vision of excellence not realized in his little world. His disillusionment and his indecent rioting were of a piece with his elaborate efforts to behave as if there were no laws human or divine, and yet his patent disgust with himself implied a suspicion that there were.

He had jeered at books but he read them none the less. Thus in 1679 he came on Burnet's *History of the Reformation*, strange book for a rake! Then, strange wish for a rake, he desired to meet Burnet, of whom he knew already as the spiritual comforter of one of his erstwhile mistresses. So the divine and the Earl talked together and exchanged letters. In his debates with Burnet Rochester tried hard to express systematically his carefully thought out attitude toward life.

Earlier he had encountered conscience, "Bedlams midnight theam." Vague remorse had sometimes bothered him when he was sick, but he saw that what he felt "were rather general and dark Horrours, than any Convictions of sinning against God." They had no effect, for he discerned shrewdly that the pangs of repentance were out of proportion to the seriousness of the offense. Sometimes he was particularly outrageous, and had no regrets; sometimes he erred in a trifle and was tormented for it. When he was urged to send for ministers to comfort him, he sometimes did so, if he was feeling very ill, but said that "it was but a piece of his breeding, to desire them to pray by him," for he did not want to join in their supplications. Yet the sage Marquis of Halifax was right when he asserted that Rochester was "too intelligent" to be an atheist, for the Earl confessed to Burnet that he had always had an impression of the existence of a supreme being. This idea, he said, he could not shake off, but he could form no conception of God. "To love God seemed to him a presumptuous thing, and the heat of fanciful men." To worship was to fall into a snare set by priests to make men believe that the clergy alone knew how to appease the Creator. To pray was to admit that God was weak enough to yield to trivial human importunities. And Wilmot was puzzled because he could not think that a truly good Almighty would make him, the Earl of Rochester, miserable.

Because his mind was clear when he was sick, he believed the soul was immortal, but he could not accept the notion that it would be rewarded or punished after death. Heaven was too high for man's deserving; Hell too severe a penalty for his frailty. He thought the soul must begin again after the body perished, with no memory of what had gone before. As for morality, he confessed that if he ever seemed to praise it he did so only as a polite mode of speech. Public opinion and his own self-interest were all that restrained him and, he thought, everyone else, from being as immoral as the slightest whim might decree. In empty protestations of friendship, lovers' exaggerated vows, and gentlemen's slighting of creditors, he saw sufficient proof that what passed for reality was but sham.

All this had consistency, and Burnet found in his noble pupil a man who had pondered much about the meaning of human existence and, better still, was ready to discuss his problem with a divine whom he respected. He swore that he would talk with Burnet not for victory in controversy nor to show his wit, but to explain candidly "what stuck with" him. He exposed his creed, propounded his difficulties, and got in return a series of miniature sermons, expert presentations of the conventional tenets of the pious.

What Rochester wanted was some single harmonious system for understanding and living in this world; what Burnet offered was a skilful statement of the case for religious feeling as a partial substitute for mere logical thought, an exposition of the alleged rational validity of religious experience and of the revealed truths of religion. The bishop discoursed on the need for man's internal regeneration by the action of some principle higher than mere expediency, law, or reasonable precept. This Wilmot succinctly dubbed "*Enthusiasme or Canting*," declaring that he could form no idea of any such process and could not understand it. He did understand the dictates of "*Reason* and *Philosophy*," he said, but nothing more mysterious was within his ken. Burnet cited cases of men saved by prayer from temptation; Rochester retorted, "This must be the effect of a heat in Nature: it was only the strong diversion of the thoughts, that gave the seeming Victory. I doubt not but if one could turn to a *Problem* in *Euclid*, or to Write a Copy of Verses, it would have the same effect." Why, he asked cogently, should man be so dependent upon nebulous intimations from on high, uncertain revelations, emotions, or the dubious interpretations of mental states? "Why . . . could not this be rectified by some plain Rules given?" What were miracles but tricks of men who wished to seem to speak in the name of God? Wilmot felt that no one could believe in the Christian mysteries, for no one can believe what he cannot comprehend. Burnet, like Falkland, thought that Christian revelation was consonant with reason and gave axioms from which logical conclusions could develop. Rochester could not agree. The Anglican rationalists, like the group at Great Tew, for all their pious professions, had made reason the master of faith. Therefore when science and materialistic criteria challenged much that they had believed to be divinely revealed, their assumptions became debatable, and the scepticism implicit in their intellectual scrutiny of religious truth taught the next generation to question the premises on which they most relied. Wilmot was open-minded, but again and again he protested that all Burnet's talk of revelation and religious feeling begged the question. "I understand nothing of it," he cried and then in a single sentence bared the root of his disease: "I think those are very happy who are under the power of religious impressions, since they have somewhat on which their thoughts centre and rest."

Without this he might seem a self-sufficient materialist, seeking no more than his senses and the physical world could supply; with it he appears, as he was, a man at war with himself, groping for a "Sun at noon" in the warmth of which he could live. Lady Falkland had discovered one in the authority of an ancient faith; her son vainly had sought his in a conception of reason, humanly applicable but divine in essence. Rochester had found none, and was "smothered and stupified" in anguish because he had not. He told Burnet that he thought those who could find truth in religion were the happiest of men. In his own words, "They were happy that believed; for it was not in every man's power," and, "If a man says he cannot believe, what help is there? For he is not master of his own Belief." The key to Wilmot's bitterness is in his despairing admission that he, the sovereign intellectual, the Earl of a thousand graces, "the Bold, the Witty, and the Gay," would give "all that he was Master of" to be able to believe and to taste the joys he knew must flow from faith.

In a different time and place, and less sensitive to human ugliness, he might, like Falkland, have built out of traditional theories some abstract principles and have tried to live by them. Perhaps had he seen less of the court, which he came to liken to "a hog-sty," and more of the Englishmen whom he considered beneath him, he might have fared better. But, like Falkland, he was bred as a courtier, and had little chance to know the standards of any class but his own. This cut him off from realizing that there might be persons happier and less foolish, though less fashionable, than his intimates; it made it fatally easy to assume that, except for the rich and well-born, whose vices he saw all too clearly, there were only vagabonds or stupid slaves. Those, naturally, he disregarded; the others, though they were his friends, did little to protect youthful illusions about mankind. By inheritance prepared to love wine and adventure, by training made loyal to the King, he came to a thoughtless court where faith was a jest, where honor was talked about but rarely defined except as a kind of selfishness, where sensual realities ranked highest, where imagination was less than cleverness, and beauty subservient to artifice and sterile form. His hot head got him into trouble; his loyalty and love of danger took him to war. There he found brave men and also foolish ones, and learned what it is to fight, as he did at Bergen, in a cause foredoomed to defeat by the stupidity of those in high place. Dr. Balfour had made him love books and the classics; he found London paying homage at the shrine of an artificial and bombastic heroic drama. If he was romantic in love, most of the women he knew—even Mrs. Barry—were not, and most of what passed for love in Restoration London satisfied only the flesh. Inevitably he came to believe that men were usually fools or knaves, and that to look beyond physical pleasure for tests of value was to give up substance for shadow. Inevitably it was hard to cling to abstract maxims for conduct, when in practice excess and riot prospered. He was forced to doubt what he most wanted to accept.

Pleasure did not satisfy him, as it might coarser clay. He longed to believe and could not, and so his desire for revenge on the world that swindled him, on the men who fell short of what he wanted to think was good, on verse-makers who betrayed the Muses, made him lash out furiously at everything about him. In his deeds as well as in his words, he satirized human folly. His abortive duel was a mockery of a silly code, and he wrote where everyone might read that all men would be cowards if they dared. Revenge became his central passion —revenge upon false morality, false laws, false men and women, even his own falseness to what he vainly tried to convince himself was best. His malady was common in the Restoration period. Its germs were in the struggle to build out of a reaction against pious fanaticism and out of weariness with the shibboleths of doctrinaires, a new faith, founded on the concrete and expedient, which might make life endurable in a vastly imperfect world. Rochester's tragedy lay in the persistence of his yearning for some of the values of an older creed even while he tried passionately to live wholly by the new.

Burnet's formal arguments helped him very little. He grew sicker. His body was twisted with pain, and his mind racked with questions and forebodings. The Bishop of Oxford came to see him; so did Dr. Marshal, priest of the parish. They did their best, but it was Robert Parsons, the chaplain, who at last brought Wilmot what he craved. He read him one day the fifty-third chapter of Isaiah, as part of an argument to prove that Christ's coming was prophesied "many Ages before it was done." As he heard the splendid lines on the "man of sorrows, and acquainted with grief," he was suddenly moved. Parsons read:

"He was wounded for our trangressions, he was bruised for our iniquities . . .

All we like sheep have gone astray; we have turned every one to his own way; and the Lord hath laid on him the iniquity of us all . . .

For the trangression of my people was he stricken.

And he made his grave with the wicked, and with the rich in his death; because he had done no violence, neither was any deceit in his mouth . . .

304

Therefore will I divide him a portion with the great, and he shall
divide the spoil with the strong; because he hath poured out his
soul unto death: and he was numbered with the transgressors;
and he bare the sin of many, and made intercession for the
transgressors."

The poetry beat in upon the Earl like the glare of the sun.
The magnificent dignity of the phrases, and the poignancy—
perhaps even the irony—of the prophet's vision, woke a new
and profound sensation. "He felt an inward force upon him
. . . that he could resist . . . no longer: For the words had an
authority which did shoot like Raies or Beams in his Mind."
He was gripped "by a power which did . . . constrain him"; he
believed in "his Saviour, as if he had seen him in the Clouds."
What if this was but a "heat of Nature?" What if it was but
one more deceitful prompting of mere sense? It was worth
being cheated to be able to throw off uncertainty, dread,
hatred, physical frustration; to be swallowed up in the exquisite bliss of surrender; to let the power of a dream—if
dream it was—quiet the tortured writhing of his tired brain.
Cynicism had led to misery; lust, to weariness; pleasure, to
satiety; doubts, to fear—in this strange new sensation might
at last be the clue to peace, the ultimate security he had sought
so long. To it he yielded himself as helplessly as a child.

He was conquered by overwhelming experience, and paid at
last his debt to instinctive feelings that had pursued him even
when he had sought refuge in chilly indifference or in feverish
intoxication with the sensual. He breathed the one warmth
that could blunt the icy needles of his challenging and condemning mind—the same warmth breathed more than fifty
years before by Elizabeth, Lady Falkland. Like her, he rejoiced in hope that things which could not be proved were
more true than those which could. Like her, he felt that God
came to him, "not as in the dawning of the day, not as in the
bud of the spring, but as the Sun at noon." In its light he saw

promise of escape from the "wayes of fortune, or understanding" in which he had been "clouded and eclypsed, damped and benummed" till now.

The end came quickly. "My lord Rochester, a very profane wit," who had sneered at religion and those who taught it, now wanted them constantly with him to keep his new confidence alive. One night he called for Burnet, and Burnet did not come. He cried out, "Has my friend left me? Then I shall die shortly!" The next morning he was dead. Only in giving up his vengeful struggle against life by giving up life itself did he finally achieve content.

NOTES ON AUTHORITIES

THESE notes do not purport to be a complete bibliography of all the works consulted and used in the preparation of this book, but include references only to those most specifically referred to and most often quoted.

To several I owe more than can be adequately indicated by a mere listing in the following paragraphs. Among these are Longueville's entertaining and useful *Falklands*; Sir John Marriott's *Life and Times of Lucius Cary*, justly regarded as the standard biography of Falkland; J. Prinz's study of Rochester; and V. De Sola Pinto's *Rochester*, which contributes both to knowledge of the Earl's life and to understanding of his poems. For the general history of the period I have found Gardiner's great studies indispensable, and have constantly used also the admirable shorter books by Godfrey Davies and I. Deane Jones, and John Buchan's brilliantly written life of Cromwell. And, like every student of the seventeenth century, I have found riches in the pages of Falkland's friend, Edward Hyde, Earl of Clarendon, who eulogized him with a dignity and beauty never since equalled, and told the story of his time with shrewdness of observation and splendor of phrase.

CHAPTER II

The chief source for Elizabeth Cary's life is *Life*. For its author-ship see pp. v, vi. P. 105n. gives evidence that notes for it were made by one of Lady Cary's sons. See also prefatory matter in J. Du Perron, *The Reply . . . to the . . . King of Great Britaine* (Douay, 1630), and dedications in: John Marston, *Works* (London, 1633); Michael Drayton, *Englands Heroicall Epistles* (London, 1597, and later eds.); and in 2d. ed. of *Englands Helicon* (London, 1614); poem in John Davies, *Muses Sacrifice* (London, 1612); sonnet in W. Basse, *Poetical Works* (ed. R. W. Bond; London, 1893), pp. 145, 147. *CSP, Domestic*, for the years from 1603 to 1639, is rich in material bearing on Lady Falkland and her husband, as is *CSP, Ireland, 1615–1625, 1625–1632*. For modern accounts of her life see *DNB*, articles on Sir Henry Cary and Sir Lawrence Tanfield; Georgiana Fullerton, *Life of Elizabeth, Lady Falkland* (London, 1883); J. Gillow, *Literary and Biographical History or Bibliographical Dictionary of the English Catholics* (London, 1885–1902), II, ix-xiii; (F. Harrison), *The Devon Carys* (N. Y., 1920), II, 407n.-410n.; Longueville; and Marriott. *Complete Peerage* has useful data. Other authorities used for this chapter are Clarendon, *History*, III, 180-181; J. S. Brewer and W. Bullen, eds., *Calendar of the Carew Manuscripts* (London, 1867–1873), VI, 432; J. Cosin, *Correspondence* (ed. G. Ormsby; Durham, 1869–1872), I, 101; P. Gawdy, *Letters* (ed. I. H. Jeayes; London, 1906), p. 161; R. H. Gretton, *Burford Records* (Oxford, 1920), p. 274; W. H. Hutton, *The English Church from the Accession of Charles I to the Death of Anne* (London, 1903), pp. 61, 350; B. Jonson, *Poems* (ed. B. H. Newdigate; Oxford, 1936), p. 21 (Epigram LXVI); A. B. Grosart, ed., *The Lismore Papers, First Series* (London, 1886), II, 103; D. Lloyd, *State-Worthies, Or, The States-men And Favourites of England* (2d. ed.; London, 1679), p. 938; J. Rous, *Diary* (ed. M. A. E. Green; London, 1856), p. 75.

CHAPTER III

In this chapter and the next five, on Lucius Cary, my chief authorities for his life are *Athenae*; Aubrey; Clarendon, *History*; Clarendon, *Life*; *DNB*, article on Lucius Cary; T. Lewis, *Lives of*

the *Friends and Contemporaries of Clarendon* (London, 1852),
Vol. I; *Life*; and, of course, Longueville and Marriott. I have also
drawn material in this chapter from the following works, referred
to as general authorities in the notes to Chapter I: W. Basse,
Poetical Works; *CSP, Domestic, 1619–1623, 1629–1631, 1631–1633,
1633–1634*; *CSP, Ireland, 1615–1625, 1625–1632*; *Complete Peerage*;
A. B. Grosart, ed., *The Lismore Papers, First Series*; (F. Harrison),
The Devon Carys; B. Jonson, *Poems*. Other authorities used are
*Cabala, Sive Scrinia Sacra: Mysteries of State and Government, in
Letters* (3d. ed.; London, 1691); Gardiner, *History*; J. T. Gilbert,
History of the Irish Confederation and the War in Ireland (Dub-
lin, 1882); *Hist. Mss. Comm.*, Report II, Appendix, p. 157, Report
IV, Appendix, p. 285, Report XII, Appendix 9, p. 126; W. A. Shaw,
Knights of England (London, 1906). For Burford and Great Tew
see M. S. Gretton, *Burford Past and Present* (Oxford, 1920); R. H.
Gretton, *Burford Records*; W. J. Monk, *History of Burford* (Lon-
don, 1891); E. C. Williams, *Companion into Oxfordshire* (London,
1935). For Cary's elegy, K. B. Murdock, "An Elegy on Sir Henry
Morison, By Lucius Cary, Viscount Falkland" in *Harvard Studies
and Notes in Philology and Literature*, XX (Cam., 1938),
29-42. For Trinity College, G. D. Burtchaell and T. U. Sadleir,
eds., *Alumni Dublinienses. A Register of the Students . . . of
Trinity College, in the University of Dublin* (London, 1924);
G. P. Mahaffy, *An Epoch in Irish History, Trinity College, Dublin . . . 1591–1660* (2d. ed.; London, 1906); W. R. W. Roberts,
"Viscount Falkland" in *Peplographia Dublinensis: Memorial Dis-
courses Preached in the Chapel of Trinity College, Dublin, 1895–
1902* (London, 1902); W. Urwick, *Early History of Trinity College,
Dublin* (London, 1892). For the Boyles, *DNB*, articles on Richard
Boyle, 1566–1643, and Richard Boyle, 1612–1697; D. Masson,
Life of John Milton (London, 1875–1880), III, 658-660, V, 229-
234, 278-279, VI, 455-458, 638, 724, 724n.; C. F. Smith, *Mary
Rich, Countess of Warwick (1625–1678): Her Family and Friends*
(London, 1901); D. Townshend, *Life and Letters of the Great
Earl of Cork* (London, 1904). On the Morisons, C. Hughes,
*Shakespeare's Europe. Unpublished Chapters of Fynes Morison's
Itinerary* (London, 1903), introduction; A. R. Maddison, ed.,

Lincolnshire Pedigrees in Harleian Society Publications L-LII (London, 1902–1904), II, 693-694; W. C. Metcalfe, Book of Knights Banneret (London, 1885), pp. 209-210; J. Nichols, History and Antiquities of the County of Leicester (London, 1795–1811), I, 425, 458, 567, IV, 875; Virginia Magazine of History and Biography, II (Richmond, 1894–1895), 383-385, XX (Richmond, 1912), 70-71; William and Mary College Historical Magazine, IX (Richmond, 1901), 119-120. On the Haringtons, H. Chauncy, Historical Antiquities of Hertfordshire (London, 1826), pp. 534-535; E. Gosse, Life and Letters of John Donne (London, 1899), II, 43-45; J. Harington, Letters and Epigrams (ed. N. E. McClure; Philadelphia, 1930), p. 3; J. A. Manning, Memoirs of Sir Benjamin Rudyard (London, 1841); J. Wright, History and Antiquities of the County of Rutland (London, 1684), pp. 48, 51, 52, 55, 56.

CHAPTER IV

For this chapter I have used the following, already cited in the "Notes on Authorities" for earlier chapters: Athenae; Aubrey; CSP, Domestic; CSP, Ireland; Clarendon, History; Clarendon, Life; Complete Peerage; DNB; Gardiner, History; Gosse, Life and Letters of John Donne; (F. Harrison), The Devon Carys; Hist. Mss. Comm., Report VI, Appendix, p. 312b; Jonson, Poems; T. Lewis, Lives; Life; Lloyd, State-Worthies; Longueville; Mahaffy, An Epoch in Irish History; Manning, Memoirs; Marriott; Monk, History of Burford; Murdock, "An Elegy"; Virginia Magazine of History and Biography, II. Other works quoted or referred to are: F. Bacon, "Of Judicature" in Works (ed. J. Spedding, R. L. Ellis, and D. D. Heath; Boston, 1861), XII, 270; W. D. Briggs, "Studies in Ben Jonson" in Anglia, XXXVII (Halle, 1913), 474-479; G. Bromley, Collection of Original Royal Letters (London, 1787), pp. 142-143; J. Buchan, Oliver Cromwell (London, 1934); T. Carew, Poems (ed. A. Vincent; London, 1899); L. Carey [sic], Poems (ed. A. B. Grosart; n.p., 1871); S. Cressy, An Epistle Apologetical of S.C. to a Person of Honour (n.p., 1674), p. 84; T. Crosfield, Diary (ed. F. S. Boas; London, 1935), p. 63; G. Davies, The Early Stuarts, 1603–1660 (Oxford, 1937); J. Donne,

Letters to Severall Persons of Honour (ed. C. E. Merrill, Jr.; N. Y., 1910); T. Fuller, *The Church History of Britain* (ed. J. S. Brewer; Oxford, 1845), VI, 163; C. Gildon, ed., *Miscellaneous Letters and Essays* (London, 1694), pp. 85-86; M. A. E. Green, "Life of Elizabeth, Eldest Daughter of James I" in *Lives of the Princesses of England from the Norman Conquest*, Vols. V and VI; C. H. Herford and P. Simpson, *Ben Jonson, The Man and His Work* (Oxford, 1925); I. D. Jones, *The English Revolution* (London, 1931); B. Jonson, *Volpone*; H. Killigrew, *Pallantus and Eudora* (London, 1653), "The Publisher to the Reader"; L. C. Knights, *Drama and Society in the Age of Jonson* (London, 1937), which contains a very stimulating summary of some of the conflicts between new ideals and old, especially economic, in Falkland's day, and has given me much for this chapter; D. Mathew, *Catholicism in England, 1535–1935* (London, 1936); *The Records of the Honorable Society of Lincoln's Inn* (London, 1896); Rushworth; T. Strafford, Earl of Wentworth, *Letters and Dispatches* (ed. W. Knowler; London, 1739), I, 163; J. Suckling, *Works* (ed. A. H. Thompson; London, 1910); T. Triplet, prefatory epistle in L. Cary, *Discourse of Infallibility* (London, 1660); E. Waller, *Poems* (ed. G. Thorn-Drury; London, 1893); R. F. Williams, ed., *The Court and Times of Charles the First; Illustrated by Authentic and Confidential Letters* (London, 1848), II, 16. There are essays on Earle and Hales in A. C. Benson, *Essays* (N. Y., 1896). For Lettice Cary, see C. Barksdale, *Characters and Historical Memorials* (London, 1662); J. Duncon, *The Vertuous, Holy, Christian Life and Death of the Late Lady Lettice, Vi-Countess Falkland* (3d. ed.; London, 1653).

CHAPTER V

For this chapter see the following authorities already cited for previous chapters: *Athenae*; Aubrey; F. Bacon, *Works*, Vol. VI; W. D. Briggs, "Studies in Ben Jonson"; J. Buchan, *Oliver Cromwell*; L. Carey [sic], *Poems*; Clarendon, *History*; Clarendon, *Life*; S. Cressy, *Epistle Apologetical*; *CSP, Domestic, 1635, 1636–1637, 1637–1638, 1639–1640*; DNB; J. Duncon, *The Vertuous, Holy Christian Life*; Gardiner, *History*; (F. Harrison), *The Devon*

Carys; Life; D. Lloyd, State-Worthies; Manning, Memoirs; Marriott; J. Suckling, Works; T. Triplet, prefatory epistle; R. F. Williams, The Court and Times of Charles the First.

Other works quoted or referred to are: G. Burnet, History of His Own Time (Oxford, 1833), I, 320-321; F. Cheynell, The Rise, Growth, and Danger of Socinianisme (London, 1643); W. Chillingworth, Works (Oxford, 1838); G. N. Clark, The Seventeenth Century (Oxford, 1929), pp. 322-323; Serenus (or Hugh) Cressy, Exomologesis (2d. ed.; Paris, 1653), pp. 499-500, 529, and Fanaticism Fanatically imputed to the Catholick Church (n.p., 1672); P. Des Maizeaux, An Historical and Critical Account of the Life and Writings of Wm. Chillingworth (London, 1725); J. Earle, Micro-Cosmographie (ed. Arber; London, 1904); H. C. Foxcroft, A Supplement to Burnet's History of My Own Time (Oxford, 1902), pp. 67-68; M. Freund, Die Idee der Toleranz im England der Grossen Revolution (Halle, 1927); G. P. Gooch, English Democratic Ideas in the Seventeenth Century (2d. ed.; Cambridge, 1927), and Political Thought in England from Bacon to Halifax (London, 1915); J. Hales, Golden Remains (3d. ed.; London, 1688); J. D. Hyman, William Chillingworth and the Theory of Toleration (Camb., 1931); W. K. Jordan, The Development of Religious Toleration in England . . . 1603–1640 (Camb., 1936); H. J. Laski, The Rise of Liberalism (N. Y., 1936); P. Meissner, "Die Rationalistische Grundlage der Englischen Kultur des 17 Jahrhunderts" in Anglia, LV (Halle, 1931); A. O. Meyer, "Der Toleranzgedanke im England der Stuarts" in Historischen Zeitschrift, CVIII (Munich, 1912), p. 269; F. C. Montague, History of England from the Accession of James I to the Restoration (London, 1907), (Vol. VII of W. Hunt and R. L. Poole, eds., Political History of England), pp. 189-190; P. E. More, "Sir Thomas Browne" in Shelburne Essays, Sixth Series (N. Y., 1909); Sir P. Pett, ed., The Genuine Remains of that Learned Prelate Dr. Thomas Barlow (London, 1693); G. Santayana, Reason in Religion (N. Y., 1905), p. 172; A. A. Seaton, The Theory of Toleration under the Later Stuarts (Cambridge, 1911), p. 51; J. Selden, Table-Talk (ed. E. Arber; London, 1905); J. Swift, "A Letter to a Young Clergyman Lately Entered into Holy Orders" in Prose Works (ed. T. Scott; London,

1898–1908), III, 201-202; J. Tulloch, *Rational Theology and Christian Philosophy in England in the Seventeenth Century* (2d. ed.; London, 1874); A. Wood, *The Life and Times of*, (ed. A. Clark; Oxford, 1891–1900), III, 358. For Cary's writings on infallibility, see *The Coppy Of A Letter Sent from France by Mr Walter Mountagu to his Father the Lord Privie Seale, with his answere thereunto. Also a second answere to the same Letter by the Lord Faulkland. Imprinted, 1641.*; his letter to Morison in (C. Gataker), *Five Captious Questions, Propounded by a Factor for the Papacy: Answered by a Divine of the Church of God in England . . . To which is added, An occasional Letter of the Lord Viscount Falkland, to the same Gentleman* (London, 1673), reprinted in Gataker's *The Papists Bait* (London, 1674); and his *Discourse of Infallibility*, printed according to Grosart in Oxford, 1645. It was reprinted in 1646 in Henry Hammond, *A View of Some Exceptions Which Have Beene Made By a Romanist to The Lord Viscount Falkland's Discourse of the Infallibilitie of the Church of Rome* (Oxford, 1646), and in the 2d. ed. of the same, London, 1650. In 1651 the *Discourse* was issued with a prefatory letter by Thomas Triplet and a preface by I. P. With it appeared in this edition *An Answer to The Lord Faulkland's Discourse of Infallibility* and *The Lord of Faulklands Reply*. In a 2d. ed. of this volume (London, 1660) the preface is ascribed to John Pearson (1613–1686, Bishop of Chester) and the Answer to Thomas White (1593–1676) who wrote *An Apology for Rushworth's Dialogues Wherein the Exceptions of the Lords Falkland and Digby are answer'd* (Paris, 1654). For Falkland's and Chillingworth's use of Daillé, and for the nature of Daillé's work, first published in 1631, see J. Daillé, *A Treatise Concerning the Right Vse of the Fathers* (London, 1651), prefatory note by T. S.; J. Daillé, *Ioannis Dallaei de Vsv Patrum* (Geneva, 1656), dedicatory epistle, and the edition of the *Treatise* by G. Jekyll (London, 1841), pp. xiii-xiv; W. Warburton, *Julian* (London, 1750), preface; (E. Hyde, Earl of Clarendon), *Animadversions Upon a Book, Intituled Fanaticism, etc.* (London, 1673), pp. 183ff. For Falkland and Cowley, see A. Cowley, *Poems* (ed., A. R. Waller; Cambridge, 1905); J. Loiseau, *Abraham Cowley, Sa Vie, Son Oeuvre* (Paris, 1931), pp. 59-61;

A. H. Nethercot, *Abraham Cowley, The Muse's Hannibal* (Oxford, 1931), pp. 59-60; T. Sprat, "Account of the Life of . . . Cowley" in J. E. Spingarn, *Critical Essays of the Seventeenth Century* (Oxford, 1908–1909), II, 123.

Chapter VI

For this chapter see the following authorities already cited for previous chapters: *Athenae*; Aubrey; J. Buchan, *Oliver Cromwell*; L. Cary, "Reply" in *Discourse of Infallibility* (London, 1660); Clarendon, *History*; Clarendon, *Life*; *CSP, Domestic*, 1639; G. Davies, *The Early Stuarts*; *DNB*; J. Duncon, *The Vertuous, Holy, Christian Life*; Gardiner, *History*; (F. Harrison), *The Devon Carys*; *Hist. Mss. Comm.*, Report XII, Appendix 2, p. 270, Appendix 4, pp. 510, 511; I. D. Jones, *The English Revolution*; T. Lewis, *Lives*; D. Lloyd, *State-Worthies*; Marriott; D. Masson, *Life of John Milton*; J. Rous, *Diary*; Rushworth; J. Suckling, *Works*. Other works quoted or referred to are: R. Baillie, *Letters and Journals* (ed. D. Laing; Edinburgh, 1841–1842); J. Bastwick, *The Letany of John Bastwick* (n.p., 1637), p. 6; H. Craik, *The Life of Edward Hyde, Earl of Clarendon* (London, 1911); S. D'Ewes, *Journal* (ed. W. Notestein; New Haven, 1923); H. Hickman, Πατρο-σχολαστικο-δικαιωσις *Or A Justification of the Fathers and Schoolmen: Shewing That they are not Selfe-condemned* for denying the *Positivity of Sin* (2d. ed.; Oxford, 1659), preface, pp. 40-41; T. Hobbes, *Behemoth* (London, 1682); C. H. McIlwain, *The High Court of Parliament* (New Haven, 1910); W. A. Shaw, *A History of the English Church . . . 1640–1660* (London, 1900); J. R. Tanner, *English Constitutional Conflicts of the Seventeenth Century* (Cambridge, 1928), pp. 101-103; W. H. Terry, *Life and Times of John, Lord Finch* (London, 1936), pp. 386-387; W. C. and C. E. Trevelyan, eds., *The Trevelyan Papers, Part III* (London, 1872), p. 201; F. P. Verney, *Memoirs of the Verney Family During the Civil War* (London, 1892); R. Verney, *Verney Papers. Notes of Proceedings in the Long Parliament* (ed. J. Bruce; London, 1845); N. Wallington, *Historical Notices of Events* (London, 1869), I, 212; P. Warwick, *Memoires of the Reign of King Charles I* (2d. ed.; London, 1702).

NOTES ON AUTHORITIES

CHAPTER VII

For this chapter see the following, already cited for previous chapters: F. Bacon, *Works*, Vol. XII; J. Buchan, *Oliver Cromwell*; L. Cary, *Discourse* (1660); Clarendon, *History*; Clarendon, *Life*; *CSP, Domestic, 1641–1643*; G. Davies, *The Early Stuarts*; Gardiner, *History*; (F. Harrison), *The Devon Carys*; *Hist. Mss. Comm.*, Report VII, Appendix, Report XII, Appendix, Part 2, Report on the Manuscripts of Lord Montagu of Beaulieu; J. D. Hyman, *William Chillingworth*; I. D. Jones, *The English Revolution*; H. J. Laski, *The Rise of Liberalism*; T. Lewis, *Lives*; D. Lloyd, *State-Worthies*; D. Masson, *Life of John Milton*; Sir P. Pett, ed., *The Genuine Remains*; Rushworth; W. A. Shaw, *History of the English Church*; J. Swift, *Prose Works*, Vol. X; J. R. Tanner, *English Constitutional Conflicts of the Seventeenth Century*; W. H. Terry, *Life of Lord Finch*; R. Verney, *Verney Papers*; P. Warwick, *Memoires*. Other works quoted or referred to are: J. Forster, *The Debates on the Grand Remonstrance* (London, 1860); Gardiner, *Great Civil War*; J. Nalson, *An Impartial Collection of the Great Affairs of State* (London, 1682–1683), II, 816; (W. Seward), *Anecdotes of Some Distinguished Persons* (London, 1795–1797), IV, 381-382; T. Woodcock, *Extracts from the Papers of*, (ed. G. C. Moore Smith; London, 1907), p. 56. Falkland's speech on the bishops is included in the 1660 edition of his *Discourse of Infallibility*.

CHAPTER VIII

For this chapter I have used the following authorities already cited for previous chapters: *Athenae*; Aubrey; Clarendon, *History*; Clarendon, *Life*; *CSP, Domestic, 1641–1643*; Des Maizeaux, *Historical and Critical Account*; Gardiner, *Great Civil War*; *Hist. Mss. Comm.*, Report II, Appendix, p. 36, Report V, Appendix, p. 49; T. Lewis, *Lives*; J. Loiseau, *Abraham Cowley*; Marriott; D. Masson, *Life of John Milton*; K. B. Murdock, "An Elegy"; Sir P. Pett, ed., *The Genuine Remains*; Rushworth; (W. Seward), *Anecdotes*; J. Swift, *Prose Works*, Vol. X; D. Townshend, *Life* and *Letters;* E. Waller, *Poems;* P. Warwick, *Memoires;* T. Wood-cock, *Extracts.* Other works quoted or referred to are: W. Cobbett, ed., *The Parliamentary History of England* (London, 1806–1820), III, 121-129; A. Collins, ed., *Letters and Memorials of State* (London, 1746); J. Denham, *Poetical Works* (ed. T. H. Banks, Jr.; New Haven, 1928), p. 99; W. D. Fellowes, *Historical Sketches of Charles I* (London, 1828), pp. 214-215; T. Fuller, *Good Thoughts in Bad Times, Good Thoughts in Worse Times, Mixt Contemplations in Better Times* (London, 1841), pp. 199, 232; K. F. Gibbs and W. Briggs, eds., *The Parish Records of Aldenham, Hertfordshire* (St. Albans, 1902), p. 190; C. R. Gillett, *Burned Books* (N. Y., 1932), I, 187-189; A. Harbage, *Sir William Davenant, Poet, Venturer, 1606–1668* (Philadelphia, 1935); (E. Hyde), *State Papers Collected by Edward, Earl of Clarendon* (Oxford, 1767–1786), II, 155, 166; *Journals of the House of Commons;* W. Money, *The First and Second Battles of Newbury* (2d. ed., London, 1884); "A Narrative of Some Passages in . . . the Long Parliament" in W. Scott, ed., *A Collection of . . . Tracts . . . Particularly . . . Of the Late Lord Somers* (London, 1809–1815), VI, 574; S. Pepys, *Diary* (ed. H. B. Wheatley; London, 1924), VIII, 111 and note; *A Perfect Diurnall of the Passages in Parliament,* No. 15, 19 Sept.–26 Sept., 1642; W. Sanderson, *A Compleat History of the Life and Raigne of King Charles* (London, 1658), pp. 609, 632; (E. Sandys), *His Declaration in Vindication* (London, 1642); J. L. Sanford, *Studies and Illustrations of the Great Rebellion* (London, 1858); *A Vindication of Col. Sandys's Honour and Loyalty* (London, 1642); C. Vivian, *Some Notes for a History of the 'Sandys' Family* (ed. T. M. Sandys; London, 1907); E. Warburton, *Memoirs of Prince Rupert and the Cavaliers* (London, 1849); J. Webb, *Memorials of the Civil War . . . as it Affected Herefordshire* (ed. T. W. Webb; London, 1879), I, 306; S. H. Werlein, Jr., *Edmund Waller: A Study of His Life and Works* (manuscript; Camb., 1919); B. Whitelocke, *Memorials of the English Affairs* (Oxford, 1853); C. Wilkinson, *Prince Rupert, The Cavalier* (Philadelphia, 1935). I have also quoted from letters of Falkland to Lady Dungarvan, owned by the Right Honorable Earl Spencer, who courteously allowed me to have photographs

made of them by my colleague, Professor Perry G. E. Miller. Cf
Hist. Mss. Comm., Report II, Appendix, p. 19.

CHAPTER IX

I have relied constantly on J. Prinz, *John Wilmot, Earl of
Rochester, His Life and Writings* (Leipzig, 1927); V. De Sola
Pinto, *Rochester, Portrait of a Restoration Rake* (London, 1935);
J. Hayward, introduction in his *Collected Works of John Wilmot,
Earl of Rochester* (London, 1926); and, of course, G. Burnet,
*Some Passages of the Life and Death Of the Right Honourable
John, Earl of Rochester* (London, 1680). I have also found useful
(T. Longueville), *Rochester and Other Literary Rakes* (2d. ed.;
N. Y., 1903), and have been stimulated, as anyone interested in
Rochester must be, by the interpretations of him in B. Dobrée,
Rochester, A Conversation (London, 1926), and, especially, C.
Williams, *Rochester* (London, 1935). For the text of Rochester's
poems I have followed Hayward's edition. I have used the follow-
ing authorities already cited: *Athenae; Aubrey;* G. Burnet, *History;
CSP, Domestic*, for the years from 1660 to 1680; J. Denham,
Poetical Works; Hist. Mss. Comm., Report VI, Appendix, Report
VII, Appendix, Part 1, Report VIII, Appendix, Report XII, Ap-
pendix, Part 5, Part 7, Report XV, Appendix, Part 2, Calendar
of the Manuscripts of the Marquis of Bath, Report on the Manuscripts of the Duke of Buccleuch and Queensberry . . . at Montagu
House, Report on the Laing Manuscripts; S. Pepys, *Diary;* E.
Waller, *Poems.* Other works quoted or referred to are: E. Chambers, *Sir Henry Lee, An Elizabethan Portrait* (Oxford, 1936); J.
Evelyn, *Diary* (ed. A. Dobson; London, 1906); F. Fane, dedication to "Love in the Dark" in J. Malone, *Critical and Miscellaneous Prose Works of John Dryden* (London, 1800); T. Flat-
man, *Poems and Songs* (3d. ed.; London, 1682), pp. 146-147; H.
C. Foxcroft, ed., "Some Unpublished Letters of Gilbert Burnet"
in *Camden Miscellany*, XI (London, 1907), p. 14; R. G. Ham,
Otway and Lee, Biography from a Baroque Age (New Haven,
1931); Anthony, Count Hamilton, *Memoirs of Count Gramont*
(ed. A. Fea; London, 1906); N. Lee dedication of "Nero" in
Works (London, 1713); J. G. Longe, *Martha, Lady Giffard* (Lon-

don, 1911); E. Marshall, *Supplement to the History of Woodstock Manor* (Oxford, 1874), p. 29; A. Marvell, *Poems and Letters* (ed. H. M. Margoliouth; Oxford, 1927), II, 322, 356; D. Ogg, *England in the Reign of Charles II* (Oxford, 1934); R. Parsons, *A Sermon Preached At the Funeral of the R^t Honorable John Earl of Rochester* (Oxford, 1680); J. Sheffield, *Works* (London, 1723), II, 8-10; "Some Memoirs of the Earl of Rochester," ascribed probably erroneously to St. Evremond, reprinted in J. Wilmot, *Poetical Works* (ed. Q. Johns; The Haworth Press, 1933); E. M. Thompson, ed., *Correspondence of the Family of Hatton* (London, 1878), I, 133-134.

ABBREVIATIONS USED IN THE FOOTNOTES AND THE LIST OF AUTHORITIES

Athenae: Wood, Anthony, *Athenae Oxonienses* (ed. P. Bliss; London, 1813–1820).

Aubrey: Aubrey, John, *'Brief Lives,'* chiefly of Contemporaries, set down by John Aubrey, between the Years 1669 & 1696 (ed. A. Clark; Oxford, 1898).

Clarendon, History: (Hyde), Edward, Earl of Clarendon, *The History of the Rebellion and Civil Wars in England Begun In The Year 1641*, Re-edited from A Fresh Collation of the Original Ms. in the Bodleian Library by W. Dunn Macray (Oxford, 1888).

Clarendon, Life: (Hyde, Edward), *The Life of Edward Earl of Clarendon, Lord High Chancellor of England . . . in Which is Included A Continuation of his History of the Grand Rebellion*. Written by Himself. A New Edition (Oxford, 1827).

Complete Peerage: C., G. E., *The Complete Peerage of England, Scotland, Great Britain and the United Kingdom Extant, Extinct or Dormant*. New edition, revised and enlarged (ed. V. Gibbs and H. A. Doubleday; London, 1910–).

CSP: *Calendar of State Papers, Domestic Series . . . Preserved in the State Paper Department of the Public Record Office* (various dates and editors); and *Calendar of State Papers Relating to Ireland . . . in the Public Record Office* (various dates and editors).

DNB: Dictionary of National Biography (ed. L. Stephen and S. Lee; reissue; N. Y. 1908–1909).

Gardiner, Great Civil War: Gardiner, S. R., History of the Great Civil War, 1642–1649 (London, 1893).

Gardiner, History: Gardiner, S. R., History of England From The Accession of James I. to The Outbreak of the Civil War, 1603–1642 (London, 1883–1884).

Hist. Mss. Comm.: Royal Commission on Historical Manuscripts, Reports (various dates, editors, and places).

Life: The Lady Falkland: Her Life. From a MS. in the Imperial Archives at Lille (London, 1861).

Longueville: (Longueville, T.), Falklands (London, 1897).

Marriott: Marriott, J. A. R., The Life and Times of Lucius Cary, Viscount Falkland (2d. ed., London, 1908).

Rushworth: Rushworth, J., Historical Collections of Private Passages of State, Weighty Matters in Law, Remarkable Proceedings in Five Parliaments (London, 1721).

In listing places of publication, I have used "Cambridge" to indicate Cambridge, England; and "Camb." to indicate Cambridge, Mass., U. S. A.

INDEX

This index includes the more important references to persons in the text, but omits some of those mentioned only incidentally. Authors quoted in the text, or cited in the List of Authorities, are not ordinarily included. The title "Sir" is omitted in indexing the names of knights and baronets, and other titles are included only when they seem desirable to aid in identification of the persons concerned.

INDEX

INDEX

INDEX

INDEX

This index was prepared for the author by Henry D. Reck, of Cambridge, Massachusetts.